T0385580

SPEAKING THE TRUTH
ABOUT ONESELF

THE CHICAGO FOUCAULT PROJECT

Arnold I. Davidson, Henri-Paul Fruchaud & Daniele Lorenzini
SERIES EDITORS

The wide-ranging and groundbreaking works of Michel Foucault (1926–1984) have transformed our understanding of the human sciences and shaped contemporary thought in philosophy, history, critical theory, and more. In recent years, the publication of his lectures, seminars, and public discussions has made it possible not only to understand the trajectory of his work but also to clarify his central ideas and to provide a better overall perspective on his thought. The aim of the Chicago Foucault Project is to contribute to this enterprise by publishing definitive English-language editions of these texts and fostering an ongoing appreciation of the lasting value of Foucault's oeuvre in the English-speaking world.

"Discourse and Truth" and "Parrēsia"
> EDITED BY Henri-Paul Fruchaud & Daniele Lorenzini
> INTRODUCTION BY Frédéric Gros
> ENGLISH EDITION ESTABLISHED BY Nancy Luxon

About the Beginning of the Hermeneutics of the Self:
Lectures at Dartmouth College, 1980
> EDITED BY Henri-Paul Fruchaud & Daniele Lorenzini
> INTRODUCTION AND CRITICAL APPARATUS BY Laura Cremonesi,
> Arnold I. Davidson, Orazio Irrera, Daniele Lorenzini & Martina Tazzioli
> TRANSLATED BY Graham Burchell

MICHEL FOUCAULT

SPEAKING THE TRUTH ABOUT ONESELF

LECTURES AT VICTORIA UNIVERSITY, TORONTO, 1982

EDITED BY
Henri-Paul Fruchaud & Daniele Lorenzini

ENGLISH EDITION ESTABLISHED BY
Daniel Louis Wyche

The University of Chicago Press • Chicago and London

The University of Chicago Press, Chicago 60637
The University of Chicago Press, Ltd., London
© 2021 by The University of Chicago
All rights reserved. No part of this book may be used or reproduced
in any manner whatsoever without written permission,
except in the case of brief quotations in critical articles and reviews.
For more information, contact the University of Chicago Press,
1427 E. 60th St., Chicago, IL 60637.
Published 2021
Printed in the United States of America

30 29 28 27 26 25 24 23 22 21   1 2 3 4 5

ISBN-13: 978-0-226-61686-5 (cloth)
ISBN-13: 978-0-226-62305-4 (e-book)
DOI: https://doi.org/10.7208/chicago/9780226623054.001.0001

Originally published as *Dire vrai sur soi-même.*
Conférences prononcées à l'Université Victoria de Toronto, 1982
Édition, introduction et apparat critique par Henri-Paul Fruchaud et Daniele Lorenzini
© Librairie Philosophique J. Vrin, Paris, 2017. http://www.vrin.fr.

Library of Congress Cataloging-in-Publication Data

Names: Foucault, Michel, 1926–1984, author. | Fruchaud, Henri-Paul, editor. |
Lorenzini, Daniele, editor. | Wyche, Daniel Louis, editor. | Foucault, Michel,
1926–1984. Works. Selections (University of Chicago. Press). English.
Title: Speaking the truth about oneself : lectures at Victoria University,
Toronto, 1982 / Michel Foucault ; edited by Henri-Paul Fruchaud and
Daniele Lorenzini ; English edition established by Daniel Louis Wyche.
Other titles: Lectures. Selections. English
Description: Chicago : University of Chicago Press, 2021. | Series: The Chicago
Foucault Project | Includes bibliographical references and index.
Identifiers: LCCN 2021005205 | ISBN 9780226616865 (cloth) |
ISBN 9780226623054 (ebook)
Subjects: LCSH: Self (Philosophy) | Hermeneutics. |
Subjectivity. | Truth. | Subject (Philosophy)
Classification: LCC B2430.F724 A5 2021 | DDC 194—dc23
LC record available at https://lccn.loc.gov/2021005205

♾ This paper meets the requirements of ANSI/NISO Z39.48-1992
(Permanence of Paper).

CONTENTS

INTRODUCTION

FROM MAY 31 THROUGH JUNE 26, 1982, Michel Foucault participated in the Third International Summer Institute for Semiotic and Structural Studies at Victoria University, Toronto. Foucault came to Toronto at the invitation of Paul Bouissac, professor of semiotics and one of the organizers. There Foucault gave a series of six lectures in English,[1] entitled "The Discourse of Self-Disclosure," and led a seminar of the same name.[2] Among the other notable participants at the Institute that summer were John R. Searle and Umberto Eco, as well as Daniel Defert, who presented an analysis of the strategies of description used in travel narratives from the "age of discovery" up to the eighteenth century.[3]

Not long before arriving in Toronto, from January through March of 1982, Foucault had completed his 1981–1982 Collège de France lecture series, "The Hermeneutics of the Subject." The latter were devoted to "the culture of the self" in Greco-Roman antiquity, which Foucault examined through the notions of the care of the self and "techniques of the self."[4] The "Hermeneutics" lectures also mark the first appearance in Foucault's work of the notion of *parrēsia* (a concept traditionally translated as "frank-speaking" or even "free speech"), to which he would devote his final investigations in 1983 and 1984.[5]

The theme of the ancient culture of the self that Foucault addresses at Toronto has its origins in an entire series of previous interventions. At a lecture at the University of Grenoble in May 1982, Foucault gave his first comprehensive account of *parrēsia* within the framework of the study of Greco-Roman philosophy, from the perspective of the care of the self.[6] At Toronto several weeks later, he would present the lectures and seminar that constitute the present volume. In October 1982, Foucault held a seminar entitled "Technologies of the Self" at the University of Vermont,[7] in which he returned to the themes of the Toronto lectures in a more concise manner. Following this seminar, in April 1983, Foucault lectured on the culture of the self[8] at the University of California, Berkeley. The Berkeley lectures are nearly identical in subject to the first three Toronto lectures, although Foucault explicitly reframed the content in terms of the perspective opened by the historico-critical question inherited from Kant, "What are we now?"[9] Finally, the second and third volumes of *The History of Sexuality* appeared in May and June of 1984, each devoted to Greco-Roman antiquity,[10] with the second chapter of volume 3, *The Care of the Self*, entitled "The Culture of the Self."[11]

IN THE INTRODUCTORY LECTURE OF the Toronto series, Foucault explains that his goal is to study "the development of the hermeneutics of the self successively in two contexts quite different the one from the other, but nevertheless presenting a certain historical continuity." It is for him a question "first of all of Greco-Roman philosophy at the imperial period; and then of Christian spirituality at the period in which monastic principles and institutions were developing."[12] Foucault specifies that he has come to pose these kinds of questions by observing, within the context of his investigations into the history of sexuality, the relationship within Western societies between prohibitions in sexual matters and the obligation to speak the truth about oneself.

The study that Foucault carries out in the Toronto lectures is situated at the nexus of three of the major inflection points of his thought that appear at the beginning of the 1980s: first, the question of the subject; second, that of the truth; and third, the historical framework of these analyses.

Even though the question of the subject, or more precisely of subjectivation, is by no means new to Foucault's work at this point, he begins to approach it from a new angle at the beginning of the 1980s. It is no longer only a question of understanding the ways in which the subject is constituted in and by mechanisms of power-knowledge, but also of exploring the ways in which one constitutes oneself though a series of techniques of the self. From this point on, Foucault's work is inscribed within a genealogy of the modern (Western) subject.[13] It is a genealogy that seeks to analyze the ways in which the latter subject is historically constituted, and is at the same time designed to be a "historical ontology of ourselves"[14] marked by an explicitly critical dimension.[15]

The second inflection concerns the fundamental role that Foucault confers upon the relationship between the subject and truth within this historical process: truth-telling is one of the matrices of subjectivity. Indeed, it is above all through these "truth acts"[16]—in particular, in speaking the truth about oneself, though with equal regard to (and vis-à-vis) speaking the truth about others—that subjects constitute themselves, modify their relationships to themselves, and modify themselves by tying themselves to the truths that they speak. Among the forms of truth-telling that Foucault studies, two occupy a central place: the confession of faults, or more precisely the Christian confession of sins; and the risky, courageous, and sometimes insolent form of truth-telling called *parrēsia*.

The third inflection coincides with Foucault's expansion of the historical framework of his studies, which leads to his interest in the ancient Greco-Roman culture of the self, and the first two centuries of the Roman Empire in particular. There Foucault discovers practices of subjectivation and relations between the subject and truth quite different from the model that he found in early and medieval Christianity, as well as modern forms of subjectivity. This is not only the point of departure for the final version of his history of sexuality,[17] but an entire domain of study in its own right, to which he will devote his last several courses at the Collège de France. The reference to Greco-Roman antiquity is in fact what allows Foucault to clearly bring to light the rupture represented by Christianity in the genealogy of the (modern) Western subject.[18]

These three dimensions of the genealogy of the subject, of the relationship between the subject and the truth, and a renewed interest in Greco-Roman antiquity allow us to situate Foucault's remarks in the Toronto lectures. He seeks to describe the very specific type of knowledge of oneself and relation to oneself through which the subject is constituted in Greco-Roman antiquity. Further, to understand how, in the first centuries of the Christian period (and within the monastic communities in particular), the reversal that led to the birth of a hermeneutic of the self had operated. According to Foucault, it is this hermeneutics of the self that, despite numerous modifications, in many respects remains ours today.

Foucault had already studied the emergence of the hermeneutics of the self within the ancient Greco-Roman and early Christian contexts in the autumn of 1980, in two different lecture series: first, at the University of California, Berkeley, under the title "Truth and Subjectivity" (which Foucault noted should have been "The Origins of the Hermeneutics of the Self");[19] second, and with some modifications, his lectures at Dartmouth College, entitled "Subjectivity and Truth" and "Christianity and Confession."[20] There is, however, a fundamental difference between these lectures and those given at Toronto. In 1980, the ancient culture of the self did not constitute the object of an extensive study for Foucault. It is for this reason that he limited his analyses to a comparison of the examination of conscience and confession within Greco-Roman antiquity and the early centuries of Christianity. At Toronto, by contrast, the field of inquiry is far vaster, comprising the ancient culture of the self in its entirety, which is then compared to the Christian hermeneutic of the self as it was constituted within the first monastic communities.

WE HAVE, UNFORTUNATELY, ONLY A fragmented and uneven image of Foucault's Toronto lectures, because of the state of the sources available. Complete versions of the first three lectures—

indeed several different versions of each of these lectures—have survived. Lectures IV and V, which are either principally or in part devoted to Christianity, are incomplete, however. Lecture VI, in which Foucault intended to propose "some marking points for a possible history of the hermeneutics of the self in Western culture,"[21] could not be recovered, and indeed may not have been given. Consequently, the first part of the cycle, devoted to the culture of the self in antiquity, occupies an outsized place here, to the detriment of Foucault's discussions of the birth of the Christian hermeneutics of the self, which was certainly not the case in the lectures as they were actually given. To be sure, the autumn 1980 lectures at UC-Berkeley and Dartmouth College, and perhaps above all Foucault's seminar on the technologies of the self at the University of Vermont, can provide us with some information regarding the missing pieces of the final lectures at Toronto. Nevertheless, the approach to the Christian hermeneutics of the self that Foucault developed at Toronto included certain themes that he would not subsequently develop.

It is for this reason, then, that we must be clear that the Toronto lectures are not *centrally* concerned with the ancient culture of the self, even as they may seem to be at first glance. They are rather an even account of two forms of knowledge of the self, and two very different forms of the relation to oneself, even despite certain crucial continuities.

Foucault's analyses of the Greco-Roman culture of the self in the first half of the Toronto lectures are quite similar to those developed several months earlier in "The Hermeneutics of the Subject." Alongside the "Socratic moment" (or rather, the Platonic-Socratic moment), Foucault focuses on the first two centuries of the Roman Empire, which he considers the golden age of the culture of the self. But Foucault does not study this period exclusively in terms of the opinions of philosophers. Rather, he is inclined toward those concrete practices actually taken up in the service of "caring for oneself." And in order to characterize the care of the self as it was practiced at its apogee, Foucault takes as his benchmark a text that precedes this period by several centuries: Plato's *Alcibiades*. It is here that this notion of the care of the self makes its first appearance, and Foucault systematically compares the Platonic-Socratic conception of the care of the self with the understanding current during the first two centuries of the empire. Between the two, he identifies four significant differences.

First, in the *Alcibiades*, the care of the self only concerns a single category of people at a precise moment in their lives: ambitious young aristocrats just on the verge of entering political life. Moreover, and for this very reason, the care of oneself is here tied directly to the care of the city. One must, after all, care for oneself in order to learn how to govern others well. However, by the first two centuries of the Roman imperial period, the care of the self had become widespread across society. One had to practice it not only in youth, but throughout one's life, as it would culminate only in old age. In this way, it was not a question of a simple preparation for (political) life, but rather an entire form of life, so much so that the care of oneself could be dissociated from the care of the city—to the extent that it could even, for some at least, entail the renunciation of political life itself.

Second, in the *Alcibiades*, the care of the self was meant in part to compensate for a defective pedagogy. It would allow the young man to discover principles of good government that he would not have otherwise encountered, and which he could later put into practice. In the imperial period, this pedagogical function disappeared and was replaced by several others: a critical function (to disabuse oneself of false opinions), a combative function (to engage in spiritual combat), and a medical function (to assuage one's passions).

Third, for Plato, the care of the self is identified with self-knowledge. It is by contemplating his soul that the young man will discover, through recollection (*anamnesis*), justice and the principles of good government. In the culture of the self of the early imperial period, it is rather the care of the self that plays the principal role: the primary goal is to insure that the individual is equipped with an ensemble of truths that will allow him to face the outside world. Self-knowledge is thus subordinated to the care of the self, and the former simply allows one to measure the degree to which the subject has advanced in the assimilation of these truths.

Finally, in the *Alcibiades* the care of the self is practiced within the framework of an eroto-philosophical relationship with a master. In

the imperial period to the contrary, while the presence of another
was still indispensable to the care of the self, the erotic relationship
was effaced. From this point forward, the relationship of education,
of direction, or of counsel, which could be accompanied, though not
necessarily, by bonds of friendship, would be exercised in multiple
forms—in schools, lectures, private counsel, or philosophical communities such as the Epicureans—and would rely upon more stan-
dardized practices.

Foucault thus traces the appearance of a form of the relationship
to the self quite different from that of the Platonic-Socratic care of
the self. A new form of subjectivity is thus constituted through practices such as reading, writing, and retreat to the country, as well as a
series of exercises or tests such as the *praemeditatio malorum*, forms
of abstinence, the permanent surveillance of internal representations,
and the meditation on death. The implementation of the culture of
the self in the imperial period occurs by way of practices whose goal
is not simply the subject's acquisition but the *assimilation* of truths,
which must constitute a permanent matrix for his conduct, and which
must be available to him as the need arises.[22] Within such an apparatus, self-knowledge merely occupies a subsidiary place: "Its aim is
to control the process of acquiring true discourses, of making them
a part of ourselves, of transforming ourselves through them." Foucault adds, further, that "it is not a question of making the self appear
in its reality in true discourses; it is a question of making the true
discourses transform the self by a permanently controlled appropriation of the truth."[23] Taking up a term he had already invoked in
1980 at both Berkeley and Dartmouth, Foucault thus qualifies this
self-knowledge as "gnomic."[24]

In the second half of the Toronto lectures, Foucault opposes this
"gnomic" self-knowledge to the Christian hermeneutic of the self,
such as it appeared in the first monastic communities of the fourth
and fifth centuries. In order to define the inversion that constitutes
this new mode of subjectivation, Foucault introduces a rather complex distinction between two forms of ascesis (one that he would
not, incidentally, refer to again a few months later in his seminar at
the University of Vermont). There are what he calls "truth-oriented"
forms of ascesis on the one hand, and "reality-oriented" forms of

ascesis on the other. The "ethopoetic" goal of the truth-oriented ascesis characteristic of the ancient culture of the self is to allow one to establish "a relationship of possession and of sovereignty" with oneself,
and to provide one with the kind of "preparation . . . which permits
[one] to confront the world."[25] Conversely, "reality-oriented" ascesis
has a "metanoetic" function, insofar as here one transforms oneself
with the goal of renouncing this world in order to accede to eternal
life in the next: "Christian asceticism has as a goal escaping this world
and obtaining the other world. Christian asceticism is a 'rite of passage,' from one reality to another, from death to life, through an apparent death which is a real access to real life. I should say, in a word,
that Christian asceticism is reality-oriented."[26]

And yet this "reality-oriented" Christian ascesis itself presup-
poses, as a necessary precondition, a "truth-oriented" ascesis. In fact,
according to Foucault, Christianity imposes two different yet indisso-
ciably linked "obligations of truth." And it is through these obligations
that the subject transforms himself in his relationship to the truth:
first, in the obligation to believe in a revealed truth (the dogma, the
Text), followed by an obligation for the subject to know himself in
his reality, to explore the depths of his interiority in order to ferret
out anything that maintains his attachment to this world. This hermeneutic self-knowledge is thereby the condition of self-renunciation.
Thus, contrary to that of pagan antiquity, a form of truth emerges with
Christianity that must not only be assimilated but *decoded*.

Foucault thus distinguishes two forms of hermeneutic knowledge within Christianity. First, an "interpretive hermeneutic," which
seeks out the truth of the Text through different forms of knowledge
(historical, allegorical, anagogical, tropological). Second, a "discriminative hermeneutic," which is concerned with the movements of
thought and which, through an exercise of discrimination, seeks to
identify their origin, whether in God or Satan. Foucault locates its
appearance in a text drawn from the *Conferences* of Cassian, which
he analyzes at length. However, the manuscript is interrupted at the
end of this analysis, and we can unfortunately only speculate as to
what followed in Foucault's analyses. It is nevertheless probable that
the description of the two forms of Christian hermeneutics was fol-

lowed by a discussion of *exagoreusis*, such as one finds in Cassian. It is through this operation that the monk enacts the practice of hermeneutic discrimination in which he reveals to his superior even the most miniscule movements of his thought.[27] In this study of the ancient culture of the self and the Christian hermeneutic of the self, Foucault particularly insists on a permanent balancing act between the care of the self and self-knowledge, between the precepts of "caring for yourself" and "knowing yourself," which appear directly tied to one another, and which each take primacy in their turn. In the *Alcibiades*, the care of the self that is required of ambitious young men in preparation for entry into political life explicitly takes the form of self-knowledge. In conformity with Platonic doctrine, it is by contemplating one's soul that one accedes to the Ideas, such as those of justice and good government. To the contrary, among the philosophers of the first two centuries of the Roman Empire, it is instead the care of the self that takes pride of place. Here, self-knowledge is subordinate, and relegated to the simple function of controlling the process by which the subject assimilates those true discourses that constitute the matrix of his conduct.

Finally, with Christianity, we see yet another reversal: self-knowledge, understood in terms of exploring and deciphering the interiority of the subject, now takes pride of place, thus effacing the care of the self. Foucault explains that this preeminence would not be displaced in its turn. Rather, it has been maintained in the history of Western societies in several ways. First, by the transformation of moral principles, such that it is not possible to base a rigorous morality on the precept that one must accord oneself greater importance than all the rest. Second, by the importance accorded to self-knowledge by "theoretical" philosophy since Descartes. Finally, by the development of the human sciences, which constitute the human being, first and foremost, as an object of knowledge.[28]

THE SEMINAR THAT FOUCAULT LED at Toronto, whose meetings were interspersed between the lectures, engaged the same subjects, though with a different function and goals. In the first lectures of "The Hermeneutics of the Subject" in 1982, Foucault announced his intention to systematically devote the first hour of each lesson to a general exposition and the second to the explication of texts.[29] He did not ultimately follow this organizational principle through to the end of the course, but it can still be seen, in a somewhat different form, a few months later in Toronto. While the lectures themselves were devoted to theoretical exposition, in the seminar meetings Foucault proceeds through detailed analyses of certain texts referenced during his talks. These analyses, specifically those devoted to certain passages drawn from the *Discourses* of Epictetus, demonstrate the depth of Foucault's understanding of these texts, the essential aspects of which he returned to in his courses and books. There is thus a continuous reciprocation between the lectures and the seminar, which together constitute a genuine whole. Moreover, Foucault is extremely attentive to the questions and reactions of the students who attended the lectures and seminar, consistently seeking to further specify anything that may not have been fully understood and to situate the themes of the lectures within his work overall.

Foucault also devotes the third meeting of the seminar and the beginning of the fourth to a long exposition on the theme of *parrēsia*. *Parrēsia* first appears in Foucault's work in *The Hermeneutics of the Subject*, where it was tied directly to the notion of the care of the self: in order to care for oneself as one must, the aid of another person (a friend or a master) to whom one speaks the truth about oneself, is absolutely required; this other must possess *parrēsia*. In the *Hermeneutics*, Foucault defines *parrēsia* as "impressionistically, the frankness, freedom, and openness that leads one to say what one has to say, as one wishes to say it, when one wishes to say it, and in the form one thinks is necessary for saying it."[30] Soon after, first at a lecture in Grenoble,[31] and then in the Toronto seminar,[32] Foucault considerably expanded the field of study by analyzing the different significations that *parrēsia* held in Hellenistic and Roman antiquity. Despite many similarities, there is nevertheless one important difference between the interventions at Grenoble and Toronto: whereas at Grenoble Foucault was addressing an audience of specialists in ancient philosophy, his presentation at Toronto was far more didactic, occasionally referring to different ancient texts and authors.

At Toronto, Foucault begins with a definition of *parrēsia*, in which he introduces the notion of danger, expanding the field within which it is exercised to the political domain. *Parrēsia* is at once the freedom and the obligation to speak the truth within the domains of ethics *and* politics. It is characterized by a situation in which the one who speaks the truth has less power than the one, or ones, who listen (the assembly, the prince, those who are directed). *Parrēsia* thus presents a danger to the speaker to the extent that he ties himself directly to this truth. Foucault investigates this notion in three different contexts. First, within the Athenian democracy, wherein *parrēsia* is the right, enjoyed by every citizen, to freely say what he believes to his fellow citizens. Second, within monarchic regimes where Foucault introduces the idea of the "parrhesiastic pact": if the counselor must evince *parrē-sia* when speaking to the prince, the latter must, in return, accept the truths, even the unpleasant truths, that must be spoken. Finally, in the context of the care of the self. Here, the question arises of the criteria that allow one to recognize the true *parrēsiastēs*, of which one is in need. The response is found (at least for Plutarch or Galen) in the unique schema of the life of the *parrēsiastēs*, and in the conformity of his *logos* with his *bios*, of his discourse with his way of life.

Aspects of these analyses can be found in Foucault's work on *parrēsia* in 1983–1984.[33] However, the study of Socratic *parrēsia*, Cynic *parrēsia*, and the idea that *parrēsia* constitutes a stage in the genealogy of the critical attitude do not yet appear at Toronto (or at Grenoble, for that matter).[34] But alongside the analysis of speaking the truth about oneself, it is striking to see Foucault develop the beginnings of his inquiries into a new form of relation of the subject to the truth. Specifically, truth-telling with regard to (and vis-à-vis) the other, or others, which would become the nearly exclusive theme of his final researches.

Henri-Paul Fruchaud & Daniele Lorenzini

Translated by Daniel Louis Wyche

NOTE ON THE
RECONSTRUCTION
OF THE TEXT

THIS VOLUME PRESENTS THE CYCLE of lectures as well as the seminar, all delivered in English, by Michel Foucault at the Third International Summer Institute for Semiotic and Structural Studies, Victoria University, Toronto, in June 1982.

Foucault indicates at the end of section 3 of Lecture I that he had initially planned six lectures,[1] on the following themes:

1. The inaugural lecture on the care of the self
2. The fundamental traits of the culture of the self in the Roman imperial period
3. The forms of knowledge and interpretation of the self that emerged within the culture of the self in the first centuries of the empire
4 & 5. The technology and interpretation of the self within the framework of fourth- and fifth-century Christian asceticism
6. Several landmarks for a possible history of the hermeneutics of the self in Western culture

However, whether or not Foucault gave a sixth lecture, no trace of one could be found in the archives.[2] There are no preliminary writings in French for the last three lectures (it is possible that Foucault planned to prepare them once he arrived in Toronto), and there are only incomplete extant versions of Lectures IV and V. Further, Foucault extensively and thoroughly revised and modified Lectures II and III. In the final version of Lecture III (reproduced here), he most notably introduces a distinction between two forms of ascesis: reality-oriented ascesis and truth-oriented ascesis. He uses these concepts to distinguish the Christian and ancient philosophical forms of ascesis, and he develops the distinction further in Lectures IV and V (though he would not subsequently retain this distinction). With these difficulties in mind, the present volume has been established as follows.

THE LECTURES

WITH THE EXCEPTION OF LECTURE II, none of the lectures were recorded. The audio recording of Lecture II is of very precarious quality, though invaluable. Outside of this case, the texts that constitute the present volume have been reconstructed from handwritten manuscripts and typescripts, archived at the Bibliothèque nationale de France,[3] and (in the case of the French version of the first lecture) at the University of California, Berkeley and the Institut mémoires de l'édition contemporaine (IMEC).

Numerous media are available for the first three lectures, and the choices made by the editors regarding which to include have been difficult. Most importantly, these choices differ from those made for the French edition of this book: in this English edition, we decided to reproduce the versions of the lectures that Foucault actually presented at Toronto in English, instead of the French typescripts. The situation is quite the inverse for the last three lectures: only incomplete manuscripts have survived for Lectures IV and V, and no materials related to a possible sixth lecture have been preserved.

Before coming to Toronto, Foucault seems to have written a preliminary version of the first three lectures in French.[4] These three texts were then translated into English by someone other than Foucault, most likely students at Victoria University (this is corroborated by the nature of the documents, the odd style, and several interpretive errors in these documents). Foucault then reedited and altered these translations himself in English:

1. The new version of the first lecture, preserved in a folder with the title "The Technology of the Self" written on it, is most likely the lecture that Foucault actually gave. At very least, a remark by one of the auditors in the seminar regarding the "four technologies" referenced in Lecture I, section 2, leads us to believe that this is the case.

2. Foucault clearly based the version of Lecture II that is preserved in the audio recording on the revised second English version.

3. Foucault also substantially rewrote Lecture III for the English version, the beginning of which significantly departs from the original manuscript. He may also have rewritten the end of that lecture, though this is only a hypothesis, as the text is incomplete.

Further, thanks to Clive Thomson, we know that on this same visit to Canada, Foucault gave a lecture at Queen's University, Kingston on the culture of the self. However, we were unable to identify this text, which does not seem to have been preserved. It is possible that Foucault reused the text of Lecture I, "The Technology of the Self," or that the Kingston lecture at least draws from the section of the first Toronto lecture of the same name.

FOR THIS ENGLISH EDITION, WE have chosen to present the English version of Lecture I, edited and revised by Foucault himself; the English revised version and a transcript of the audio recording of Lecture II; and both the first and second English versions of Lecture III, because of the quite radical differences between the two. Finally, we have presented the extant, incomplete English versions of Lectures IV and V.

THE SEMINAR

UNLIKE THE LECTURES, AN OFFICIAL audio recording was made of the seminar, with copies held by the Victoria University library and IMEC. However, no manuscript could be recovered. The text of the seminar has been reestablished from the recording, from a transcription by Davey K. Tomlinson. The text has been established here in the most literal way possible. We have only removed repetitions or rectified incorrect phrases when absolutely necessary, and have reproduced or summarized questions by seminar participants to the best of our ability. We have also done our best to retain Foucault's more casual, verbal style in English, including his jokes and exchanges with the auditors, to the greatest extent possible.

COMPLETE LIST OF ARCHIVAL MATERIALS RELATED TO *SPEAKING THE TRUTH ABOUT ONESELF*

LECTURE I

- French typescript (Berkeley, BANC 90/136z, 1:10), omitted here but reproduced in Michel Foucault, *Dire vrai sur soi-même: Conférences prononcées à l'Université Victoria de Toronto, 1982* (Paris: Vrin, 2017).
- English manuscript (BnF NAF 28730, box 29, folder 5), entitled "The Technology of the Self"; reproduced here. This text is very similar to the first part of the seminar "Technologies of the Self," given at the University of Vermont in October 1982.[5]

LECTURE II

- Typescript of the first version of the lecture in French (BnF NAF 28730, box 29, folder 2); omitted here, but reproduced in *Dire vrai sur soi-même*.
- Typescript of the first English translation, not by Foucault (BnF NAF 28730, box 29, folder 3), including many interpretive errors; omitted here.
- English typescript, modified and corrected by Foucault, supplemented with several manuscript pages (BnF NAF 28730, box 29, folders 3 and 6), reproduced here (manuscript incomplete). The text of this version is overall very similar to the first English translation,

though typed on a different machine, and including edits and corrections by Foucault.

• Audio recording of the English lecture. This audio recording, which partially overlaps with the second English version, has been transcribed and reproduced here. Notes have been added to mark variations from the English typescript, and verbal mistakes, filler words, discourse markers, and sentences that are incomplete because of the fragile nature of the recording have been either noted, edited, or removed for clarity and readability.

LECTURE III

• Typescript of the first version of the lecture in French (BnF NAF 28730, box 29, folder 8); omitted here but reproduced in *Dire vrai sur soi-même*.

• Typescript of the English translation (not by Foucault) of the French manuscript of the lecture (BnF NAF 28730, box 29, folder 8). This version was not presented at Toronto, but we chose to reproduce it here because of the many relevant differences with the version that Foucault actually presented.

• English lecture manuscript, including several typed pages (BnF NAF 28730, box 29, folder 7); reproduced here. It is this version that Foucault presented at Toronto.

LECTURE IV

• English lecture manuscript (BnF NAF 28730, box 29, folder 4); reproduced here (incomplete).

LECTURE V

• English lecture manuscript (BnF NAF 28730, box 29, folder 9); reproduced here (incomplete).

THE SEMINAR

• Audio recording held by the Victoria University library and IMEC.

THE EDITORS WOULD LIKE TO thank Clive Thompson, who co-organized the Third International Summer Institute for Semiotic and Structural Studies and assisted in Foucault's lectures. He has provided indispensable aid throughout this project, notably including the discovery of the audio recording of Lecture II. We would also like to express our gratitude to Alan O'Connor, who agreed to share the recording with us.

Finally, we wish to thank the Bibliothèque nationale de France, which allowed us to consult the documents within the Foucault archive from which this volume has been primarily reconstituted.

Henri-Paul Fruchaud & Daniele Lorenzini

ABBREVIATIONS OF WORKS BY MICHEL FOUCAULT

AB   *Abnormal: Lectures at the Collège de France, 1974–1975* (New York: Verso, 2003)

ABHS *About the Beginning of the Hermeneutics of the Self: Lectures at Dartmouth College, 1980*, ed. Henri-Paul Fruchaud and Daniele Lorenzini, trans. Graham Burchell (Chicago: University of Chicago Press, 2016)

AC   *Histoire de la sexualité*, vol. 4, *Les aveux de la chair* (Paris: Gallimard, 2018)

BC   *The Birth of the Clinic: An Archaeology of Medical Perception* (New York: Pantheon, 1973)

CCS   *Qu'est-ce que la critique?* suivi de *La culture de soi*, ed. Henri-Paul Fruchaud and Daniele Lorenzini (Paris: Vrin, 2015)

CS   *The History of Sexuality*, vol. 3, *The Care of the Self*, trans. Robert Hurley (New York: Pantheon, 1986)

CT   *The Courage of Truth: Lectures at the Collège de France, 1983–1984*, ed. Frédéric Gros, trans. Graham Burchell, English series ed. Arnold I. Davidson (New York: Palgrave Macmillan, 2011)

DE II *Dits et écrits II, 1976–1988*, ed. Daniel Defert and François Ewald, with the collaboration of Jacques Lagrange (Paris: Gallimard, 2001)

DP   *Discipline and Punish: The Birth of the Prison*, trans. Alan Sheridan (London: Allen Lane, 1977)

DT   *Discourse & Truth,* in *"Discourse and Truth" and "Parrēsia,"* ed. Henri-Paul Fruchaud and Daniele Lorenzini, English edition established by Nancy Luxon (Chicago: University of Chicago Press, 2019)

EW 1   *The Essential Works of Foucault, 1954–1984,* vol. 1, *Ethics, Subjectivity, and Truth,* ed. Paul Rabinow (New York: New Press, 1997)

EW 3   *The Essential Works of Foucault, 1954–1984,* vol. 3, *Power,* ed. James D. Faubion (New York: New Press, 2000)

GL   *On the Government of the Living: Lectures at the Collège de France, 1979–1980,* ed. Michel Senellart, trans. Graham Burchell, English series ed. Arnold I. Davidson (New York: Palgrave Macmillan, 2014)

GSO   *The Government of Self and Others: Lectures at the Collège de France, 1982–1983,* ed. Frédéric Gros, trans. Graham Burchell, English series ed. Arnold I. Davidson (New York: Palgrave Macmillan, 2010)

HIST   *The History of Sexuality,* vol. 1, *An Introduction,* trans. Robert Hurley (New York: Random House, 1978)

HM   *The History of Madness,* ed. Jean Khalfa, trans. Jonathan Murphy (New York: Routledge, 2006)

HS   *The Hermeneutics of the Subject: Lectures at the Collège de France, 1981–1982,* ed. Frédéric Gros, trans. Graham Burchell, English series ed. Arnold I. Davidson (New York: Palgrave Macmillan, 2005)

LWL   *Lectures on the Will to Know: Lectures at the Collège de France, 1970–1971,* ed. Arnold I. Davidson (New York: Palgrave Macmillan, 2013)

OT   *The Order of Things: An Archaeology of the Human Sciences* (New York: Vintage Books, 1994)

P   *Parrēsia,* in *"Discourse and Truth" and "Parrēsia,"* ed. Henri-Paul Fruchaud and Daniele Lorenzini, English edition established by Nancy Luxon (Chicago: University of Chicago Press, 2019)

PP   *Psychiatric Power: Lectures at the Collège de France, 1973–74,* ed. Jacques Lagrange, trans. Graham Burchell, English series ed. Arnold I. Davidson (New York: Palgrave Macmillan, 2006)

ST   *Subjectivity and Truth: Lectures at the Collège de France, 1980–1981,* ed. Frédéric Gros, trans. Graham Burchell, English series ed. Arnold I. Davidson (New York: Palgrave Macmillan, 2017)

STP *Security, Territory, Population: Lectures at the Collège de France, 1977–1978,* ed. Michel Senellart, trans. Graham Burchell, English series ed. Arnold I. Davidson (New York: Palgrave Macmillan, 2007)

UP *The History of Sexuality,* vol. 2, *The Use of Pleasure,* trans. Robert Hurley (New York: Pantheon, 1985)

WDTT *Wrong-Doing, Truth-Telling: The Function of Avowal in Justice,* ed. Fabienne Brion and Bernard E. Harcourt, trans. Stephen W. Sawyer (Chicago: University of Chicago Press, 2014)

LECTURE I

The Technology of the Self

I

ONE THING STRUCK ME WHEN I started studying the rules, duties, obligations, and prohibitions concerning sexuality in the Christian societies of the West: what strikes me is the fact that the interdictions against doing certain kind of things, the interdictions against
having such and such relations, had very constantly been associated
with certain obligations to speak, to tell the truth—more precisely
to tell the truth about oneself.

Better still: this obligation to tell the truth about oneself is concerned not simply with the acts (permitted or forbidden) which one
might have committed, but with feelings, with representations, with
thoughts, with desires that one might experience. This obligation
drives the individual to seek within himself any feeling which might
be hidden, any movement of the soul which might escape the perception, any desire which might be disguised under illusory forms.

I think that there is a very significative difference in our societies
between the interdictions concerning sexuality and other great systems of prohibition: the former—[the]* interdictions about sex—
have been coupled with the obligation to tell the truth, and with the
obligation to undertake a certain deciphering of oneself.

* Conjecture; manuscript illegible.

Of course I am very aware of two facts. One is that confession and avowal had played a very important role in penal and religious institutions: and not only for sexual faults, but for any kinds of sins, offenses, crimes. But it is obvious that the task of analyzing one's own thoughts or desires has always been more important in matters of sexual faults than for any other kind of sin (with an exception, maybe, for pride).

And I am also aware, on the other hand, that sexual behavior, more than any other kind of behavior, has been submitted to very strict rules of secrecy, decency, and modesty.

So that sexuality, in our society, is related, in a rather strange and complex way, both to verbal prohibitions and to truth obligations. Sexuality is related to the obligation to hide what one does and to the obligation to decipher what one is.[1]

This association of prohibitions concerning deeds and words and strong invitations to speak about sex is a constant feature of our culture.

We have to remember that psychoanalysis[2] was born in the middle of the Victorian Age. But we have also to remember the long history of the direction of conscience, cure of souls, and penitential practice, since the Middle Ages.[3] And even more we have to remember primitive Christianity, and the great ascetic movement of the fourth century which tied together the theme of renunciation of the flesh and the principle of deciphering more or less imperceptible movements of the soul.[4] And perhaps one finds already in Greco-Roman philosophy the main lines of the relationship between an interdiction on doing and an obligation of saying (of telling the truth about oneself).[5]

It is thus that I have conceived the perhaps rather odd project of studying not the evolution of sexual behavior (specialists in social history do this, and do it very well), but the history of the link between these interdictions and these obligations: how, in our societies, has the subject been led to decipher himself with regard to that which was forbidden?

You see that it is a question of coming back, with regard to a precise problem, to the very old question of the relations between asceticism and truth. But it seems to me that in the tradition of Max

Weber (such at least as some of his successors have understood him) the question was posed in the following manner: if one wants to behave rationally, to regulate one's action according to true principles, what should one forbid oneself? What part of oneself should one renounce? To what kind of asceticism should one submit? Briefly, what is the ascetic price of Reason?[6]

Now I should like to ask the opposite question: how have certain kinds of knowledge constituted the price to be paid in order to validate an interdiction? If one is to renounce such and such a thing, what must one know about oneself?

It is in asking this kind of question that I have been led to study the hermeneutic technology of the self in pagan and Christian antiquity. The hermeneutics of myths and legends was a common practice in ancient culture; the principles and methods of this hermeneutics have already often been studied. The hermeneutics of the self, on the contrary, is relatively less well known. There are several reasons for this. One is that Christianity has been more willing to interest itself in the history of its beliefs and institutions than in the history of its real practices. The second is that this practice of the hermeneutics of the self has never been organized into a body of doctrines, like textual hermeneutics (although it has been extremely precise in its practices). The third reason is that, too often, this hermeneutics of the self has been confused with philosophy, or with doctrines of the soul, of the Fall, of sin, of concupiscence. Finally it seems to me that this hermeneutics of the self has been diffused across Western culture through extremely numerous channels; little by little, it has been integrated with models of experience, types of attitudes proposed to individuals; to the point that it is often difficult to isolate it and to separate it from what we believe to be our spontaneous experience of ourselves. Our experience of ourselves seems to us, no doubt, to be that which is most original and immediate; but we have to remember that it has been constituted through historically formed practices. And what we believe we see so clearly in ourselves and with such transparency is in fact given to us via techniques of deciphering laboriously constructed in the course of history.

II

LET ME RECALL IN A few words the context in which I am studying the hermeneutics of the self.

My objective has been for a rather long time to sketch out a history of the different ways by which, in our culture, human beings developed knowledge about themselves. And this through several practices, like economics or grammatics,[7] like psychiatry or medicine,[8] like penal institutions.[9]

But the main point for me is not to value this knowledge, to recognize if it is a science or an ideology; it is not to show—which is [a] truism—that this kind of knowledge always has an economical importance and a political role.

My purpose is to analyze those so-called sciences, as very specific "truth-games" related to specific techniques that human beings use towards themselves.

It seems to me that one can distinguish in general four major types of technology. Those which permit one to produce, to transform, to manipulate things. Those which permit one to use sign systems. Those which permit us to determine the conduct of individuals, to impose certain wills on them and to submit them to certain ends or objectives. That is to say: technologies of production, technologies of meaning, technologies of domination.

But there are also, I believe, in all societies whatever they are, techniques which permit individuals to effect by their own means, and with the help of others (or under the direction of others), a certain number of operations on their own bodies, on their own souls, on their own thoughts, on their own conduct; and this, in a manner so as to transform themselves, to modify themselves and to attain a certain state of perfection, of happiness, of purity, of enlightenment; to become a sage, a sorcerer, to break through to the light, to immortality, to insensibility.[10]

These four great types of technology hardly ever function separately; there is no technology of production which can do without applying sign systems; one knows very well also that every technique of production is associated with specific processes of domination: a certain K. Marx, in the second book of *Capital*, has said on this subject things much more precise and interesting than the costly distinction between infra- and superstructure.

And one could add that every technology of production implies certain modes of training and modification of individuals, not only in the obvious sense that they must be made to acquire a certain skill, but in the sense that they must be made to acquire a certain attitude towards themselves and towards the environment, as well as towards other people.

One could take up each of these major matrices of practical reason—the technology of production, the technology of the sign, the technology of power, and the technology of the self—and show at the same time their specific nature and their constant interaction.

In order to situate my work with respect to this totality, I will say that above all it has been these last two technologies—that of domination and that of the self—which have kept my attention [and] occupied me. Most frequently when one studies the history of sciences, it is with reference to the first two technologies, be it the reference to the technologies of production (economic and social history of the sciences of matter, of life and of man) or be it the reference to the technologies of signs (analyses of symbols and formal structures of scientific discourse). I have tried, in order to balance the picture, to produce a history of knowledge and of organizations of knowledge which are tied to processes of domination and of technology of the self.

For example, with regard to madness I have not tried to measure psychiatric discourse by reference to criteria of formal sciences nor to explain its birth by reference to exploitation in industrial societies. But I have wanted to show how the type of management of individuals inside and outside the asylums had made possible this strange discourse so as to make comprehensible its economic meaning and its formal aberrations (which are only apparently absurd).[11]

But perhaps I had insisted too much on the technologies of power and domination. In any case, I have more and more been brought to interest myself in technologies of the self. More precisely in the points of interaction between the one and the other, where the tech-

nologies of the domination of individuals over one another have recourse to processes by which the individual acts upon himself. This
contact point where the way individuals are driven and the way they
conduct themselves are tied together is what one can call, I think,
"governmentality."[12]
My aim is to analyze the history of hermeneutics of the self in the
framework of this governmentality.

III

I SHOULD LIKE TO STUDY the development of the hermeneutics of the self successively in two contexts quite different from one
another, but nevertheless presenting a certain historical continuity.
It is a question first of all of Greco-Roman philosophy in the imperial period; and then of Christian spirituality in the period in which
monastic principles and institutions were developing.

But I do not want to study it only in its theoretical formulations,[13]
but in relation to a set of practices which had a great importance in
late antiquity—at least among the social groups who were the main
agents of culture at this moment.

These practices constituted what in Greek was called *epimeleia
heautou*, in Latin *cura sui*.[14] It is not very easy to translate these terms:
"the concern with oneself," in French "le souci de soi." The verbal
form *epimeleisthai heautō* means something like "to be concerned
with oneself, to take care of oneself," "s'occuper de soi-même."[15]
[...]*
I know very well that all that is nothing more than a point of departure. A point of departure for some possible analysis about the care
of the self throughout our culture. The aim of such studies would be
to analyze the relationships between the care of the self, in its different forms, and the different forms of the self-knowledge: these relationships are constitutive of our subjectivity.

For us now the notion is faded and obscure. To that extent that if

---

* Foucault removed a passage here and inserted it in the text later; see
infra, p. 9.

we are asked what was the most important moral principle and the most characteristic in ancient philosophy, the answer which comes immediately to mind is not *epimele seautō*, but *gnōthi seauton*, the Delphic precept "know thyself." Perhaps our philosophical and historical tradition has somewhat overrated the importance of the *gnōthi seauton*. [Now, it must be remembered that before being a philosophical principle, the Apollinian precept was technical advice, a rule to be observed for the consultation of the oracle: something like, according to some commentator (Defradas): do not suppose yourself to be a god;[16] or according to other commentators: be aware of what you really ask to the oracle.[17]]* But one must remember that the rule of having to know oneself was constantly associated with that of concerning oneself with oneself.

And more than that: to know oneself was considered a means for taking care of oneself.

This association is explicit in the Socratic dialogues of Plato, in the *Memorabilia* of Xenophon;[18] it is explicit also in Epictetus, and all along through the Neoplatonic tradition from Albinus in the second century to Proclus. And this association, for the most part, was a subordination: it was because one had to be concerned with oneself, it was because one had to occupy oneself with oneself that the Delphic principle *gnōthi seauton* was brought into action.

And this for almost a thousand years of ancient culture. Let us look at some marking points of this long period.

First, Socrates himself. In the *Apology*, we see him present himself before his judges as the master of the concern with oneself. It is he who addresses passers-by and tells them: you concern yourselves with your riches, your reputation, and your honors; but you do not concern yourselves with your virtue or with your soul. It is Socrates who watches over his fellow citizens to make sure that they take care [of] themselves. Now, with regard to this role, a little further on Socrates says, in the same *Apology*, three important things: this role is a mission which has been conferred on him by the god, and which he

---

* The passage in brackets appears in the French manuscript but seems to have been crossed out in the English version, though it is not clear.

will not abandon except with his last breath; it is also a disinterested task, for which he demands no reward, he accomplishes it out of pure benevolence; finally it is a useful function for the city, more useful even than an athlete's victory at Olympia, for in teaching people to occupy themselves with themselves (rather than with their possessions) one teaches them also to occupy themselves with the city itself (rather than with its material affairs). Instead of condemning him, his judges would do better to reward him for having taught others to concern themselves with themselves.[19]

Eight centuries later, the same notion of *epimeleia heautou* appears with a role equally as important with Gregory of Nyssa, but with a deeply different meaning. By this term, he does not mean the movement by which one takes care of oneself and of the [city]*, he means the movement by which one renounces marriage, detaches oneself from the flesh, and by which, thanks to a virginity of heart and body, one recovers the immortality of which one had been deprived.[20] In another passage of the *Treatise on Virginity*, Gregory makes the parable of the lost drachma the model of concern with oneself.[21] You will remember the verses from Saint Luke's Gospel: for a lost drachma, you must light a lamp, turn the whole house over, search in every corner, until, gleaming in the shadows, one sees the coin's metal.[22] In the same way, in order to recover the effigy which God has printed in our soul, and which the body has tarnished, one must take care of oneself, light the lamp of Reason, and search every corner of the soul. We can see clearly that Christian asceticism, like ancient philosophy, places itself under the sign of concern with oneself and makes the obligation to know oneself one of the elements of this essential preoccupation.

Between these two extreme points of reference—Socrates and Gregory of Nyssa—one can state that the concern with oneself constituted not only a principle, but also a constant practice. I am going to take two other examples, very removed from one another in their mode of thought and type of moralizing. An Epicurean text which was to serve as a manual of morals, the *Letter to Menoeceus*, begins thus: "It is never too early or too late to occupy oneself with one's soul.

* Conjecture; manuscript illegible.

One should therefore philosophize when one is young and philosophize when one is old."²³ Philosophy is here assimilated to the care of the soul (the term is even very precisely medical: *hugiainein*), and this care is a task which must be carried on throughout one's life.

[And although we know very few things about the Epicurean circles of the Hellenistic period or of the late republican period in Italy, the information we can get through Philodemus²⁴ shows very clearly that in those circles teaching and everyday life were organized in order to incite everyone to take care of oneself. The entire community—teachers and fellows—had as an objective to help every member of the group in this task of *epimeleisthai heautō, to di' allēlōn sōzesthai,* the mutual salvation.]*

In the *Treatise on the Contemplative Life,*²⁵ we know that Philo describes a group about which we have no other information than the very succinct information which he gives himself; Philo calls them the "Therapeutes." It is a question, in any case, of a group very marked by religiosity and which is in the confines of Hellenistic and Hebraic culture; these people lived in austere retreat, not very far from Alexandria, gave themselves over to reading, to meditation, to individual and collective prayer; they met at regular intervals for a kind of spiritual banquet. All this stemmed from a principal task, which was, according to the text, the *epimeleia heautou,* the concern with oneself.†

[We cannot simply rest here, however. It would be an error to believe that the care of the self was an invention of philosophical thought, or that it constitutes a precept particular to the philosophical life. It was in fact a general precept of life that was very highly valorized in Greece. Plutarch thus cites an Lacedaemonian aphorism which, from this point of view, is very significant. One day, Alexandrides was asked why his compatriots, the Spartiates, entrust

---

* The passage in brackets denotes the text that Foucault removed from an earlier part of the lecture and included here; see *supra,* p. 6.

† The following several pages, from this point until the end of section 3, are missing from the English manuscript. The text has been supplemented with a translation of the corresponding material from the French version, in brackets.—DLW (Daniel Louis Wyche).

the cultivation of their lands to slaves, rather than performing this work themselves. The response was "Because we prefer to occupy ourselves with ourselves."[26] To occupy oneself with oneself is a privilege. It is the mark of a social superiority, in opposition to those who must occupy themselves with others in order to serve them, or who must still occupy themselves with a trade or craft in order to live. The advantages of riches, status, and high birth result in the fact that one has the opportunity to occupy oneself with oneself.

It can be noted that the Roman conception of *otium* is very similar: the "leisure" designated by it is the time that one passes in occupying oneself with oneself *par excellence*. In this sense, philosophy, in Greece as in Rome, simply transposed a widespread social ideal into the interior of its own exigences. We can also see how philosophy, in representing itself as the art of occupying oneself with oneself, could be at once an aristocratic activity (as in Platonism) *and* the democratization of an aristocratic ideal (as among the Epicureans and later in Stoicism).

But in making such an important place for the care of the self, philosophy did not simply interiorize and transform a traditional social ideal. It also seems to have inherited very specific practices from "foreign" milieux. I am thinking here of the hypothesis of E. R. Dodds, taken up in France by J.-P. Vernant. According to this argument, around the seventh century, the Greeks first came into contact with the civilizations of eastern Europe, and from them inherited some of the diverse practices that can be found within shamanistic cultures.[27]

These practices, which underwent numerous transformations, became very important for the history of the relations that we are undertaking here. They constitute what might be called an archeology of philosophy. In a very schematic fashion, we can describe them in the following way. They include exercises of abstention—alimentary abstention and sexual abstinence, which at once aimed to insure a purification of the body *and* a perfect mastery of that same body. They also include exercises of endurance, by which one trains the body in insensitivity, which diminishes its dependence on the view of the exterior world, and permits a concentration of thought and attention to interior objects. To these we must also add practices of the retention of breath and of apparent death intended to allow the individual to escape death and put them in contact with divine powers. And yet it is not difficult to encounter these practices within a philosophy that, we must always remember, had been an activity and form of life in antiquity. It is in this way that we again find the rules of abstinence and austerity capable of purifying the soul and rendering it capable of contemplating the truth. We again see the rules of concentration and thought which permit one to detach oneself from the exterior and fix one's gaze on more interior, or more elevated, realities. And finally, we once more find the famous *meletē thanatou*, which has been translated, for better or worse, as the "meditation on death." But it is in fact a real exercise of death, by which one tries to actualize death in oneself in order to place oneself in communication with the immortality of the gods.

Consider Socrates, as he appeared in certain dialogues of Plato. He was one of those people who, through work exercised upon themselves, had acquired a power that was more than human. It was Socrates who endured the cold at the battle of [Potidaea];[28] it was Socrates who could resist the beauty of Alcibiades;[29] it was Socrates who, on the way to the banquet, remained unmoving, insensible to all that was occurring around him.[30] But it is also Socrates who recommends to everyone that they occupy themselves with themselves through a form of practice that will become that of philosophy. In the transformation of these ancient techniques of the self into the form of philosophical vigilance towards oneself, Socrates (with the Pythagoreans, incidentally) represents an important moment.

In any case, even having become a philosophical principle, the care of the self remains a form of activity. The very term *epimeleia* does not simply refer to an attitude of conscience or a form of attention that one could focus on oneself. Rather, it designates a regulated occupation, a work which has its processes and its objectives. Xenophon, for example, employs the word *epimeleia* to describe the work of the master of the house who directs his agricultural cultivation.[31]

The activity of the sovereign who watches over the people and leads the city is also called *epimeleia*. We must therefore understand that when philosophers and moralists recommend that one take care of oneself (*epimeleisthai heautou*), that they are not simply counseling that we pay attention to ourselves, or to avoid faults or dangers, or to take refuge from the world. We can say that across philosophical antiquity, the care of the self was at once considered a duty and a technique, a fundamental obligation and a carefully elaborated ensemble of behaviors.

It is on the foundation of this ethic and this technology of the self that I try to describe the development of the hermeneutics of the subject in antiquity. In a previous work, I tried to analyze the constitution of a psychopathological knowledge on the basis of practices and institutions of internment;[32] I have also attempted to understand the formation of a criminal anthropology, beginning with punitive practices and legal punishment.[33] In the same way, I would like to understand the formation of a hermeneutics of oneself, and more precisely the formation of a hermeneutics of sexual desire and concupiscence on the basis of this technology of oneself.

In the next meeting, I will try to bring to light several of the fundamental traits of this technology of the self during a period which could be considered a veritable golden age in its history: the first two centuries of the Common Era, the era of the High Empire. Following that, I will describe the forms of knowledge and interpretation that emerged within the culture of the self during this same period. In the fourth and fifth lectures, I will return to these two questions]* — the technology and the analysis of the self—within the framework of Christian asceticism in the fourth and fifth centuries of our era. In the last lecture I shall indicate some marking points for a possible history of the hermeneutics of the self in Western culture.†

---

* As noted above, the passages in brackets are missing from the English manuscript and have been translated from the French version.—DLW.

† As noted in the introduction to this volume, this passage indicates that Foucault intended to give six lectures, though records exist for only five.

IV

BUT BEFORE CONCLUDING, I SHOULD like to ask a legitimate question. If it is true, as I have just said, that the concern with oneself, and all the techniques which have been tied up with it, had such importance in classical culture, how is it that this theme has disappeared? How is it that, not only it is no longer actual, but that one has even tended to forget its historical importance? How is it, to express things very simply, that one has preserved the memory of the *gnōthi seauton*, as one of the highest expressions of ancient thought and culture, while one has forgotten the importance which was for a long time given to the twin principle: *epimele seautō*?[34]

It seems to me that one can give several reasons.

1. First, a very profound transformation in moral principles in Western societies. It seems very difficult for us *now* to base a rigorous morality, austere and demanding, on the principle that we should give ourselves more importance than anything else in the world. We are rather more inclined to recognize in this the basis of an immorality which permits the individual to escape from all rules and to set himself up as the criterion for the validity of all possible rules. We are the inheritors of a Christian morality which, paradoxically, makes self-renunciation the condition for salvation. Equally we are the inheritors of an ethic (partly Christian, partly secular) which considers respect for the law to be the general form of moral conduct. Finally, we are the inheritors also of a social morality which seeks the rule for acceptable behavior in the relationship with others. Such traditions of thought scarcely seem able to accept the concern with oneself as the foundation of morality. It is a fact, since the sixteenth century, that the critique of established morality has been undertaken precisely in the name of the importance to be recognized of the self. The self is always that which one can object to ascetic renunciations, to the universality of the law, to the obligations which bind us to others.

2. In theoretical philosophy, knowledge of the self has taken on an ever-increasing importance. From Descartes to Husserl the principle of knowing oneself has appeared as the first principle of a theory of

knowledge. No knowledge can be considered well founded if it has not previously taken into consideration the thinking subject: be it that one demands from him the criterion for intuitive evidence, be it that, from this standpoint, one tries to establish the limits of possible knowledge. So, briefly, it can be said that there has been an inversion of hierarchy between the two principles that antiquity had associated: the concern with oneself and the knowledge of oneself. While in ancient thought the second most often appeared as the consequence of the first, it is clear that, in modern philosophy, it is the knowledge of oneself which constitutes the fundamental principle.

3. One must add to this the human sciences, which have sought to give to all preoccupation with human beings the general form of knowledge. No doubt, these human sciences are, for the most part, very distant in their form and objective from the Socratic *gnōthi seauton* or from the knowledge of the self as one finds it in the philosophers. But they translate none the less, in their own fashion, one of the most fundamental and constant features of Western culture: namely, they suppose that the relationship with the self is and ought to be essentially a relationship of knowledge.

One more thing: no doubt, one sees, since the nineteenth century, the signs of a new development of the culture of the self; one could follow this movement across diverse phenomena, more often aesthetic than political. But it is to be noted that even when it has taken the form of revolt and struggle against established morality, it has as its goal the liberation of the self. But maybe the self has to be considered not as a reality which has to be liberated or excavated; but the self has to be considered as the correlate of technologies built and developed throughout our history. Then the problem is not to liberate the self, but those technologies, that means, the self.[35]

LECTURE II

(*Second English Version*)[1]

I

THE FIRST PHILOSOPHICAL ELABORATION OF the principle "you must concern yourself *with* yourself" is to be found in Plato's *Alcibiades*.[2]

As you know, commentators hesitate in proposing a date for this dialogue. Some are in favor of supposing that the text dates from Plato's youth: the characters would suggest this, and also the type of interrogation, the slowness of the dialogue, and many of the themes which are touched upon. Others would suggest a rather late date, particularly because of the extremely "metaphysical" conclusion to the discourse concerning the contemplation of oneself in the divine essence. Let us put aside this debate, which I am not competent to discuss.

Let us simply keep in mind the solution suggested by the Neoplatonists. This solution is interesting insofar as it shows clearly the sense which was given, in the classical tradition, to this dialogue, and the importance assumed by the theme of "concerning yourself with yourself" as a primary consideration.

As you know, one of the targets of the Neoplatonist school, in the first centuries of our era, was to organize Plato's writings both as a *cursus* for studies (following a pedagogical model) and as a matrix for an encyclopedic knowledge. From these two points of view, the *Alcibiades* was considered as *the* first dialogue:

—the first to be read by students,

—the first to be explained by commentators.

A second-century author, Albinus, said that every "naturally gifted man" who has reached the age for "philosophizing" and who wanted to stand apart from the perturbations of politics and practice virtue should begin by studying the *Alcibiades*. Later, Proclus said that this text should be considered as *archē apasēs philosophias*, the principle and point of departure for all philosophy. Olympiodorus, comparing the ensemble of Platonic thought to a sacred arena, made of the Alcibiades the *propylaea* of the temple of which the *aduton*, the central and sacred part, would be the *Parmenides*.[3]

It is not my intention to study the details of this text. I would like simply to point out some principal features of this notion of *epimeleia heautou* which constitutes its center.

1. HOW IS THE QUESTION INTRODUCED into the dialogue? It is brought in by the project of Alcibiades to begin his public life; more precisely to "speak before the people," to be better than Pericles as a political figure and to become all-powerful in the city.

At the moment at which Socrates comes across Alcibiades and declares his love for him, the latter is at a point of transition. This point of transition is something common to every young aristocratic Athenian. It is the moment where he starts taking part in the political life with his peers, his equals. It is also the moment where he cannot be an *eromenos* anymore, and he has to become an *erastēs*, a lover; he has to become active in the love game.

Alcibiades is at this well-known transition point both in the political and in the erotic life. But the way he goes through this transition point is different from the others. Alcibiades wishes to bring the political transition about in a very special way: he does not want to be satisfied with the privileges given to him by his birth, fortune, and status; he says specifically that he does not want to "spend his life" profiting from all this with his equals and at the same level as his [peers].* He wishes to gain the advantage over all the others inside the city, and outside also over the kings of Sparta and over the Persian sovereign; those are for him not simply the enemies of his country but also his personal rivals.

From the erotic point of view also, Alcibiades is at a transitional point: during his adolescence he was desirable and had a crowd of followers; now he has arrived at the age when his beard is growing and his lovers wish to separate themselves from him. But, [unlike] the others, when he was still in the full bloom of his beauty, he had rejected all those who paid court to him, not wishing to give in to them, wishing to remain "dominant" (*kreittōn*). The ambivalence between the political and erotic vocabulary, which is constant in Greek, here becomes essential. And now Socrates presents himself. And, without being interested in Alcibiades' body, he succeeds where all others have failed; he is going to show Alcibiades that he is stronger than him; he is going to make him submit, but in a completely different sense. That's the point: in order to become the first in the political life, he has to submit to a lover, but not in the physical meaning of the word.

It is at the point of intersection of the young man's very particular political ambition (a personal ambition) and of the master's very particular love (a philosophical love) that the question of concerning oneself with oneself is to appear.

2. WHY SHOULD ALCIBIADES CONCERN HIMSELF with himself?

Socrates asks Alcibiades what his ambition consists in. Or rather what he considers to be his personal capacities. Does he know what it is to govern well? Does he know what the word "justice" means? Or "concord" within the city? Of all this he knows nothing and finds himself incapable of replying. Socrates, then, invites Alcibiades to compare himself with his rivals outside the city. The Spartan kings receive a very formal education which teaches them the indispens-

* Conjecture; manuscript illegible.

able virtues. And insofar as the Persian king is concerned, from the age of fourteen he is given over to four instructors, who teach him, the first wisdom (*sophia*), the second justice (*dikaiosunē*), the third temperance (*sōphrosunē*), and the last courage (*andreia*). And Alcibiades, what education has he received? He has been given over to an old slave, completely ignorant, and his tutor Pericles has not even been able to bring up his own sons properly!

So in order to gain the upper hand over his rivals, Alcibiades should acquire a *technē*, a know-how; he must apply himself to this— *epimeleisthai*. But, as we have seen, he does not even know what he should apply himself to, because he has no knowledge at all about justice, concord, right government. Alcibiades is consequently in the greatest embarrassment. He despairs. But Socrates intervenes and tells him this important thing: if you were fifty years old the situation would be serious; then it would be too late to *epimeleisthai seautō*. Here is the first time this expression appears in the text. It is highly significant that the principle of having to concern oneself with oneself is directly related to a defective pedagogy and to a precise moment in life. Just at the moment when the youth is to start with political life.

3. ALL THE LAST PAGES OF the dialogue are devoted to the answer to the third question: What [does] this "concern with oneself" consist in? More precisely there are two problems: What is this "self" one has to take care of? What [does] this care consist in?

I will quickly run over the long discussion which offers an answer to the first question. The self which is in question does not, obviously, consist in the things which we can own, such as our possessions, our clothing, our tools; nor does it consist in our body, which is an occupation for the doctor or the teacher of gymnastics. We should occupy ourselves with that which is able to use our belongings, our tools, our body: that means our soul, in fact.[4]

But in order to occupy yourself with your own soul you must know what this soul consists in. And in order for your soul to know itself, it is necessary for it to look in a mirror which has the same constitution *as* itself, that is to say that it has to look in the divine element. And it is in this contemplation that the soul will be able, while occupying itself with itself, to discover the principles and essences on which just action can be founded and which will establish the rules for political action.

There are several reasons why this passage deserves to be noticed. Firstly because it bears all the signs of late Platonism. But above all, for another reason which I should like us to keep in mind: that concern with oneself is in some way absorbed into knowledge of oneself. For the whole length of the dialogue the principle of concern with oneself, which was the main theme of the discussion, has gravitated around the Delphic principle of having to know oneself. Several times, directly or indirectly, the *gnōthi seauton* has been mentioned alongside the *epimele seautō*. But it is clear at the end of the dialogue that it is the "know thyself" which occupies the whole field opened up by the principle that you must concern yourself with yourself. For Plato, at least in the *Alcibiades*, the concern with oneself consists in knowing oneself.

I have spent some time over this text whereas most of the documents which I shall subsequently study are much more later in date. I have done so because this [dialogue] seems to bring out very clearly several of the fundamental problems in the history of being occupied with oneself; the solutions will often be very different from those given in the *Alcibiades*, but the problems will remain:

1. The problem of the relationship between being occupied with oneself and political activity. Socrates asked Alcibiades to concern himself with himself insofar as he claimed to be concerned with others and to direct them. Later, and particularly under the empire, the question is more inclined to present itself in the form of an alternative: would it not be better to turn away from political activity in order to concern oneself with oneself?

2. The problem of the relationship between being occupied with oneself and pedagogy. In Socrates' proposal, being occupied with oneself is presented as the duty of a very young man whose education is insufficient. Later, being concerned with oneself will be presented as the duty of an adult—a duty to be followed through for the whole of one's life.

3. The problem of the relationship between concern with oneself and knowledge of oneself. We have seen the privileged position accorded by Plato's Socrates to the *gnōthi seauton*, and this privileged position will be one of the characteristic features of all the Platonic movements. In the contrary, it would seem that concern with oneself in Hellenistic and Greco-Roman philosophy assumed a certain autonomy, perhaps even a certain privileged status with respect to self-knowledge. In any case it often happens that the philosophical accent is put on the concern with oneself—self-knowledge being consequently only an instrument, a method for concerning oneself correctly with oneself.

II

LET US NOW TURN TO the first two centuries of the empire; more precisely from the Augustan dynasty to the end of the Antonines. These 150 or 200 years constitute, as is well known, one of the strongest periods of ancient civilization. They also mark a privileged moment, a kind of golden age in the practice and theory of the concern with oneself.[5]

From this point of view Epictetus is significant. [...]* [He is a Socratic *persona*, who wishes to follow the lessons and methods of Socrates. And it is to be noted that the Socrates he evokes in the *Discourses* (*Diatribai*) is above all the master of this concern with oneself, who calls upon his fellow citizens, from the street corners, to tell them that they must be occupied with themselves.[6] But more generally, Epictetus makes the concern with oneself the distinguishing mark of the human being, that which indicates his superiority and offers him a task. Nature, he explains in the ... *Discourses*,[7] has provided the animals with everything that they need, so much so that they do not need to occupy themselves with themselves. Is this to say that humans do so insofar as Nature has neglected them and deprived them of that which is necessary? No. To have to be occupied with oneself is to be

---

* Foucault inserted additional text here in a manuscript page that has been lost.

understood as a supplementary gift which has been bestowed: Zeus has confided us to ourselves, thus giving us the possibility and the duty to be free. Epictetus often insists on the necessity of knowing oneself. But the change of perspective from the *Alcibiades* is noticeable. It is rather in the concern with oneself than in the possibility of looking at oneself in the mirror of oneself that the being proper to man is manifested, and his relation to the divine.]*

Today I don't want to remain with these [early]† theoretical references. In the early imperial period at which Epictetus invokes Socrates, the theme of vigilance over oneself had taken on a considerable amplitude. A long development had prepared this apogee. The first and second centuries are not a point of departure, rather a long-term development.

Amongst those philosophers who claimed to be advisers on life and guides on existence, the principle of "occupying oneself with oneself" was almost universally accepted. Following their master, the Epicureans repeat that it is never too early or too late to occupy oneself with one's soul.[8] Amongst the Stoics, Musonius Rufus says: "It is in constantly paying attention to oneself that one assures one's salvation";[9] or Seneca: "You must attend to your soul, attend to yourself, lose no time in doing so"; "Retire into yourself and stay there."[10] Plutarch recommends introspection and "bringing to bear upon yourself all the attention of which you are capable." Dio Chrysostom gives one lecture over to the *anachōrēsis*, the retreat into oneself.[11] And Galen, recalling how much time is necessary to train a doctor, an orator, or a grammatician, thinks that even more time is necessary to become a good man: years and years, he says, spent in occupying yourself with yourself.[12]

But this was not simply a piece of abstract advice given by a few philosophers and technicians of the body and soul. Occupying yourself with yourself was an extremely widespread activity [in cultivated

---

* This passage was partially crossed out by Foucault. It is likely that the missing text noted above was meant to replace it. In the absence of the missing material, we have conserved this passage.

† Conjecture; manuscript illegible.

circles, but, no doubt, even more widespread if one thinks]* of the fairly popular recruitment of certain Epicurean groups, or of those who listened in the streets to the Cynics. Certain well-established supports reinforced this zeal concerning oneself: schools, private or public teaching establishments, lectures, more or less closed discussions amongst disciples. Vigilance concerning oneself is to be found in extremely structured groups and takes the form of an ordered life in common: such as with the Pythagoreans, or, to take an example at once famous and obscure, on the frontiers of Greco-Roman culture, the "Therapeutae" described by Philo of Alexandria;[13] but there were also much more flexible groups who met around a guide or simply a type of philosophy, a *forma vitae*. One went to certain masters for a visit or a course; there were also the masters who came to you and took up residence: the Roman aristocracy loved these counselors on life. Certain of these activities were paid, others free, but all of them presupposed a network of obligations and service. All this activity brought about considerable competition: between those who held fast to a rhetorical teaching and those who preferred to turn souls towards a concern with themselves; amongst the latter, the different schools confronted one another, despite objectives and procedures which were often very close to one another; finally there were those who simply contended with one another for clients. Lucian, who didn't particularly like philosophers, presents a picture of this practice which is scarcely flattering.[14] The dialogue *Hermotimus* presents one of these persons converted to the concern with himself and who prides himself, in speaking to a friend whom he meets, on the fact that he has had the same master for twenty years; it has ruined him but given him the hope that he may arrive at happiness in the next twenty years.[15]

But not everything was pretense and charlatanism in these practices from which certain people certainly profited. Certain individuals sincerely applied themselves to a personal act of concerning oneself with oneself. It was a good idea to set aside at least a few moments

---

* We have reestablished the passage in brackets, which seems to have been mistakenly omitted, from the first English translation of Lecture II, where it does appear.

every day; one might even consecrate a certain period of time, several weeks or months: this is what Pliny advises a friend, and he himself liked to practice these country retreats, which were also retreats into himself. And if such leisure time could be described as *scholē* or *otium*, nevertheless it must be borne in mind that this was an active leisure, a time of study: reading, conversation, diverse activities of meditation and preparation for misfortune or death, which implied a certain abstinence. Writing also played an important role; occupying oneself with oneself also implied taking notes about what one has read or listened to; one collated what the Greeks called *hupomnēmata*, notebooks which offered the possibility of being read again and committed to memory. One wrote treatises for friends, corresponded with them, which was a way of helping them in their own undertakings, but also a way of reactivating for oneself the truths one needed.[16]

The importance of writing is one of the main features of this culture of the self. As you know, reading and writing were widespread in Greek and Roman society. But in the political life, the oral culture was largely dominant. It is a fact that the development of administrative structures and bureaucracy increased the role of writing in the imperial government. But we must keep in mind that very early in the government of the self the role of writing has been determinant. The self as something which one had to take care of was a theme of a constant writing activity.

Subjectivity as a theme of writing activity is not a modern discovery: neither a discovery due to Romanticism, nor an innovation of [the] Reformation. It is one of the most ancient traditions of the West. And this tradition was well established and deeply rooted when Augustine started with his *Confessions*.

At the same time as these practices spread, it would seem that the experience of oneself was, by virtue of this very fact, intensified and widened. This introspection becomes more attentive and more detailed. The letters of Seneca[17] and Pliny,[18] the correspondence between Marcus Aurelius and Fronto,[19] show this vigilance and this*

---

* The page on which this material would have appeared in the second English version has been lost, and we have thus reestablished the text from the corresponding passage in the first English manuscript.

meticulousness with regard to the attention which one should pay to oneself. It often concerns the details of daily life, nuances of health and mood, the small physical malaises that one experiences, the movements of the spirit, one's reading, quotations that one remembers, reflections on such and such an event. A certain way of relating to oneself and a whole field of experience are to be seen where in earlier documents they are absent.

From this point of view, the *Sacred Discourses* of Aelius Aristides[20] constitute a remarkable witness. These texts are expressions of gratitude towards Asclepius, the god of health,* hence they are to be associated with the traditional genre of steles which speak of a healing or an act of gratitude. But while this traditional framework is maintained, Aelius unfolds an account seething with illnesses, malaises, sufferings, diverse feelings, premonitory dreams or those which offer advice, medicines tried out, and improvements sometimes obtained. Are the limits of the principal hypochondriacal symptoms reached? It's certain. But the problem is not to know to what point Aelius was ill. Rather what is important is to recognize the means which the culture of his time gave him in order to formulate his personal experience of this illness and to transmit it to others.

FORGIVE ME FOR PASSING OVER this so quickly. I wanted to suggest that the theme of concerning oneself with oneself at this period, that of the High Empire, is not to be found within any one particular philosophical doctrine. If it is not a universal precept at least it is extremely common. Many individuals respond to its call; it is a practice which has its institutions, its rules, its methods, and also a mode of experience—individual experience but also collective experience with its means and its forms of expression.

To resume: occupying yourself with yourself is confirmed in its recognized validity, it is formalized in ordered practices, it opens up a field of experience and of expression. One may legitimately speak of a "culture of the self."[21]

---

* The typescript mistakenly records "the god of war" here.

Next Tuesday I shall try to show the place which the principle of *gnōthi seauton* occupies in this culture of the self; I shall try to analyze the forms of knowledge of the self, of the deciphering of oneself, the examination of oneself which is developed at this period and within the framework of this culture.

Today I should like simply to point out the great differences between this concern with oneself as it is formulated in the *Alcibiades* and the practices used in the first and second centuries of our era.

III

1. SOCRATES, YOU WILL REMEMBER, RECOMMENDED to Alcibiades to profit from his youth and occupy himself with himself: at fifty it would be too late. Epicurus on the contrary said: "When you are young you must not hesitate in philosophizing, and when you are old, you must not hesitate in philosophizing. It is never too early or too late to concern yourself with your soul (*pros to kata psuchēn hugiainon*)."[22] It is this principle of perpetual attention to oneself, throughout one's life, which very clearly gains the upper hand. Musonius Rufus, for example, says: "You must take care of yourself without ceasing if you are to lead a life conducive to well-being."[23] Or Galen: "In order to become an accomplished man, each one needs, so to speak, to exert himself all his life," even if it is true that it would be better "to have kept watch over one's soul since one's earliest age."[24]

It is a fact that the friends to whom Seneca or Plutarch give advice are no longer the ambitious and desirable adolescents whom Socrates addressed himself to: they are men, sometimes young (like Serenus),[25] sometimes fully mature (like Lucilius, who had the important position of procurator in Sicily when he and Seneca exchanged a long spiritual correspondence).[26] Epictetus keeps a school for young pupils, but sometimes he has occasion to speak with adults and even "consular figures"—to remind them of their task of occupying themselves with themselves. When Marcus Aurelius brings together his notes, he is exercising the function of emperor, and for him it is a question of "coming to his own aid."[27]

Being occupied with oneself is not therefore a simple momentary preparation for life, it is a life form. Alcibiades realized that he should occupy himself with himself insofar as he wanted consequently to occupy himself with others. Now it is a question of occupying yourself with yourself and *for* yourself.

It is from this fact that the idea of changing one's attitude towards oneself (*ad se convertere*) comes, the idea of a movement in one's existence by which one turns back on oneself (*eis heauton epistrophein*).[28] You will tell me that the *epistrophē* is a typically Platonic theme. But, as [it] has already been seen in the *Alcibiades*, the movement by which the soul turns towards itself is also, following the Platonic doctrine, a movement by which its gaze is attracted towards "that which is on high"—towards the divine element, towards the essences and the supercelestial world where the latter are visible. The turning back to which one is invited by Seneca, Plutarch, and Epictetus is quite different: it is a kind of turning round on the spot, it has no other end or conclusion than "taking up residence in oneself" and staying there. The final objective of the conversion to oneself is the establishing of a certain number of relations with oneself:

—Sometimes these relations are conceived of according to a juridico-political model: being sovereign over oneself, exercising complete mastery over oneself, being fully independent, being completely one's own (*fieri suum*, Seneca often says).[29]

—They are also often represented according to the model of enjoyment of possessions: (literally) to "enjoy oneself," take pleasure in oneself, find the satisfaction of one's desires in oneself.

2. A SECOND BIG DIFFERENCE IS concerned with pedagogy. In the *Alcibiades*, the concern with oneself was necessary because of faults in pedagogy, complementing teaching or substituting itself for it; a question in any case of offering a "training."

From the moment when concern with oneself has become an adult practice which one must undertake all along one's life, its pedagogical role tends to be effaced, and other functions present themselves.[30]

a. Firstly, a critical function. The cultivation of the self should permit one to get rid of all bad habits, all false opinions derived from the crowd, bad masters, but also relatives and entourage. To "un-learn" (*de-discere*) is one of the important tasks of the development of oneself.

b. But it also has the function of a struggle. The practice of oneself is conceived as a permanent fight. It is not simply a question of train-ing a man of valor for the future. One most give to the individual the arms and the courage which will permit him to fight all his life. You are aware no doubt of the frequency of these two metaphors: that of the athletic contest (in life one is like a wrestler who must free himself from successive adversaries and who must keep in training even when he is not in combat) and that of war (the [soul]* must be organized like an army which may at any moment be assailed by an enemy).

The great Christian theme of the spiritual combat of the soul is already a fundamental principle of the cultivation of the self in an-cient pagan times.

c. But above all this cultivation of the self has a curative and ther-apeutic function. It is much nearer to the medical model than the pedagogical one. One must of course remember some extremely an-cient facts about Greek culture: the existence of a notion such as that of *pathos*, which signifies a passion of the soul as well as an illness of the body; the breadth of a metaphorical field which permits the ap-plication to the body and the soul of expressions such as cure, look after, amputate, scarify, purge. One must remember also the principle familiar to the Epicureans, the Cynics, and the Stoics, that the role of philosophy is to heal the maladies of the soul. Plutarch could say one day that philosophy and medicine constitute *mia chōra*, a single area, "a single field."[31]

But I would also wish to insist on the practical correlations be-tween medicine and the cultivation of the self. Epictetus did not want his school to be considered simply as a training place, but rather as a doctor's consulting room, an *iatreion*; he wanted it to be a dispen-sary for the soul. He wanted his pupils to [become] conscious of the fact that they were ill: "One of them," he said, "with a shoulder out of joint, a second with an abscess, a third with a fistula, another with

---

* Manuscript illegible; corrected to conform with the French version.

a headache."[32] "You wish to learn syllogisms? Then first cure your wounds, stop the flow of your humors, calm your spirits."[33]

Inversely, a doctor such as Galen considers it to be within his competence to heal the soul from the passions, that is to say, from "disordered energies, rebels to reason," but also "the errors which are born of false opinions." In the treatise *On the Passions and Errors of the Soul*, he quotes cures he has undertaken and been successful in: he has cured one of his companions inclined to anger, he has helped a young man whose soul was troubled by events of little importance.[34]

[All these ideas may appear very familiar; and in fact they are, since they have been constantly transmitted in Western culture. All the more reason for giving them an historical importance. In effect it is important for the history of subjectivity in the West that the relation to oneself should have become a permanent task in existence, for on this point Christianity has not rejected the lessons of the pagan philosophers. Equally it is important to see that this relation with the self has been defined as a critique, relation of combat, and medical practice: here also the West has not renounced the forms of the old cultivation of the self.]*

3. [FINALLY,] I SHOULD LIKE TO quickly indicate the third great difference between the occupation with oneself in the *Alcibiades* and the practice of the self in the culture of the imperial period. In Plato's dialogue, the erotico-philosophical relationship with the master was

---

* Foucault crossed out this paragraph in the manuscript, but we have maintained it because the text with which he replaced it has not been preserved. It is possible that the missing text is similar to what Foucault says in his lectures on the culture of the self at Berkeley: "All those ideas may appear now very familiar, and in fact they are so, but I think it is very important for the history of subjectivity in the West to catch the first links between the experience of the self and the medical practice. It is important to catch at which moment and under which conditions those relations between the medical practice and the experience, the inner experience of oneself, [have] been related one to the other."

essential; it constituted the framework within which Socrates and Alcibiades together took in hand the soul of the young man. In the first and second centuries the relation to the self has come to always be considered as relying on the relationship with a master, a director, or in any case to someone else, but more and more independent of a more or less marked amorous relationship.[35]

It is very generally admitted that one cannot occupy oneself with oneself without the help of another. Seneca said that nobody is sufficiently strong to free himself from the state of *stultitia* in which he is: "He needs someone to hold out his hand and pull him."[36] In the same way Galen said that a man loves himself too much to be able to be cured of his passions; he had often seen men staggering when they had not consented to put themselves under the authority of another.[37] This principle is true for beginners, but it is also true for what follows and up to the end of one's life. The attitude of Seneca in his correspondence with Lucilius is characteristic: it is of no avail to be old, he still needs to be directed; he gives advice to Lucilius, but he asks for it too and congratulates himself on the help which he finds in this exchange of letters.

What is remarkable in this practice of the soul is the multiplicity of social relations which can serve as its support.

— There are strictly scholastic organizations. The school of Epictetus can serve as an example: there a passing audience was received alongside pupils who stayed for a longer course, but teaching was also given to those who wanted to become philosophers themselves and soul directors; certain of the discourses reassembled by Arrian of Nicomedia are technical lessons for future practitioners of the cultivation of the self.

— One finds also, and above all in Rome, private counselors: installed in the entourage of some great personage, part of their group or of their clientele. They gave political advice, directed the education of young people, helped in important circumstances in life. Thus Demetrius in the entourage of Thrasea Paetus, when the latter committed suicide — he was a member of the opposition to Nero — in a certain way Demetrius himself advises the suicide and occupies the last moments of the man's life with a discourse on immortality.[38]

But there are many other forms according to which the direction of souls is exercised. The latter reduplicates and animates an ensemble of other relationships: family relationships (Seneca writes a consolatory letter to his mother at the time of his own exile);[39] protective relationships (the same Seneca is concerned at the same time with the soul and the career of the young Serenus, a cousin from the provinces who has just arrived in Rome); relationships of friendship between two persons close in age, culture, and situation (Seneca and Lucilius); relationships with a highly placed person towards whom one fulfills one's obligations by presenting useful advice (thus Plutarch with Fundanus, to whom he sends urgent letters containing the notes which he has made himself on the tranquility of the soul).[40]

One could see developing what one might call "a soul service," which is brought into effect by a variety of multiple social relationships. The traditional *eros* plays only an occasional role in this, which does not imply that relationships of affection were not often intense. No doubt, our modern categories of friendship and love are in themselves inadequate to decipher them. The correspondence of Marcus Aurelius with his master Fronto can serve as an example of this intensity and complexity.[41]

To resume: I wanted to show you today the permanence of the principle of "concern with oneself" nominally in the thought but also in the general culture of the ancient world. This permanence does not exclude certain profound changes. In particular, during the imperial period, one witnesses an extension of the cultivation of the self which gives it very different forms from those to which the first Platonic dialogues attest.

The relationship with the self becomes here a complex activity which is permanent, in which the subject is for himself the object of a critique, the arena of [a] combat, the center of a pathology. But this activity which has no other end than the self is nevertheless not solitary; it develops within a constant nexus which implicates a complex field of social relations.

LECTURE II

(*Recorded Version*)*

I

THE THEME [OF THE LECTURE] is the culture of the self, as I call it, in the first two centuries of the Roman Empire.[1] And by this rather pretentious expression, "culture of the self," I mean the concern with oneself insofar as this concern is, first, a way of life; secondly, a permanent relationship with oneself and a personal experience; thirdly, a type of relationship to the others; and also—the fourth point—a set of techniques. Well, today I'll put aside this last aspect of the culture of the self, I mean the techniques, and I'll try to develop it in the next lecture. Today I'll try to develop the first three points: the concern with oneself as a way of life, as a permanent relationship with oneself, and as a relationship to the others.

Well, first, I have prepared a lecture for two hours, but I think it would be really tiring for me and for you to sit here for two hours, so we can make a stop after one hour, and if you want to ask ques-

---

* As noted above, this manuscript has been reconstructed from a very fragile audio recording of the English lecture. Words in brackets denote missing sections that have been filled in through the editors' best guesses based on the audio, context, and Foucault's speaking style. Notes have been added to the text to mark variations from the English typescript.

tions, either during my lecture or after the first hour or after the second hour, of course please do it as soon and as frequently as possible.

Well, I think it is an important fact that the Latin and Greek moralists who have been most influential on Christian and modern ethics, those moralists were also, in the ancient culture, the most representative of this culture of the self. For instance, when a Christian writer of the greatest importance, Clement of Alexandria, writes certain chapters of the *Paedagogus*[2] (or several of his *Stromateis*),[3] he recopies *mot à mot* Musonius Rufus, who was a Stoic, one of the main figures of Stoicism in the early Roman Empire. You are well aware that Augustine speaks of Seneca as "our" Seneca. And it also happens that for centuries and centuries the *Enchiridion* of Epictetus[4] [was] attributed not to Epictetus but to a Greek Christian Father, Saint Nil. Even in the nineteenth century the *Enchiridion* was still attributed to Saint Nil: in the great patristic collection edited in the middle of the nineteenth century in France by Migne[5] you find the *Enchiridion* itself, but among the works of Saint Nil. We must also add that these same Greek and Latin moralists—Seneca, Epictetus, Marcus Aurelius, and so on—those Latin and Greek moralists have been used by modern culture, from the Renaissance on, either against Christianity and Christian ethics or at least as an alternative to it. So, [one] can say that, either through Christian culture or through non-Christian culture, the culture of the self has been transmitted to us: we are, for a large part of our ethics, the inheritors of this culture of the self.

Most of the historians of ancient philosophy are concerned with the [development] of metaphysics and ontology from Parmenides to Aristotle through Plato. [For their part], most of the historians of science or historians of ideas are interested in the [rise]* of rational thought in the Greek mathematics, in Greek cosmology, in the Greek natural sciences. But I think that it could also be [interesting] to study the [rise]† of a certain type of subjectivity, of a certain type of relation to oneself in this Greco-Roman, Greco-Latin culture of the self. For

* Foucault says "raise"; the French manuscript says "développement."
† Again Foucault says "raise"; the French manuscript says "développement."

we could say that Greek metaphysics has been determinant for our relation to being; that Greek science, Greek rationality has been determinant, [in] our history, for our relationship to the world, to the physical world; and that the Greco-Latin culture of the self has been determinant for our relationship to ourselves.[6] Of course one could ask why this last aspect of the ancient tradition has been much more neglected than the others, why historians of philosophy have been so deeply interested in the [rise] of metaphysics or in the [rise] of rationality, and why they haven't been interested in this [rise] of the culture of the self. Well, I won't try to give or to sketch out an answer today. I'll try to do it in one of the last exposés.

Today I'd like to present you a draft of this culture of the self. You remember that the last time we met I insisted on two or three items. The first was that the principle of concerning oneself with oneself was not a pure philosophical precept. [Rather,] I think it was—and we have a lot of witnesses showing that, this principle of concerning oneself with oneself—a widespread social act. The second point I underlined last time was that this theme was not characteristic of a period, a period of decline, of social, political, or cultural decay. [On the contrary,] the theme that one has to be concerned with oneself, this theme appears . . . as a very archaic precept related to archaic techniques. The third idea I underlined last time was that the concern with oneself is not to be identified with the knowledge of the self: it is a fact that these two principles, *gnōthi seauton* and *epimele seautō*, those two principles are related, but the [former] (know yourself) seems to be part or consequence of the [latter] (be concerned with yourself). Well, that was the three points that I tried to underline last time.

In spite of that, we must [. . .] recognize that in the early Greek classical period we can find the strictly philosophical formulation of this obligation to concern oneself [with oneself], and in this formulation, in this philosophical formulation, the *gnōthi seauton* is given a primary importance. This first philosophical formulation is of course to be found in Plato, in the *Alcibiades*.[7] And I will use today this text as a kind of point of departure, as a guide mark in order to make clear the differences between the strictly Platonist theory and the general forms of the culture of the self.

So the first philosophical elaboration of the principle "you must concern yourself with yourself," this first philosophical elaboration is to be found in the *Alcibiades*.

As it is well known (or not [well known]), commentators hesitate in proposing a date for this dialogue. Some of the commentators are in favor of supposing that the text dates from Plato's youth: the *dramatis personae** would suggest this, as would the type of interrogation, the slowness of the dialogue and of the discussion, and many of the themes which are touched upon. [On the contrary], other commentators would suggest a rather late date, particularly because of the extremely dogmatic and "metaphysical"† conclusion to the discourse concerning the contemplation of oneself in the divine essence, which is, as you know, the theme of late Platonic thought.

Well, let's put aside this debate, which I am not competent to discuss. But we must be aware that this dialogue, the *Alcibiades*, is something really strange in Plato's work, and at this point that some commentators have doubts [about its] authenticity. I think that most of the modern commentators agree now to accept this text as a Platonic text, but the place, the exact place of this work in Platonic thought, [...] and so on, is still very [...] enigmatic for us. But the Neoplatonists in the first centuries of our era had a very elegant solution for the problem of the *Alcibiades*. This solution is interesting insofar as it shows clearly the sense which was given, in the classical tradition, to this dialogue, and the sense also which was given to the theme, to the precept "concern yourself with yourself" [as a principal preoccupation].‡ Well, what was this solution?

As you know, one of the main objectives of the Neoplatonic school, from the second century to the fifth and sixth centuries of our era, was [...] to publish Plato's writings and to organize Plato's writings both as a *cursus* for studies (following [the] pedagogical model), and also as a matrix for an encyclopedic knowledge. Plato and the edi-

---

* Foucault has written "Les personnages" in the margin.

† In quotes in the typescript.

‡ The bracketed text appears in the typescript, though not in the recording.

tions of Platonic works were for the Neoplatonic school both a kind of university *cursus* and an encyclopedia of all the knowledge. From this point of view, [...] in this Neoplatonic tradition, the *Alcibiades* was considered *the* first dialogue: the first which had to be read by students and the first to be explained by commentators.

For instance, a second-century author, a Neoplatonist, Albinus, said that every "naturally gifted man," I quote, every "naturally gifted man" who has reached the age for "philosophizing" and who wanted to stand apart, I quote, "from the perturbations of politics" and who wanted "to practice virtue" ... so, a "naturally gifted man," somebody who wanted to stand apart "from the perturbations of politics" and who wanted "to practice virtue," this kind of guy should begin by studying the *Alcibiades*. And why should he start [with] the *Alcibiades*? Because in the *Alcibiades* he could learn to, I quote, "turn toward oneself and to decide what should be the object of one's [...] preoccupations." Later on, in the fifth century, Proclus said that this text of the *Alcibiades* should be considered as *archē apasēs philosophias*, which means that the *Alcibiades* should be considered as the principle, the point of departure and the fundament of all philosophy. And in the sixth century, Olympiodorus, comparing the ensemble of Platonic thought to a kind of temple or sacred arena, made the *Alcibiades* the *propylées* of the temple, of which the *aduton*, which means the central and sacred part of the temple, would be the *Parmenides*. So to walk through this sacred arena to the temple, to the *aduton* of Platonic thought, this guy should start with the *Alcibiades* and go to the *Parmenides*.[8]

It is not my intention to study the details of the *Alcibiades*. I would like simply to point out some principal features of this notion of *epimeleia heautou*, of concern with oneself, which constitutes the first formulation, the first philosophical formulation ... Well, [...] this text, [in] so far as we find in this text the first philosophical formulation of the principle "concern yourself with yourself."

First question: how this precept, "concern yourself with yourself," how this precept is introduced into the dialogue.

This precept is brought in by the project of Alcibiades to begin his public life; more precisely Alcibiades has the project to, I quote, "speak before the people," to be better, to be stronger, to be greater, [...] than Pericles [as a political personage]* and to become all-powerful in the city.

Well, at the moment at which Socrates comes across Alcibiades, just at the beginning of the dialogue, and proposes that he [undertake] an examination of himself, Alcibiades is at a point of transition in his own life. This point of transition is something very well known, very common to every young aristocratic Athenian. It is the moment where the young aristocratic Athenian starts taking part in the political life with his peers, with his equals. It is also the moment where he cannot be an *eromenos* anymore, he cannot be still beloved, and he has to become an *erastēs*, a lover; so he has to become at this moment active both on the political scene and in love, in the erotic game.

Alcibiades is at this well-known transition point in both political and erotic life. But the way he goes through this classical transition point, which is common to every young Athenian, is I think very different from the others. Alcibiades in fact wishes not only to take part with his peers in political power; Alcibiades wishes ... but is not satisfied with the privileges given to him by his birth, fortune, and status; he says very specifically that he does not want to "spend his life" profiting from all this with his equals and at the same level as his peers. He wishes to gain advantage over all the others inside the city, and outside also over the kings of Sparta and over the Persian sovereign; those (the kings of Sparta, the Persian sovereign) are for him not simply the enemies of his country but also his personal rivals. So you see that, on the political scene, Alcibiades wants to appear not only as one among the aristocrats who have exercised the power in Athens; he wants to be the only one and to have a relationship of personal power with his citizens, and he wants to have personal *rivalité* with the enemies of his country. That's the difference between Alcibiades and the other young aristocrats.

From the erotic point of view also, Alcibiades is at the transitional point [which I just spoke of]:† during his adolescence he was desir-

* Text in brackets was written in the margins by Foucault.
† Conjecture; the phrase is inaudible.

able and had a crowd of followers; now he has arrived at this age when his beard is growing, and so his lovers wish to separate themselves from him. But, [unlike] the others, when he was still in the full bloom of his beauty, Alcibiades had rejected all those who paid court to him, not wishing to give in to them, wishing to remain, as he says, *kreittōn,* "dominant." The ambivalence between the political and the erotic vocabulary, which is constant in Greek, here becomes essential. And now Socrates presents himself. And, without being interested in Alcibiades' body, or at least renouncing [...] Alcibiades' body, Socrates succeeds where all others have failed; he is going to show Alcibiades that he is stronger than him; he is going to make him submit, but in a completely different sense. Alcibiades will be obliged to submit his soul and his will to Socrates in order to become the first in the city. That's the point: in order to become the first in political life, he has to submit to a lover, but not in the physical meaning of the word, but in the spiritual meaning of the word. So you see that Alcibiades meets Socrates ... Socrates meets Alcibiades at this strategical point of the life of the young Athenian, Socrates seizes Alcibiades at this moment [...] the transition from the status of the youth to the status of the adult; this transition is not experienced by Alcibiades in the same way as the other young aristocrats.

And I think that it is exactly at this point of intersection of the young man's very personal political ambition and of the master's very particular love (a philosophical love) that the question of concerning oneself with oneself is to appear.

So here comes the second question: [...] why is he [Alcibiades] obliged to concern [himself] with himself?

Socrates asks Alcibiades what his ambition consists in. Or rather what Alcibiades considers to be his personal capacities. Does he know what it is to govern the city well? Does he know what the word "justice" means? Does he know what "concord" within the city means? Of all this Alcibiades knows nothing, as a classical, familiar Socratic [youth],* he knows nothing and finds himself incapable of replying. This kind of situation, you find [it] in nearly every ... early Platonic

---

* Conjecture; the phrase is inaudible.

dialogue. Well, Socrates then invites Alcibiades to compare himself with his rivals, the rivals with whom he wanted to fight, his rivals outside the city, the Spartan kings and the Persian king. And Socrates tells Alcibiades: "Well, you know very well that the Spartan kings receive a very formal education which teaches them the indispensable virtues. And insofar as the Persian king is concerned, from the age of fourteen this young prince is given over to four instructors, who teach him, the first teaches him wisdom (*sophia*), the second teaches him justice (*dikaiosunē*), the third *sōphrosunē* (temperance), and the last *andreia* (courage). Four Platonic virtues which appear only in the last dialogues of Plato, and that's still . . . proof that it's very difficult to give a date for this dialogue. Anyway, the Persian king receives a very good, complete, and Platonic education. But Alcibiades, what education has he received? He has been given over to an old slave completely ignorant, and his tutor, Pericles, his tutor has not been able even to bring up his own sons properly!

So in order to gain the upper hand over his rivals, Alcibiades should acquire a *technē*, a know-how (a *savoir-faire*); he must apply himself to this—he must *epimeleisthai*. And we are now approaching the central discussion [of the dialogue]. But, as we have seen, he does not even know what he should apply himself to, because he has no knowledge at all about justice, or concord, about right government. Alcibiades is aware that he has to apply himself to something, but he does not know what he must apply [himself] to. Alcibiades is consequently in the greatest embarrassment. He despairs. But Socrates intervenes then and tells him this capital thing: if you were fifty years old the situation would be serious and even desperate; then it would be too late; what you have to do now is *epimeleisthai seautō* (take care of yourself).

Here is the first time this expression appears in this text and maybe in Plato's writings, [keeping in mind the discussion of the emergence of this point . . .].* Well, it is the first time this notion appears, at least in this sense. It is highly significant that the principle of having to concern [oneself] with oneself is, you see, directly related to a false

---

* Conjecture; the phrase is inaudible.

pedagogy, directly related to a defective pedagogy, and it is highly significant also that this obligation to take care of oneself must be applied at a precise moment of life: just at the moment when the youth is to start with political life.

Now, after Socrates explains that Alcibiades [has to] take care of himself, then comes the third question, or more precisely two last problems: [what is the "oneself" with which one must occupy oneself? What does occupying oneself with oneself consist in?]*

In order to occupy yourself with your own soul you must of course know what this soul consists in. And in order for your soul to know itself, it is necessary for it to look in a mirror which has the same constitution as itself, that is to say, you have to look to your own soul in the divine element which your soul is a part of. And it is in this contemplation of the soul through . . . the divine element that you will be able to discover the principles and essences on which just action can be founded and which will establish the rules for political action. So that you know now why Alcibiades had to be concerned with himself, [in] so far as he wanted to become the leader of the city. If he wants to know what the principles of just political action are, he has to look at his own soul through the divine element . . . in which he can see the eternal essences.

Well, there are of course several reasons why this passage deserves to be noticed. Firstly, because it bears all the signs *not* at all of early Platonism, but of late Platonism. But above all, the reason why I think this passage deserves attention is that the concern with oneself is in some way seen as exactly the opposite of what I said last time: the concern with oneself in this text is absorbed in the knowledge of oneself. For the whole length of the dialogue, the principle of concern with oneself, which was the main theme of the discussion, has gravitated around the Delphic principle: having to know oneself. Several times, directly or indirectly, the *gnōthi seauton* has been mentioned alongside the *epimele seautō*. But it is clear that, at the end of the dialogue, when Alcibiades is told that he has to look at the divine essence as in a mirror, it is clear that at this point the "know thyself," the

---

* There is an interruption in the recording here.

gnōthi seauton, occupies the whole field opened up by the principle that you have to concern yourself with yourself. For Plato, or at least in this dialogue, the *Alcibiades,* the concern with oneself consists in knowing oneself.

Well, I have spent some time [on] this text whereas most of the documents which I shall subsequently study are much later in date. I have done so because . . . this text seems to bring out very clearly several of the fundamental problems in the history of being occupied with oneself: the solutions [. . .] will often be very different from those given in the *Alcibiades,* but I think that we can find the same problems with different solutions all along this Greek-Hellenistic, this Greco-Roman civilization, culture, and philosophy.

There are three main problems.

First, the problem of the relationship between being occupied with oneself and political activity. As you have seen, Socrates asked Alcibiades to concern himself with himself insofar as Alcibiades claimed to be concerned with others and to direct them. In this dialogue, Alcibiades has to concern himself with himself because he wants to govern other people: *epimeleisthai heautō, epimeleisthai allois,*[9] he has to take care of himself because he has to take care of the others. Later, and particularly under the empire, this question of the relationship between being occupied with oneself and political activity, this question will be still very different. But the question at this moment, during the beginning of the empire [. . .], is much more inclined to present itself in the form of an alternative: would it not be better to turn away from political activity in order to concern oneself with oneself? The relation is a relation of implication between concern with oneself and political activity in the *Alcibiades*; [it] will take the shape, the form of an alternative in the later [. . . Hellenistic and Greco-Roman age].*

The second problem that you find all along this ancient culture is the problem of the relationship between being occupied with oneself and pedagogy. In Socrates' proposal, being occupied with oneself is presented as the duty of a very young man whose education is insuf-

---

* Conjecture; the phrase is inaudible.

ficient. Later, during the Roman imperial period, being concerned with oneself will be presented not only, and not at all as the duty of young men [as] their . . . formation [is still insufficient],* it will be presented as the duty of an adult, of every adult—a duty to be followed through the whole of one's life.

The third problem you meet in the *Alcibiades* and we meet in the later philosophy is the problem of the relationship between concern with oneself and knowledge of oneself. We have seen the privileged position accorded by Plato's Socrates to the *gnōthi seauton*, and this privileged position will be one of the characteristic features of all the Platonic or Neoplatonic movements. But on the contrary, it would seem that concern with oneself assumed in the most part of Hellenistic and Greco-Roman philosophy, this principle of being concerned with oneself, acquires a certain autonomy, perhaps a certain privileged status with respect to self-knowledge. In any case it often happens that the philosophical accent is put on the concern with oneself—self-knowledge being consequently only an instrument, a method for concerning oneself correctly with oneself.

That is the point of departure for what I would like now to analyze with [more] precision, that is the culture of the self during the first two centuries of the empire; more precisely I chose as chronology the end of the Augustan dynasty . . . from the end of the Augustan dynasty to the end of the Antonines. These 150 or 200 years constitute, as is well known, one of the strongest periods of the ancient civilization. But they mark also, I think, a privileged moment, a kind of golden age in the practice and in the theory of the concern with oneself.

Of course from this point of view Epictetus is significant. I think in fact that it is possible to find in the *Discourses* of Epictetus a real complete theory of the concern with oneself. Epictetus shows very clearly that this concern is both an obligation, a duty, and a privilege, the privilege of human beings compared to animals; for Epictetus human beings are [the] kind of beings who are able to take care of themselves and who have to do it. In the next seminar, in the first

---

* Conjecture; the phrase is inaudible.

seminar [which will take place on Friday], I will try to read with you
several pages of Epictetus about this theme.[10]

But today I don't want to remain with these strictly theoretical and
philosophical references. In the period at which Epictetus resumes
the principle of being concerned with oneself, the theme of vigilance
over oneself had taken on a considerable amplitude. A long development has prepared this apogee. The first and second centuries are not
of course a point of departure; it is rather a long-term development.

Among those philosophers who claimed to be advisers on life
and guides on existence, the principle of looking after one's own in-
terests, not of course in the material sense of the term, this principle
was almost universally accepted. Following their master, the Epicureans, for instance, repeat that it is never too early and never too late
to occupy oneself with one's soul.[11] Musonius Rufus, from amongst
the Stoics, says also: "It is in constantly paying attention to oneself
that one assures one's salvation";[12] and Seneca: "You must attend to
your soul, you must attend to yourself, you must lose no time in doing so"; "Retire into yourself and stay there."[13] Plutarch recommends
introspection and "bringing all of your attention on yourself." Dion
Chrysostome, [Dio Chrysostom . . .] or Dio of Prusa . . . gives one
lecture on the theme of the *anachōrēsis eis heauton, eis heauton*, the
retreat into oneself.[14] And Galen . . . recalling how much time is necessary to train a doctor, an orator, or a grammatician, thinks that even
more time is necessary to become a good man: years and years, he
says, spent in occupying yourself with yourself.[15]

[. . .] But this was not simply a piece of abstract advice given by
a few philosophers or several technicians of the body and the soul.
Occupying yourself with yourself was an extremely widespread activity [in cultivated circles, but, no doubt, even more widespread if
one thinks] of the fairly popular recruitment of certain Epicurean
groups, or of those who listened in the streets to the Cynics. Certain well-established supports reinforced this zeal concerning oneself: there where schools where you [were taught] to take care of
the self, schools, private or public teaching establishments, lectures,
more or less closed discussions amongst disciples. Vigilance concerning oneself is to be found in extremely structured groups and takes

the form of an ordered life in common, such as with the Pythagoreans or this strange group described by Philo of Alexandria which I
spoke of last time;[16] but there were also much more flexible groups
who met around a guide or simply around a type of philosophy, a
forma vitae. One went to certain masters for a visit or a course, for instance, Pliny, when he was sent in Asia Minor for his kind of military
service, rushed to visit Euphrates, who was well known and one of
the main figures of Stoicism at this moment; he spent the last part of
his military service taking care of his own soul under the direction
of Euphrates.[17] There were also the masters who came to you and
took up residence in your house, and the Roman aristocracy loved
these counselors of life. [...] For instance, Demetrius had been the
court philosopher of Thrasea Paetus, and when Thrasea Paetus was
obliged to kill himself, Demetrius was there beside him to give him
lessons about the immortality of the soul, and the last *regard*, the last
glance, of Thrasea Paetus was for Demetrius speaking of the immortality of the soul.[18]

Certain of these activities were paid, others were free, but all of
them presupposed a very large network of obligations and of services.
All this activity brought about considerable competition: considerable competition, first, between those who held fast to a rhetorical
teaching and those who preferred to turn souls towards a concern
with themselves; this point is very important, and of course I will
come back to this question several times. The opposition, the polarity
between the rhetorical formulation and the philosophical formulation as far as it is concerned with the care of oneself, I think that this
opposition is one of the main features of the ancient culture [in] this
period, the beginning of the empire. Among the people who tried to
teach others to concern [themselves] with themselves, there were of
course different schools [who were] rivals one to the other, despite
the fact that objectives and procedures were most of the time very
close to one another. Finally there were those who simply contended
[with] one another for clients.

And Lucian, who belonged to the Second Sophistic, at the end
of the second century, Lucian, who did not particularly like philosophers, presents a picture of those practices, of those *rivalités,* [a] pic-

ture which is scarcely flattering. And if you want to have an idea not exactly of those practices but of the satirical picture of those practices, you have to read the dialogue written by Lucian, *Hermotimus*, which presents one of those persons who had been converted to the concern with himself, and this guy, Hermotimus, is very proud of it, very proud of it, and he meets one of his friends in the street and he explains that he has had a master of philosophy, [who taught] him to take care of himself, he has had this same master during twenty years; and this master of course has ruined him, because after [a lot of] money for the [. . .] consultations [. . .], the master has ruined Hermotimus, but he has given him the hope that he may arrive at happiness maybe in the next twenty years.[19]

Well, not everything was pretense and charlatanism in these practices from which certain people certainly profited. But certain individuals sincerely applied themselves to a personal *activité* of concerning oneself with oneself, and this serious aspect of this *activité* will be the theme of the next hour.

So, is there any question to ask now about what I have said, or suggestions? I'm not sure my English [. . .]

The first part of the lecture is followed by a brief discussion. The questions posed and Foucault's responses are often inaudible, and could only be partially transcribed; we have thus provided a summary of the content of the exchange based on what could be discerned from the recording.

Two questions were posed at first, though the content of the first could not be discerned. In response to the second, Foucault evokes an analogy between the relationship between master and disciple described by Lucian and between patient and analyst within the context of psychoanalytic treatment in Foucault's day.

To the third question, Foucault responds that in the ancient culture of the self, it was not possible to practice the care of the self without the aid of another person. He explains that the relation between the master and disciple took different forms with Socrates, in the Roman era, and in the early period of monastic Christianity, apropos of which he cites the proverb "Those who are not guided will fall like a dead leaf": "Well, I'll come back to this point later on. In the old . . . ancient culture it was not

possible to be concerned with oneself without the help of somebody. The
relationship to [...] people is constitutive [...]. That is very important.
[We see] it with Socrates through a specifically erotic relation. You have
this idea [...] transformed in the Roman period. And you find exactly
the same [...] in the Christian communities, in the Christian mona-
chism with the well-known precept 'Those who are not guided will fall
like the [dead leaf].'"[20]

The fourth question seems to have to do with Socrates' attitude with
regard to Alcibiades' ambition. Foucault recalls that Alcibiades wanted
to be the first in standing among the Athenians, and that Socrates said to
him that in order to do that, he must first take care of himself. The care
of the self should lead him to discover, in turn, that his personal ambition
conducts him toward tyranny, and that this is not the kind of power that
he should exercise upon the city: "[...] You see, I [can't] say that Socrates
[...] Alcibiades in his ambition [...]. Alcibiades wants to become the
first in Athens. Socrates answers [...] tells him: 'If you want to become
the first in Athens, then you have to be concerned with yourself first.' Well,
the concern, the concern with oneself will show Alcibiades later on that
to become the first in Athens [...]. Alcibiades . . . if Alcibiades [...]
put [...] what his personal ambition lead to tyranny [...] worst point
[...] concern with oneself [...] Alcibiades to something else [...]."

Foucault returns to this point later in response to a question from an
auditor during the second seminar meeting, explaining that Socrates in
some sense sets a trap for Alcibiades.[21]

II

[IT WAS A GOOD IDEA to reserve at least a few moments each
day for the case of oneself; one could even set aside a specific period
of time.]* So, this kind of retreat, during several months or several
weeks, this kind of retreat was a practice that Pliny, for instance, knew
very well: he advises a friend of [his], and he himself liked to practice
these country retreats. The country was considered at this moment
as a kind of philosophical place, [a] philosophical location, and to
make a retreat in the country was at the same time to make a retreat

---

* Missing passage reconstructed from the typescript.

into oneself. And if leisure time could be described as *scholē* or *otium*, [...] and if such leisure time could be described as *scholē* or *otium*, nevertheless it must be borne in mind that this was an active leisure, a time of study: reading, conversation, diverse activities of meditation or preparation for misfortune, exile, or death, exercises which implied a certain abstinence. We will come back to all those things.

What I would like to underline is the fact that writing also played a very important role; occupying yourself with yourself implied taking notes about what happens to you during the day, what feeling you have, what experience you have, what you have read, the books you have read, [...] the conversations you had, and so on. One collated what the Greeks called *hupomnēmata*, notebooks which offered the possibility of being read again and committed to memory.[22] One wrote treatises for friends, sent letters to them, corresponded with them, which was a way of helping them in their own undertakings, but also a way of reactivating for oneself the truths, the truths one needed. For instance, when Seneca wrote a letter to Lucilius about the death of the son of one of [his] friends, it was, I quote, "in order that this letter should be shown to the father of the youth who was dead, and [in] this [case] as a consolation for him." It was also a kind of lesson given to Lucilius to help him [in case he might] use it for his son [or one of his parents], and it was also an exercise for Seneca himself when he wrote this letter because it was a way of reactivating, a way of reactivating the truths he knows about life, death, and so on.[23]

I think that this importance of writing is very characteristic: it was the main feature of this culture of the self. As you know, reading and writing were largely, largely widespread in Greek and Roman society. Exception of course for the slaves, except the slaves, everybody, [almost] everybody could write and read in Roman and Greek society. But there is, I think, a really important and significant difference. In the political life, at least to the classical period, to the beginning of the empire, in the political life it was the oral culture which was largely dominant. Writing was not important in the political life. It is only with the development of administrative structures and bureaucracy, at the end of the empire, with the empire but after, mainly after the great crisis of the third century, that writing has been something important, one of the necessary activities of the political life. But before that, the political life, political activity, was mainly oral. But we must keep in mind that the problem of the self, the concern with the self has been sensitively, or at least [in] the Hellenistic period, this problem of the self has been one of the points where writing was absolutely necessary. The development of the use of writing and the development of . . . the culture of the self have been related, and interrelated through all [this era]. The self is something which one had to take care of through several activities, among which there were the writing activities.*

Subjectivity as a theme of writing activity is not at all a modern discovery: it is not a discovery due to Romanticism, it is not an innovation of Reformation, it is not an innovation of Augustine and of early Christian spirituality. [. . .] Subjectivity [as] a theme for this writing activity is one of the most ancient traditions of the West. And this tradition was deeply rooted when Augustine and the Christian spirituality started. And I think that, [. . .] the fact that, during the ancient culture political activity was an oral activity, but the concern with the self was for a large part an activity of writing [. . .]. And then there was the shift, during the Christian [period], where the political activity [became] a writing activity, and the culture of the self became an oral one with confession; this shift [appears with]† Cassian [. . .]. Well, so, I wanted to underline this aspect and this importance of writing.

At the same time, as these practices spread, it would seem that the concrete, the personal experience of oneself was, by virtue of this activity, intensified and widened. I think that it was not only something related to external activity, I think that the experience people

---

* In place of the passage that begins "It is only with the development of administrative structures and bureaucracy . . ." to the end of the paragraph, the manuscript reads: "It is a fact that the development of administrative structures and bureaucracy increased the role of writing in the imperial government. But we must bear in mind that the role of writing had been decisive in the government of the self very early on."

† Conjecture; the phrase is inaudible.

had with themselves, the way their relationship with themselves has been transformed by what we could call introspection—[...] the kind of attention, [one's attention to oneself] becomes much more attentive, much more detailed, much deeper than before. The letters, the letters of Seneca and Pliny, the correspondence, for instance, between Marcus Aurelius and Fronto,[24] all those letters show this vigilance and this meticulousness with regard to the attention which one should pay to oneself. It often concerns the details of the everyday life, the nuances of health and mood, the small physical malaises or diseases that one experiences; it concerns also the tiny movements of the soul, the tiny movements of the spirit, it concerns one's reading, quotations that one remembers, reflections on such and such an event. A certain way of relating to oneself and a whole field of experience are to be seen where in earlier documents they are absent.

From this point of view, the letters written by Marcus Aurelius to his friend, master, maybe lover, Fronto, and written by Fronto to Marcus Aurelius, are very *significatives*. And if I can find here an English translation of these letters [... I don't know ... French ... find translation of these letters ... translation ... but the love letters ... Fronto ... were translated always from Greek into Latin].* So, if I'll find a translation of these letters, we will read together during the seminar one or two of those letters.[25]

There is another text which has not been translated, which is really very interesting also. It is the *Sacred Discourses* of Aelius Aristides.[26] [The] *Sacred Discourses* of Aelius Aristides constitute I think a very clear witness of all that. Aelius Aristides was a very strange guy, who has written very interesting things about politics, about the constitution of Rome, about the imperial government, and so on. [All the history, *destinée*], the political *destinée* of Rome,[27] very beautiful. But besides that, during ten years, Aelius Aristides has suffered a huge amount of [diseases], he has suffered a huge amount of diverse diseases. And during ten years he ran, in the east of the Méditerranée, he ran from a country to another, from a temple to another, from an oracle to another, from a certain priest to another priest, begging for his recovery. And in fact, after ten years, he recovered.

---

* Conjecture; the sentence is partially inaudible.

He recovered, and he wrote six discourses in order to express his gratitude towards Asclepius, the god of health. These six discourses are to be associated, by their general form, with the traditional genre of the steles which speak of healing and are manifestations, expressions of gratitude to the gods. [...] It is a kind of transcription of the inscriptions: he has written as a book [...] what is ordinarily written in a few words on the stone. And inside this traditional framework, and having transformed this traditional framework in a kind of literary work, Aelius Aristides unfolds a huge, a very long amount of descriptions about his own illnesses, malaises, sufferings, diverse feelings, about his dreams, his premonitory dreams, about the dreams which offer him advice, about the medicines which he tried, about the improvements which sometimes he obtained, and so on and so on. In this case, I think that the limits of the normal hypochondriacal symptoms [... in this story], these limits are trespassed. But the problem is not at all to know if Aelius was ill. He was. What is important is to recognize the fact that inside his own culture he found the means to formulate this personal experience. And I think that [in this text you have,] first, an innovation of a very, very long literary genre, which is the récit, the narrative of illness, and he could find in his own culture the tools or at least the stimulation to make this innovation.

Well, forgive me for passing over this so quickly. I wanted only to suggest that the theme of concerning oneself with oneself at this period, that of the High Empire, is not to be found only within a particular philosophical doctrine. It is a universal precept or at least it is extremely common. Many individuals respond to its call; it is a practice which has its institutions, its rules, its methods, and also a mode of experience, of individual experience, but also of collective ... it is a kind of collective experience with its means and its forms of expression.

To resume, I would say that occupying yourself with yourself is confirmed in the [experience], in its validity, it is formalized in ordered practices, it opens up a field of personal experience and of collective expression, and that's the reason why I think we may legitimately speak of a "culture of the self."

Well, next Tuesday I shall try to show the place which the principle of the gnōthi seauton and the techniques of self-analysis occupy in this culture of the self; I shall try to analyze the forms of knowledge of the self, of the examination of oneself, deciphering of oneself, examination of oneself, which is developed at this period and within the framework of this culture.

That was my plan. But I have still several other things to tell you, but I am afraid that you are tired, so [...]. What I wanted [to explain you today] was two or three great shifts in this concern for the self from Plato to the High Empire. One is the fact that it is becoming an adult culture. [... difference in chronology ...] The second point I wanted to underline was the very deep relationships between this kind of culture of the self and [new professions which had come into being].* And the third thing I [wanted] to show you was the place of the *gnōthi seauton* in this culture. Well I don't know what to do. We could stop here and have a discussion [...].

The first problem is Socrates, as you remember, recommended to Alcibiades to profit from his youth and occupy himself with himself: at fifty it would be too late. If you compare this to other texts of the Hellenistic and Roman period, the contrast is [clear]. Epicurus, for instance, said: "When you are young you must not hesitate in philosophizing, and when you are old, you must not hesitate in philosophizing. It is never too early, it is never too late to concern yourself with your soul."[28] Musonius Rufus, who is a Stoic, says: "You must take care of yourself without ceasing if you are to lead a life conducive to well-being."[29] Or Galen says: "In order to become an accomplished man, each one needs, so to speak, to exert himself all his life," even if it is true that it would be better "to have kept watch over one's own soul since one's earliest age."[30]

It is a fact that the friends to whom Seneca or Plutarch give advice, those friends are not any longer the ambitious and desirable young boys whom Socrates addressed himself to: the friends of Seneca and Plutarch are men, sometimes quite young (like Serenus), sometimes fully mature (like Lucilius, who had the important position of procurator in Sicily when Seneca and he exchanged a long spiritual correspondence). Epictetus keeps a school for young pupils, but some-

---

* Conjecture, reconstructed from the manuscript; the sentence is partially inaudible.

times he has the occasion to speak with adults and even with consular figures—and there is a very interesting dialogue [in which] Epictetus asks his young pupils to go through the town and to play a kind of Socratic role, going to the consular figures they met in the town and remind them of the task of occupying themselves with themselves. The adults have to occupy themselves with themselves, and the young students of Epictetus have to remind the adults that they have to do that. When Marcus Aurelius brings together his notes, he is exercising the function of emperor, he is not [young], for him it is through all his life a question of "coming to his own aid."[31]

So being occupied with oneself is not therefore a simple preparation for life. I think that in the *Alcibiades*, as important as it could be the principle to be concerned with oneself, it was a simple preparation for life, or at least Alcibiades thought that it was that and nothing else. Alcibiades realized that he should occupy himself with himself insofar as he wanted consequently to occupy himself with others. Now it is a question of occupying yourself with yourself, *for* yourself and during all your life.

And it's from this fact that comes this really [important idea], the idea of changing one's attitude towards oneself, the idea of conversion to oneself (*ad se convertere*), the idea of a movement in one's existence by which one turns back on oneself (and the Greek word, the Greek expression is *eis heauton epistrephein*).[32] This notion of *epistrophē* is a typically Platonic theme. But, as we have seen in the *Alcibiades*, the movement by which the soul turns towards itself, following the Platonic doctrine, the movement to which Alcibiades was invited by Socrates, this movement is a movement by which the gaze, the eyes, are attracted towards that which is on high—towards the divine element, towards the essences, towards the supercelestial world where the essences are visible.

[On] the contrary, the turning back to which one is invited by Seneca, by Plutarch, by Epictetus, this turning back is quite different from the turning back towards the Ideas: it is a kind of turning round on the spot; it has no other end, no other conclusion than "taking up residence in oneself" and staying there. The final objective of the conversion to oneself is the establishing of a certain number of relations with oneself: some of those relations are described following a juridico-political model, for instance, you have to be sovereign over oneself, to exercise complete mastery over oneself, to be fully independent, to be completely one's own (*fieri suum*, Seneca says often).[33] Those relations are also often represented according to the model of enjoyment: literally to "enjoy oneself," to take pleasure in oneself, to find satisfaction of one's desires in oneself, and so on.

Let's speak schematically: with Plato, the movement of turning towards oneself is only a stage in the ascension which leads beyond; here it is a question of movement which leads us into ourselves, then if we meet the divine, it is in the form of the *daimon*, the *daimon* who is present in us; this form of the relation towards oneself is oriented by a kind of internal *finalité*.

The second big difference, the second shift, I think, is concerned with pedagogy. You remember in the *Alcibiades*, the concern with oneself was necessary because of a defective pedagogy [. . .], because of faults in pedagogy, and Alcibiades has to complement, to substitute this teaching with this concern with himself. Now this concern has become an adult practice which one must undertake all [throughout] one's life, and of course its pedagogical role tends to disappear, and other functions present themselves. Those functions I think [. . .] are three.

Firstly, the culture of the self has not a pedagogical function but a critical function. [It is the reverse.] The cultivation of the self should permit one not at all to get a formation but to get rid of all the bad formation he receives before, all the bad habits, all the false opinions derived from the crowd, from the bad masters, but also from the relatives, from the entourage, from the [parents]. Now there are very *significative* letters written by Seneca against the bad influence of [parents]—you have to get rid of all that.[34] The idea that the self-culture is a critical culture is something very important and which will have a very long destiny in our society through Christianity, through the Reformation, through Romanticism, and through [. . .]. To take care of oneself is a critical [. . .]. To "unlearn" (*de-discere*) is one of the important tasks [. . .].

But this culture of the self also has the function, the function of a struggle, of a fight. The practice of oneself is conceived as a permanent fight. I think that in the Platonic, early Platonic perspective, the concern of oneself had as a model a kind of sculpture, the boy has to sculpt himself—do you say that?—to sculpt himself as a piece of art. Now, the culture of the self is not ... has not as an aim to become a piece of art, it is to [arm], to fight all [his life. You no doubt know how frequent these two metaphors were: that of the athletic joust (one is in life as wrestler who must defeat his successive adversaries)]* and who must keep in training even when he is not in combat. And the metaphor also of war: one must be organized like an army, the soul must be organized like an army, which may at any moment be assailed by an enemy. The great Christian theme of the spiritual struggle, of the spiritual fight of the soul, this great theme is already a fundamental principle of the cultivation, the culture of the self in ancient pagan times.

But above all I think that this cultivation of the self has a curative and therapeutic function. It is much nearer to the medical model than the pedagogical one. One must of course remember some extremely ancient facts about Greek culture: the existence of a notion such as that of *pathos* which signifies a passion of the soul,† a metaphorical field which was like‡ cure, amputations, scarifications, purgations, and so on—you find all this in those texts. You must remember the principle familiar to the Epicureans, the Cynics, and the Stoics, that the role of philosophy is to heal the maladies, the diseases of the soul.§

But I would like to insist [not only] on [that] correlation between medicine and the culture of the self. For instance, Epictetus did not

* Interruption in the recording; the passage has been reconstructed from the manuscript.

† The typescript adds: "as well as a disease of the body."

‡ In place of "which was like," the typescript reads: "which permitted one to apply to body and soul expressions like . . ."

§ The typescript adds: "Plutarch could say one day that philosophy and medicine constituted *mia khōra*, a single region, a single domain."

want his school to be *considered* simply as a training place, [where people learn purely sophistic theories];* it was not a training place; his school for Epictetus was really a doctor's consulting room, he calls it an *iatreion* (an *iatreion* is a dispensary); he wanted his school to be a dispensary for the soul; he wanted his pupils to be conscious of the fact that they were ill: "One of them," he said, one of them "has a shoulder out of joint, a second has an abscess, a third has a fistula, another has a headache." "You wish to learn syllogisms? Then first cure your wounds, you wish to learn syllogisms? Then first cure your wounds, stop the flow of your humors, calm your spirits."[35]

And inversely a doctor such as Galen considers it to be within his competence to heal the soul from the perturbations, the passions, which are [. . .] "disordered energies, rebels to reason," which are also "errors which are born of one's false opinions." In his *Treatise on the Cure of the Passions of the Soul*, he quotes cures he has undertaken and been successful in: he has cured one of his companions inclined to anger; he has helped a young man whose soul was troubled by events of little importance.[36]

All these ideas may appear of course very familiar; and in fact they are, since they have been constantly transmitted in Western culture. All the more reason for giving them an historical importance. In effect it is important for the history of subjectivity in the West that the relation to oneself should have become a permanent task in existence. From this point [of view] Christianity has not rejected the lessons of the pagan philosophers. Equally, it is important to see that this relation with the self has been defined as a critique, as a critical relation, as a fight, as a struggle relation, and as a medical practice. Here also the West has not renounced the forms of the old cultivation of the self.

And there I would like to stress the difference between those ambitious young men [. . .] in Socrates' [entourage], and the men who exchange letters with Seneca or wrote their notebooks like Aelius Aristides or Marcus Aurelius. For the former, for the Socratic young men, the main danger was *hubris*, hubristic *pathos*, passion; [this *pathos*], this passion consists in trespassing [the limits] at the risk of

---

* Conjecture; the sentence is partially inaudible.

one's status. The danger for the Socratic youth, the danger was this overevaluation of the self [which] was called *hubris*; inside of themselves they have a relationship with a kind of excess of force. For the men who correspond with Seneca, or for Marcus Aurelius or Aelius Aristides, and so on, the danger is not any more this excessive force within themselves. The danger is [now] the weakness of the self, some *hubristic* diseases; there is a kind of pathologization, [a] great medicalization of the relation with oneself. And I think that's [very important].

And the last point, [. . .] I will be brief on it. The third great difference between the occupation with oneself in the *Alcibiades* and [the practice of the self in the culture of the imperial period] is this one: in Plato's dialogue, the erotico-philosophical relationship with the master was essential; it constituted the framework within [which] Socrates and Alcibiades together took in hand the soul of the young man. The framework is both erotic and philosophical. In the first and second centuries, the relation, the relation to the self is considered always as relying on the relationship with a master, with a director, with somebody else, but more and more independent of the amorous, [. . .] erotic relationship.[37]

It is generally admitted* (and I'll try to show you that in the seminar), [. . .] that one cannot occupy oneself with oneself without the help of another. But now the relationship between the two partners, the director and the directed, this relation is not an erotic relation any more; it is either [a] family relationship or [a] protective relationship or [a] relationship between a highly based person and somebody [who has an inferior rank]. It is a kind of soul service which is brought into effect by a variety of multiple social relationships. The traditional *eros* plays only an occasional role in this, which does not imply that those relationships of affection or sexual relationships were not often intense and present in this kind of activity, of practice.

---

* From this point to the end of the lecture, the typescript differs significantly from the recording. The manuscript also continues beyond the end of the recording for several pages, which are reproduced above in the first version of Lecture II, section 3; see *supra* pp. 29–30.

But [I think we can say that] those affective relationships between the director and the directed, this [framework?] is very different from the erotic relationships that we find in the so-called Socratic love and also different from what we call in our [. . .] experience "homosexuality." The correspondence, for instance, of Marcus Aurelius with Fronto can serve as an example of this intensity and complexity. And I think it is worthwhile to ask [if they have sex . . .] there is a very specific, a very interesting relation, an intense affective relation between both, and [it is the work of]* historians to underline, to make appear the specificity of this experience, which was an internal experience, which was a personal experience, but which can be [. . .].

So, that is only a draft of what I wanted to say about this culture of the self, and so next Tuesday I'll try to show you what the techniques of the deciphering of the self [were].†

* Conjecture; the phrase is inaudible.
† The recording ends here.

LECTURE III

(*First English Version*)

I

TODAY I SHOULD LIKE TO evoke some of the practices to which the cultivation of the self has given rise. I would wish to remind you again that these practices as they appear in the first two centuries of our era were not invented during this period; they have a long history behind them; but what is certain is that, at the beginning of the empire, they were considerably extended and took forms which were, to differing extents, "sophisticated."

Two remarks to begin with:

1. THE NAME *ASKĒSIS* WAS OFTEN given to these forms of cultivating oneself: exercise, training, asceticism.[1] Thus Musonius Rufus said (and in so saying he was only repeating a traditional teaching) that the art of living (*technē tou biou*) was like the other arts; one could not learn it only from theoretical teaching (*mathēsis*), it demanded practice and training (*askēsis*).[2] But we must not read into this word the meaning that it was to have in Christian spirituality; this would be an illusion. No doubt, certain of the ancient ascetic practices were to be used in Christian asceticism and particularly in monastic institutions (such as the exam-

ination of conscience or the uninterrupted surveillance over self-exhibition).*

However, the general sense of Christian asceticism was to be very different from that of ancient philosophy.

Schematically:

—Christian asceticism has for its ultimate aim the renunciation of the self, while that of ancient philosophy was to formulate definitively a relationship with oneself, a relationship of possession and sovereignty.

—Christian asceticism takes as its principal theme detachment from the world, while philosophical asceticism is concerned with endowing the individual with a preparation, a baggage, which permits him to confront the world.

2. THIS WORKING ON ONESELF IS tied to a knowledge of oneself. But here also, one must avoid confusion and try not to interpret everything in the light of Platonism.

—In fact, Platonism had preserved and developed the theme which is already present in the *Alcibiades*: namely, that concern with oneself should principally, if not exclusively, take the form of knowledge of oneself; and that this knowledge of oneself should take the form of an act of memory in which the soul discovers its true nature.

—In the philosophical practice of the Stoics, the Cynics, and the Epicureans, knowledge of oneself is not the principal form of the practice of oneself; and above all it does not take the form of memory, rather of preparation for the future.

Today I would wish firstly to analyze the practice of oneself as a preparation for the future; then to look at the forms of knowledge which were tied to this preparation for the future. Normally we put together a knowledge of oneself and the memory; perhaps this is the distant influence of Platonism; it is in any case the ever-present

* The term "self-exhibition" is most likely a translation error. The French text reads "le contrôle permanent des représentations," so Foucault probably means "thoughts" or "representations" here.

influence of Christianity; no doubt it is also the result of our present interest in psychoanalysis. For us, the hermeneutics of the self is always more or less a deciphering of the past. In the cultivation of the self, about which I am talking here, it is interesting to see forms of knowledge inside a completely different relationship to time: a troubled preparation which defies the future.[3]

II. *ASKĒSIS* AS PREPARATION

IN THE *DE BENEFICIIS*, SENECA quotes the text of a Cynic philosopher very near to Stoicism: Demetrius. In this passage, Demetrius resorts to the very common metaphor of the athlete: we must train as an athlete does. The latter does not learn all the possible movements, he does not try to show a useless prowess; he prepares himself for certain movements which are necessary for him to triumph in the struggle over his adversaries.[4] In the same way, we should not undertake spectacular feats (philosophical asceticism was very wary of those who vaunted the marvels of their abstinence, their fasts, their foreknowledge of the future). Like a good wrestler, we should only learn that which will permit us to stand up against possible events; we must learn not to be discountenanced by them, not to be carried away by our emotions produced by them.

What do we need to remain in control of possible events? We need the "discourse," the *logoi*, understood as a true and reasonable discourse. Lucretius speaks of the *veridica dicta* which will permit us to disperse our fears and not to be overcome by that which we believe to be misfortunes. The equipment we need to confront the future is that of true discourses. These will allow us to confront reality.

Three questions present themselves on this subject.

1. THE QUESTION OF THEIR NATURE. On this point the discussions between philosophical schools and within them were numerous. The principal point of contention concerned the necessity for theoretical knowledge. On this point, the Epicureans were completely in agreement: knowledge of the principles which govern the

world, the nature of the gods, the cause of prodigies, the laws of life
and death, is from their point of view indispensable for preparing
oneself for possible events. The Stoics were divided, according to
their proximity to the Cynic doctrines: some gave the greatest importance to the *dogmata*, the theoretical principles which complemented practical precepts; on the contrary others considered that
concrete rules for conduct should take first place. Seneca's nineti-
eth and ninety-first letters present these theses very clearly.[5] All I am
doing is mentioning them; the only thing which I would wish to indicate here is that these true discourses that we need are concerned
only with our relationship to the world, our place in the order of nature, our dependence on or our independence from possible events.
In no way are they a deciphering of our thoughts, the things which
come to mind, our desires.

2. THE SECOND QUESTION WHICH PRESENTS itself is concerned with the way in which this true discourse exists in us. To say
that it is necessary for our future is to say that we should be able to
have recourse to it when we feel that the need arises. When an unforeseen event or misfortune presents itself, we should be able to
call upon those true discourses which are pertinent, in order to protect ourselves. They must be inside us, at our disposal. For this the
Greeks have a common expression, *procheiron echein*, that the Latins
translate by *habere in manu, in promptu habere*, to be able to lay hold
of something.

It is absolutely necessary, in order to characterize the presence
within ourselves of these true discourses, to understand that the process is not simply a question of simple recollection, which one could
bring back to mind if the need arose.

Plutarch, for example, in order to express what is essential to the
presence within ourselves of these true discourses, uses several metaphors: that of medicine (*pharmakon*) which we should keep in store
to ward off the vicissitudes of life (Marcus Aurelius compares them
to the medicine bag which the doctor should always carry about with
him); Plutarch speaks of them as of those friends of whom "the most

sure and the best are those whose useful presence in adversity helps us." Elsewhere he invokes them as an internal voice which, of its own volition, makes itself heard when the perturbation of the passions begins to show itself; they must be in us like "a master whose voice is sufficient to appease the growling of dogs."[6] In a passage of Seneca (*De beneficiis*) one finds a gradation of this kind, proceeding from an instrument which one can use to the automatic action of a discourse which spontaneously takes up speech within us. Seneca, speaking of the advice given by Demetrius, says that one must "take it in both hands (*utraque manu*), never let it go, but also one must fix it, attach it (*adfigere*) to one's spirit, until one has made it a part of oneself (*partem sui facere*), and finally by daily meditation obtain that "salutary thoughts present themselves by themselves (*sua sponte occurant*)."[7]

You see that here we have a movement very different from that which Plato prescribes when he demands of the soul that it turns back upon itself in order to find again its true nature. What Plutarch and Seneca suggested was, on the contrary, the absorption of a truth given by a teaching, reading, or advice; and one assimilates it to the point of making it an internal principle, permanent and constantly brought into action. In such a practice one does not recover a truth hidden in the depths of oneself by the movement of reminiscence; one interiorizes received truths by a progressively greater appropriation.

3. A SERIES OF TECHNICAL QUESTIONS present themselves concerning the methods for this appropriation. Obviously memory plays a great role; not, however, in the Platonic form of the soul rediscovering its original nature and its homeland, but in the form of progressive exercises in memorization. We will speak of these more precisely again in a seminar to follow.[8] I would wish simply to indicate some strong points in this "ascesis" of the truth:

— The importance of listening. While Socrates asked questions and sought to make one say what one knew, without knowing that one knew it, for the Stoics and the Epicureans (as for the Pythagorean sects) the disciple must first be silent and listen. With Plutarch[9] and Philo of Alexandria[10] the process of hearing correctly is strictly regulated (the way of concentrating one's attention, physical posture, the way of retaining what one has just heard).[11]

— The importance also of writing. At this period there was a complete culture of what one might call personal writing: taking notes on reading, conversations, reflections one hears or makes oneself; the keeping of a sort of notebook on important subjects (what the Greeks called *hupomnēmata*) and which were to be reread from time to time in order to reactualize what they contained.[12]

— The importance equally of return to oneself, but in the sense of exercises in memorizing what one has learned. This is the precise technical sense of the expression *anachōrēsis eis heauton*; it is in this sense in any case that Marcus Aurelius uses the term: to come back on oneself and examine the "riches" that one has deposited; inside oneself one should have a kind of book which one rereads from time to time.[13] Here we come back to the arts of memory studied by Frances Yates.[14]

Here then is a complete *ensemble* of techniques whose aim is to bind the subject to the truth. But it must be clearly understood that it is not a question of rediscovering a truth in the subject, nor, by some relationship of essence or origin, of making the soul the place where truth resides; nor is it a question of making the soul the object of a true discourse. We are very far from what would be a hermeneutics of the subject. On the contrary it is a question of arming the subject with a truth which he did not know and which did not reside in him; it is a question of making of this truth, learned, memorized, and progressively applied, a quasi subject which has sovereign reign within us.

To put things schematically again: with Plato, the exercise, the *askēsis*, was an instrument useful in helping to come to the reminiscence which discovered the relation of the soul with the essences. In the philosophical techniques I am speaking about here, learning and memorizing are useful instruments for this *askēsis* whose objective is to make the truth speak in us and act unceasingly in us.[15]

Which is not to say that in these exercises one does not need a certain knowledge of the self. But this is very different from what the Platonic memory of the soul had been and the Christian hermeneutics of the soul was to be. This knowledge of the self presents itself in two principal forms: examination and trials.

III. THE TRIALS

HERE IT IS A QUESTION of exercises in which the subject, in thought or in reality, puts himself into a situation such that he can verify if he is capable of confronting events which present themselves and of using the true discourses with which he is armed. In a certain sense it is a question of testing the *paraskeuē*. The different [trials]* which are possible are divided between two poles. For one the Greeks employ the terms *meletē, meletan*; for the other those of *gumnasia, gumnazein.*[16]

1. THE LATINS TRANSLATE *MELETĒ* BY *meditatio.* The rather vague sense that we give to this word nowadays should not make us forget that it was a technical term. It was borrowed from rhetoric to designate the work one undertook in order to prepare an improvisation; one thought over the principal themes, useful arguments, the way of replying to possible objections; one anticipated the real situation. The philosophical meditation is of the same kind. It comprises an element of memorizing and [reactivating]† what one knows; it is also a way of placing oneself in a situation, in the imagination, where one can judge the reasoning which one would then come up with, one's way of acting—in brief, the practical use which one would make of the true principles which one knew. It is a theoretico-practical exercise of the imagination.

* In the manuscript, the word "tests" was crossed out here, but not replaced. (The French version reads "épreuves.") Several lines above, the word "tests" is crossed out and replaced with the word "trials" as the title for section 3. Following that change in the title, we have included the word "trials" here, where "tests" was crossed out.

† The typescript uses a neologism, "re-activising," which seems to be a typo.

The most famous of these exercises in thought was the *praemeditatio malorum*, the meditation on future ills.[17] It was also one of the most discussed. [The Epicureans rejected it,]* saying that it was useless to suffer in advance evils which had not yet come upon one and that it was better to recollect memories of past pleasures in order to protect oneself from present ills. The strict Stoics—such as Seneca and Epictetus—but also men such as Plutarch whose attitude towards Stoicism was extremely ambivalent, practice with great application the *praemeditatio malorum*. It must be understood in what it consists: in appearance, it is a rather dark and pessimistic prevision for the future. In fact, it is something altogether different.

—Firstly it is not a question of imagining the future as it is likely to turn out. But, in a systematic fashion, to imagine the worst which can happen even if there is very little chance of its coming about. Seneca says this about the fire which had destroyed the city of Lyon: this example should teach us to consider the worst as always certain.[18]

—Then one should not envisage things as possibly taking place in a more or less distant future, but imagine them as already present, already in the process of taking place. Let us imagine, for example, that we are already exiled, already submitted to torture.

—Finally, if we represent them as already present, it is not in order to experience in anticipation the sufferings of pains which they would cause us, but in order to convince ourselves that they are not in any way real ills and that only the opinion which we have of them makes us take them for real misfortunes.

We can see that this exercise does not consist in envisaging a possible future of real ills in order to accustom ourselves to them, but in annulling at the same time the future and the evil. The future, since we represent it as already given in an extreme present. The evil, because one makes an effort to no longer consider it as such.

2. AT THE OTHER EXTREME OF the exercises one finds those which take place in reality. That which the Greeks designate by the

---

* The English translation omits several words; the French reads: "C'était aussi un des plus discutés. Les épicuriens le rejetaient, disant . . ."

verb *gumnazein*: to train oneself. These exercises had a long tradition behind them: the practices of abstinence, of physical privation and resistance. They could have the value of purification (such as the sexual and dietary abstinences of the Pythagoreans); or witness to the "demonic" force of he who practiced them (consider Socrates enduring, without noticing it, the cold at the battle of [Potidaea][19]). But in the culture of the self, these exercises have another sense: it is a question of establishing and testing the independence of the individual with regard to the external world.

Two examples. The first in Plutarch, the *Demon of Socrates*. One of the speakers invokes a practice whose origin he attributes to the Pythagoreans. Firstly one gives oneself over to sporting activities which create an appetite; then one places oneself in front of tables laden with the most enticing dishes; and after having contemplated them one gives them to the servants while one eats the simple and frugal food of the poor oneself.[20]

In the eighteenth letter to Lucilius, Seneca recounts that the whole city is in the process of preparing the Saturnals. For reasons of convenience, he envisages participating in the festivities in some way at least. But his preparation consists, for several days, in wearing only a rough homespun garment, sleeping on a litter, and eating only rustic bread. This is not in order to give oneself a greater appetite for the festivities, but to show that poverty is not an evil and that he is altogether capable of enduring it.[21] Other passages, in Seneca himself, or in Epicurus, evoke the usefulness of voluntary trials. Musonius Rufus also recommends courses in the country: one lives like the peasants and, like them, one gives oneself over to agricultural labors.

3. BETWEEN THE POLE OF THE *meditatio* in which one trains one's thoughts and that of the *exercitatio* where one trains in reality, there is a whole series of other possible practices destined for the proving of oneself.

It is Epictetus above all who gives examples in his *Discourses*. They are interesting because very similar ones are to be found in Christian spirituality. It is a question of one might call "control over representations."[22]

Epictetus wants one to be in a permanent state of surveillance with regard to representations which may come into one's thoughts. He explains this attitude by two metaphors: that of the night watchman who does not admit just anyone into the house or the town,[23] and that of the money changer who verifies the authenticity of currency— the *arguronomos*—who, when a coin is presented to him, looks at it, weighs it, verifies the metal and the effigy.[24] The principle that with regard to one's own thoughts one should be like a vigilant money changer is to be found in more or less the same terms with Evagrius Ponticus and with Cassian.[25] But with them it is a question of prescribing a hermeneutic attitude with regard to oneself: deciphering what concupiscence may lie in apparently innocent thoughts, recognizing that which comes from God and that which comes from the Great Seducer. In Epictetus, another thing is in question: one must know if one is more or less moved by the thing which is represented and why one is or is not.

In this sense, Epictetus recommends to his pupils an exercise of control inspired by sophisticated attitudes of defiance which were so highly valued in the schools; but instead of throwing at one another questions which are difficult to resolve, one will put forward situations faced with which one is obliged to react: "Such a person's son is dead.—Answer: we can change nothing, it is not our responsibility, it is not an ill.—A certain person's father has disinherited him. What do you think?—It is not our responsibility, it is not an evil.—He is suffering as a result.—That is our responsibility, it is an evil.—He has put up with it valiantly.—That is our responsibility, it is a good."[26] Epictetus proposes also a kind of ambulatory exercise in which one exposes oneself to all the representations which might come from the external world, and we test out our way of reacting: "As soon as you go out in the morning, examine all those you see or hear and answer as if you were being asked questions. What have you seen? A good-looking man, a beautiful woman? Apply the rule: is it something independent of yourself or does it depend on you? Independent. Reject it. What have you seen? Someone who is weeping over the death of his son? Apply the rule: this death is not our responsibility. Reject it far from you. Have you met a consul? Apply the rule: what is the consulate? A thing independent of us or dependent on us? Reject it equally, it does not stand up to the test, eliminate it. If we behave in this manner and apply ourselves to this exercise every day from morning till night, something useful will come of it."[27] It can be seen that this control of representations does not have as its object the deciphering of a truth hidden beneath appearances which would be that of the subject himself; on the contrary it finds in these representations, insofar as they present, the occasion, the opportunity for recalling a certain number of true principles—concerning death, illness, suffering, political life, etc.—and by means of this reminder one can see if one is capable of acting in conformity to such principles—if they have become, according to the metaphor of Plutarch, the master's voice which raises itself as soon as the passions begin to murmur and knows how to silence them.[28]

4. THE HIGHPOINT OF ALL THESE exercises is to be found in the *meletē thanatou*—meditation, or rather exercise, on death.[29] In fact it does not consist in a simply calling to mind, even insistent, of the fact that one is destined to die. It is a way of making death present in life. Amongst other Stoics, Seneca elaborated this practice. In a certain sense it tends to make us live each day as if it were the last.

In order fully to understand the exercise that Seneca proposes, one must recall the traditionally established correspondences between the different cycles of time: the moments of the day from dawn to dusk are brought into symbolic relationship with the seasons of the year—from spring to winter; and these seasons are in their turn brought into relation with the ages of life, from childhood to old age. The exercise of death as it is evoked in the letters of Seneca (...)* consists in living the long duration of life as if it were as short as a day and to live each day as if the whole of life were to be found in it; every morning one should be in the childhood of life, but live every

---

* The manuscript contains a blank space following the word "Seneca." Foucault most likely intended to add several more precise references here, but did not.

day as if the evening was to be the moment of death. "At the moment of going to bed", he says in the twelfth letter, "let us say happily, with smiling face: I have lived."[30]

It is this same type of exercise that Marcus Aurelius is thinking of when he writes that "moral perfection (*teleiōtēs tou ēthous*) entails spending each day as if it were the last" (VII, 69).[31] He even wanted each action to be performed "as if it were the last."[32]

What gives a particular value to the meditation of death is not only that it anticipates that which opinion generally represents to be the greatest misfortune, not only that it enables one to be convinced that death is not an evil; it offers the possibility of looking back over one's life, as it were in anticipation. By considering oneself on the point of death, one can judge according to its real value each of the actions one is [in] the process of undertaking. Death, said Epictetus, seizes the laborer in the midst of his labor, the sailor in the midst of his navigation: "And you, in what occupation do you wish to be seized?"[33] And Seneca envisaged the moment of death as that in which one could in some way become one's own judge and measure the moral progress that one had made up until one's last day. In letter 26 he wrote: "On the moral progress which I might have made I shall believe death and I shall know if I have virtue on my lips or in my heart."[34]

LECTURE III

(*Second English Version*)

IN THE PREVIOUS LECTURE, I have tried to underline the importance—the social importance—of the culture of the self in the two first centuries of our era. I only proposed a draft for this historical phenomenon. My purpose, then, was simply to sketch out a framework for a more precise analysis.

My first point will be about the notion of *askēsis*, which is the general word used by the Greeks in order to indicate the practices and exercises related to cultivation of the self. The second point will be about the role of *logos* and truth in this *askēsis*. So much for the first hour.

In the second hour, I'll try to analyze two main types of exercises:
— the trials, the tests,
— and the examination, self-examination, which constitutes the center of what I want to develop in these lectures.

I

THE NAME *ASKĒSIS* WAS REGULARLY given to the diverse forms of cultivating oneself: *askēsis*, that means exercise, training. Musonius Rufus, for instance, has written in the middle of the first century a treatise about *askēsis*, a fragment of which has been preserved through Stobaeus's *Anthologia*. Musonius said (and in so saying, he was only repeating a traditional teaching) that the art of living (*technē tou biou*) was like the other arts; one could not learn it only from theoretical teaching (*mathēsis*); it demanded practice and training (*askēsis*).

Musonius makes a distinction between three types of *askēsis*:
—training and exercises concerning the body itself,
—training and exercises concerning the soul,
—and training concerning at the same time both body and soul.

And for Musonius, only those two last kinds of exercises were part of philosophical training.[1] This exclusion of gymnastics from philosophical life is characteristic of this culture. You know that Plato, even if he made (for instance, in *Alcibiades*) a very clear-cut distinction between the care for the body and the care for the soul, imposed on young men—either in the *Republic* or in the *Laws*—a very hard physical training in order to get them to be not only good soldiers but virtuous citizens.[2]

From Plato to Musonius there was obviously a shift: a shift from the body considered as a condition and an expression of the quality of soul, towards the body—or better, towards the body-mind relations and interactions considered as a dangerous domain where passions may arise. From this point of view one does not need to refer to Aelius Aristides; one needs only to read Seneca's letters: they are full of small information about his diseases, about his headaches, about the bad air he had to breathe. The correspondence between Marcus Aurelius and Fronto shows the same thing. The body-soul relations are perceived and experienced as the cradle of *pathos*, of passion. Medicine alternates with gymnastics as the main ethical care concerning the body.

But let's turn back to the general notion of *askēsis*, as one of the most important notions in this culture of the self. We must not read into this word the meaning which it was to have in Christian spirituality. This would be an illusion. Nietzsche—I am afraid—has been a victim of this illusion. And maybe Max Weber too.

No doubt, certain of the ancient ascetic practices were to be used in Christian asceticism and in monastic institutions (such as food abstinence, or examination of conscience, or the uninterrupted control of thoughts).

However, the general meaning of Christian asceticism was to be very different from that of ancient philosophy.

—Schematically: Christian asceticism has for its ultimate aims both the detachment from the world and the renunciation of the self. The Christian ascetic has to renounce himself, since his self is a part of the world which he has to detach himself from; and reciprocally he has to detach himself from this world, since his relations to the world are the expression of his self-indulgence, which turns him away from God.

—On the contrary, pagan or philosophical asceticism was to build up a relationship with oneself—a relation of possession and of sovereignty; and at the same time it had as an essential target to endow the individual with a preparation, which permits him to confront the world.

And here also there was a reciprocal relation. One has to be able to resist anything which may occur in order to maintain a completely independent relation to oneself; and he has to establish a relation to himself as strong as possible in order to be able to confront the world.

Organizing the interconnection between the relationship to the world and the relationship to oneself; more precisely: organizing the mastership over oneself and the independence towards the world, that's the specific work of philosophical asceticism. You may measure how far it is from the Christian form of asceticism.

But there is still something much more important than that.

Christian asceticism has as a goal escaping this world and obtaining the other world.

Christian asceticism is a "rite of passage," from one reality to another, from death to life, through an apparent death which is a real access to real life. I should say, in a word, that Christian asceticism is reality-oriented.

Pagan *askēsis* is, on the contrary, truth-oriented. Truth is both an aim and a means. *Askēsis* is the training through which one becomes able to acquire truth; and possession of truth is the way by which one is able to confront the world in maintaining one's own sovereignty over oneself.[3]

Let's stop for a while over this general notion of asceticism, since it is an important notion in our ethics, since it has been an important category in historical analysis since Nietzsche and Max Weber.[4]

I'll propose a definition of asceticism which, I think, is a little more general than the ordinary definition which regularly refers to a kind of renunciation: a voluntary and costly transformation of the self through a set of regulated techniques which have as an aim not the acquisition of an aptitude or of a knowledge but the transformation of the self in its way of being.

I think that there [are], or that there have been in Western civilization two major types of asceticism:

— asceticism oriented towards reality: the aim of this asceticism is to move from one reality to another,

— and asceticism oriented towards truth: the aim of this asceticism is to make truth the rule of our relationship both to ourselves and to the world.

I think that during centuries and centuries Western culture has been oscillating between those two types of asceticism:

— the truth-oriented asceticism, whose first completely developed form is to be found in the pagan "culture of the self";

— the reality-oriented asceticism, whose first completely developed form is to be found in the Christian technology of the self.

I don't mean that those two forms of asceticism are quite incompatible with each other. Most of the time, they have been interwoven. But the tension between those two types may explain—I think—several features, several elements, or several crises in our culture.

For instance, in the Renaissance, what has been interpreted as the struggle between Middle Ages and Modernity, between Reformation and Counter-Reformation, between dogmatism and new rationality, may be analyzed as a shift from a reality-oriented asceticism to a truth-oriented asceticism; or at least as an effort to find a new equilibrium between those two types. And, maybe, this great movement which arises at the Renaissance, and goes through the Enlightenment

SECOND ENGLISH VERSION   73

to today (with the ethical problem of a scientific civilization) is to be considered as the modern form, the modern transformation of the truth-oriented asceticism.

I'll take another example, at the opposite pole of our history. We can say that Platonism—much more than Aristotelianism—has been the "philosophy" of Western civilization; or at least the first and the most permanent formulation of Western ethical and theoretical problems. The reason is that Platonism has given the first and the most perfect formulation of the reciprocal adjustment of those two asceticisms, since Platonism has settled truth in the other world, and made of the move towards the other world the way of acquiring truth.

Take the great myths of our Western civilization: the Oedipian myth and the Faust myth. Both of them may be seen as the expression of the difficult relationships between those two asceticisms. The price of truth in terms of reality.

Look at an institution like psychoanalysis. It deals [clearly]* with those two problems: price of truth and price of reality.

Why do I evoke so allusively those themes? There is a general reason: I think that this perspective could open a certain field of research; or at least that it is worthwhile to get rid of this much too large notion of asceticism, which, I think, has introduced a lot of confusion in historical studies.

There is also a personal reason. After having studied the historical problem of subjectivity through the problem of madness, crime, sex, I would like to study the problem of revolutionary subjectivity. The time has come now to study revolution not only as social movement, or as political transformation; but also as a subjective experience, as a type of subjectivity. And I have the feeling that a certain light could be thrown on this revolutionary subjectivity by the interconnection and conflicts between the truth-oriented asceticism and the reality-oriented asceticism. I think that the fascination exercised by the idea of Revolution in the personal life of individuals was due [in] part to the promise that those two forms of asceticism could be practiced together: renouncing this reality, and moving towards another reality

---

* Conjecture; manuscript illegible; it may alternately read "exactly."

through the acquisition of truth and the constitution of oneself as a subject knowing the truth.[5]

WE ARE FAR FROM MUSONIUS. But some of you suggested that I should give a hint of the reasons why I have undertaken this kind of research.[6] I would like to study our cultural experience of sex not as the permanent conflict between law and desire, but from the point of view of the historical interconnection, in our culture, of the truth-oriented asceticism and the reality-oriented asceticism.

II

LET'S COME BACK NOW TO Musonius Rufus, and the notion of *askēsis* in the late pagan culture. The idea is that this training, these exercises, the work on oneself has, as a target, the acquirement of truth as preparation for confronting the world.

Three questions:

—What is this preparation? What does that mean: to get prepared?

—How truth can [be] acquired?

—What's this kind of truth, and what's the place of self-knowledge?

I'll briefly answer the first question before the break. And I'll try to give an answer to the second one after the break. The third question will be the theme of the next lecture.

While Christian asceticism has for its aim the parting of the individual from the world, the separation between soul and body, the parting from oneself, philosophical asceticism has for its task to *prepare*; it has to prepare individuals for anything which may happen. The words *paraskeuē* (preparation), *paraskeuazesthai* (to get prepared), are among the most frequent in the vocabulary of Greek asceticism.

What do these terms mean? What are we supposed to get prepared for? The answer is clear even if it is not very precise: we have to get prepared for anything which may occur and could affect us.

I don't want [to] comment any further [on] this principle, in spite of the fact that it raises a lot of problems.

I [would] rather pay* a little more attention to another question raised by this notion: Is there any moment in the life when this *askē-sis* has succeeded, when this preparation is completed? I don't want to enter into the details of the theoretical discussion about the possibility of becoming a sage. As you know, it was a theme of numerous discussions among the Stoics or between them and their adversaries.

But from the point of view which is mine—I mean from the point of view of the cultural experience of oneself—it is worthwhile to notice that there is one single moment when this *paraskeuē* can eventually be considered as completed: when one is old. Age is, from this point of view, a privileged, *the* privileged moment of life.[7] You know how ambiguous was the status of age in classical antiquity. Both the age of wisdom—and for that reason, it was praised—; and the age of weakness and dependence—and for that reason it was despised. Cicero's *De senectute* is still marked by this ambiguity.[8]

But, with Seneca, things are quite clear: old age is the most valuable moment in life; we should wish to become old as soon as possible. We must hurry up to those last years of our life.[9]

This revaluation of old age compared to youth is one of the most striking features of this culture of the self.

The mistrust towards youth is something characteristic of this new ethics. Of course it has to be related to several social phenomena.

For instance, the fact that young people did not play the role of defenders of the city anymore. The soldiers, at the border of the empire, were professional soldiers. And on the other hand political power was more and more extensively exercised by administrators, soon by bureaucrats, who went on through a long career.

But what is meaningful, for our analysis, is the new perspective people began to acquire on their own life. Life is not anymore to be compared with a circle, or with a curb raising to the peak of youth and

* The manuscript reads: "I had rather pay."

going down when age comes. It has to be experienced as a straight line, leading to a target, to a final point which takes place at the end of the life.

Everybody knows how important has been, in our scientific knowledge and in our rationality, the substitution of a linear conception of time to the cyclic conception of the world. But this change did not take place before the end of the Middle Ages.

Much earlier, a similar change happened in the internal experience, or at least in a certain ethical model of internal experience. Following this model, life has to be organized as a road, where one has to walk as fast as possible towards a conclusion, a completion. Living is continually approaching an end.

But immediately, a question [arises]: Which end do we have to approach? I think that this question, which is so obvious for us, would have sounded rather strange for a Latin and a Greek. You know that—with the exception of Pythagoreans and some of the strict Platonists—immortality, or at least personal survival after death, was not a real, an important issue for Romans and Greeks.

The end we have to prepare is not the life after death, it is not even death, since death is ontologically nothing; what we have to prepare is a permanent relationship of proximity to death; we have to prepare the immediacy of death; we have to live as close as possible to death, but on this bank of the river. That is what gives to old age its ontological privilege.

That is also the reason for the paradoxical role of suicide in this asceticism, at least in Seneca.

On [the] one hand, following Seneca, we have to be ready to commit suicide at any moment; and being permanently aware of this readiness is a way to live in the closest neighborhood of death. But, on the other hand, we must not commit suicide before it is necessary, for the reason that the completion of our life is not in death, but in [a] perpetual, a permanent, an indefinite proximity to death.

I think it could be interesting to study the art of suicide during this period.[10] Suicide was a kind of philosophical performance by which people completed their life, and gave themselves as example to the others. Some of those suicides could meet a great success, like a good piece of poetry, like a beautiful piece of art, like a prowess of a hero: for instance, the suicide of Thrasea Paetus. But other people were criticized. For instance, Seneca is very critical towards a certain Pacuvius who had the habit of drinking a lot every night; then he lay down on a funeral bed and let beautiful boys cry and mourn for him. Following Seneca, that had nothing to do with philosophy, only with debauchery.[11]

Anyway, if I have insisted maybe a little too much on these points, the reason is that I wanted to show the change in the personal experience of oneself, of one's life, of one's age, of one's temporality, through this type of asceticism.

You feel very well that it was quite another experience a young ambitious man like Alcibiades could have of himself, four centuries before, when he let Socrates convince him that he had to take care of himself.

III

I'D LIKE NOW TO ANALYZE *askēsis* as acquisition of truth.[12]

What do we need to remain in control of possible events? We need the "discourse," the *logoi*, understood as a true and reasonable discourse. Lucretius speaks of the *veridica dicta* which will permit us to disperse our fears and not to be overcome by that which we believe to be misfortunes. The equipment we need to confront the future, is that of true discourses. These will allow us to confront reality.

Three questions present themselves on this subject.

1. THE QUESTION OF THEIR NATURE. On this point the discussions between philosophical schools and within them were numerous. The principal point of contention concerned the necessity for theoretical knowledge. On this point, the Epicureans were completely in agreement: knowledge of the principles which govern the world, the nature of the gods, the cause of prodigies, the laws of life and death, is from their point of view indispensable for preparing oneself for possible events. The Stoics were divided, according to

their proximity to the Cynic doctrines: some gave the greatest importance to the *dogmata*, the theoretical principles which complemented practical precepts; on the contrary others considered that concrete rules for conduct should take [first]* place. Seneca's [ninetieth] and ninety-first letters present these theses very clearly. All I am doing is mentioning them; the only thing which I would wish to indicate here is that these true discourses that we need are concerned only with our relationship to the world, our place in the order of nature, our dependence on or our independence from possible events. In no way are they a deciphering of our thoughts, the things which come to mind, our desires.

2. THE SECOND QUESTION WHICH PRESENTS itself is concerned with the way in which this true discourse exists in us. To say that it is necessary for our future is to say that we should be able to have recourse to it when we feel that the need arises. When an unforeseen event or misfortune presents itself, we should be able to call upon those true discourses which are pertinent, in order to protect ourselves. They must be inside us, at our disposal. For this the Greeks have a common expression, *procheiron echein*, that the Latins translate by *habere in manu*, *in promptu habere*, to be able to lay hold of something.

It is absolutely necessary, in order to characterize the presence within ourselves of these true discourses, to understand that the process is not simply a question of simple recollection, which one could bring back to mind if the need arose.

Plutarch, for example, in order to express what is essential to the presence within ourselves of these true discourses, uses several metaphors: that of medicine (*pharmakon*) which we should keep in store to ward off the vicissitudes of life (Marcus Aurelius compares them to the medicine bag which the doctor should always carry about with him); Plutarch speaks of them as of those friends of whom "the most sure and the best are those whose useful presence in adversity helps

* Word missing from the typescript.

us." Elsewhere he invokes them as an internal voice which, of its own volition, makes itself heard when the perturbation of the passions begins to show itself; they must be in us like "a master whose voice is sufficient to appease the growling of dogs." In a passage of Seneca (*De beneficiis*) one finds a gradation of this kind, proceeding from an instrument which one can use to the automatic action of a discourse which spontaneously takes up speech within us. Seneca, speaking of the advice given by Demetrius, says that one must take it in both hands (*utraque manu*), never let it go, but also one must fix it, attach it (*adfigere*) to one's spirit, until one has made it a part of oneself (*partem sui facere*), and finally by daily meditation obtain that "salutary thoughts present themselves by themselves (*sua sponte occurant*)."

You see that here we have a movement very different from that which Plato prescribes when he demands of the soul that it turns back upon itself in order to find again its true nature. What Plutarch and Seneca suggested was, on the contrary, the absorption of a truth given by a teaching, reading, or advice; and one assimilates it to the point of making it an internal principle, permanent and constantly brought into action. In such a practice one does not recover a truth hidden in the depths of oneself by the movement of reminiscence; one interiorizes received truths by a progressively greater appropriation.

3. A SERIES OF TECHNICAL QUESTIONS present themselves concerning the methods for this appropriation. Obviously, memory plays a great role: not, however, in the Platonic form of the soul . . .[13]

LECTURE IV

I

THE LAST TIME WE MET, I tried to make clear the general notion of *askēsis*.

And assuming that *askēsis*, "asceticism," was not necessarily linked
to renunciation—as we ordinarily imagine, through our Christian or
post-Christian culture—I proposed a general definition of asceticism.

I proposed to call asceticism a regulated and costly technique for
transforming the self; and by "transforming the self," I don't mean
—the acquisition of aptitudes or knowledge,
—but the modification of the self in its way of being.
So that if we want to give a more general schema, we could say that,
among the techniques of the self I am just now studying, we could
make the following primary distinction:

DIAGRAM 1

---

disciplinary ~~acquisitive~~* techniques

Techniques of the self

ascetic techniques

---

* In the manuscript, the word "acquisitive" is crossed out and replaced with "disciplinary."

And of course, when I use the word "disciplinary,"* I give a very large meaning to [it]:

— It may be the acquisition of a knowledge or of an aptitude.

— But I also mean the very restrictive regulation of behavior. For instance, the strict discipline which was imposed [on] the soldiers in the seventeenth- and eighteenth-century armies belongs to a "disciplinary technique."[1] It was the acquisition of a code of behavior in order to be efficient, in order also to avoid death during the battle, or punishment during the exercises.

[Both are very often related, and it's often rather difficult to isolate one from the other.]†

— And among the ascetic techniques of the self, I think that, at least in Western culture, it is possible to make a distinction between *truth-* and *reality-*oriented asceticism. I have said [a] few things about this topic in the previous meeting.[2]

But I am afraid I [was] not clear enough last time, when I evoked this distinction. I would like to elaborate a little more.

1. I SPOKE OF THE REALITY-oriented asceticism as techniques which make the individual able to move from any type of reality to another. I should have been more precise and said that they give the individual this capacity in so far [as] they transform its own reality as a subject.‡

For instance, when we speak of Christian asceticism as a reality-oriented asceticism, we must conceive that it is not only a question of moving from this world to the world beyond, it's also at the same time a question of transforming the way of being of the subject itself.

* Here again, the word "acquisitive" is crossed out in the manuscript and replaced with "disciplinary."

† Foucault adds this sentence in the margin, in reference to the preceding statement.

‡ On an unpaginated manuscript page included in these documents, Foucault writes: "They transform its own reality as a subject. For instance, insofar [as] they transform a being devoted to death into a being able to take part to immortality."

This movement and this transformation cannot be separated nor isolated from each other.

If Christian asceticism is able to give access to heaven, and eternal bliss, it is able to do so insofar as the subject has been transformed (the problem is to know how it can be transformed; here appears the problem of grace. That's another story—or maybe the same). Anyway, in this kind of asceticism, no movement through reality without a complete transformation of the subject.

Christian authors have a word for this double change:

—for this passage from one type of reality to another,

—and for the modification of [the] subject from a way of being to another.

This word is *metanoia*.³ Etymologically: *change of mind*.

In Christian literature, it refers

1. to the change in the direction of [the] soul's eye when one's attention moves from earth to heaven, from flesh to spiritual world, from beneath to above—that's *metanoia*;

2. but the word *metanoia* also refers to a change in the status of the soul. And precisely to this change from Fall, removal from God, death to salvation, proximity to God, eternal Life.

Using this word borrowed by Christian authors from the Greek ethical vocabulary, we could say that the reality-oriented asceticism has a *metanoetic function*.

2. I WOULD LIKE ALSO TO elaborate a little more what I have said about truth-oriented asceticism.

I told you that those techniques make the individuals able to acquire truth. The words "to acquire" or "acquisition" I used last time are not exactly the right ones. When I speak of truth-oriented asceticism, I don't have in mind the procedures which put individuals in possession of knowledge. (The procedures which simply permit individuals to increase their knowledge are to be considered as "acquisitive techniques" and not at all as ascetic techniques). By truth-oriented techniques, I referred to a specific kind of technique: techniques which make the acquisition of truth able to transform the individual in his way of being and which reciprocally make the individual, through the transformation of his way of being, able to acquire truth.

This is a question more of appropriation, assimilation* of truth than of acquisition of truth, since the discovery of truth and the transformation of [the] subject are in a strict relationship: they are reciprocal and sometimes simultaneous.

I'll take the example of illumination: a radical transformation is necessary for illumination; without a previous purification the subject couldn't receive the light of the truth.

But reciprocally, the light of truth, illuminating the subject, transforms it; illuminating him does not simply increase the individual's knowledge, nor [does] it simply enlarge its insight. It changes its status; it changes an existence of darkness into an existence of light.

The Greeks had a word for this transformation of the subject in his way of being. *Ēthopoiēsis*: formation and transformation of *ēthos*.[4]

Using this word I should say that the truth-oriented asceticism has an *ethopoetic* function [see diagram 2].

So much for the general schema. Let's turn back to the analysis of the techniques used by the truth-oriented asceticism during the early imperial period.

In the previous lecture I mentioned two main instruments for acquiring truth in such a way that truth, true discourses, could become a part of the subject and not only an object of knowledge. Those two instruments were [the following]:

—listening, or more precisely the art of listening, related to an art of keeping silent;

—writing, or more precisely a kind of personal writing, which took as one of its main aspects the form of *hupomnēmata*.

As you may notice, these two techniques are at the same moment near and far from the most well-known Platonic themes.

For Plato also the problem was to find a way towards the true discourse; or better than that, he wanted to establish or discover an ontological relation between the soul and true discourses.

---

* Foucault had first written "appropriation," then "assimilation" over it, with a question mark in the margin; it seems as though he hesitated with regard to choosing the best formulation and uses the two terms interchangeably below.

DIAGRAM 2

Techniques of the Self

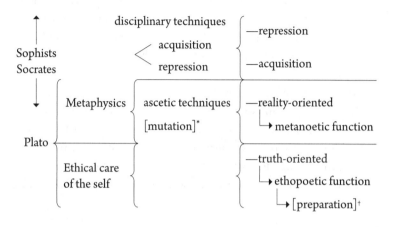

* Conjecture; manuscript illegible
† Conjecture; manuscript illegible

For this purpose, he used the art of asking and answering questions. The art of listening and keeping silent constitutes a break with this Platonic tradition. And this break has of course something to do with the professionalization and "scholarization" of philosophical teaching.

And as you also know, Plato, in order to give place to the reminiscence as a move from one reality to another, was deeply distrustful towards writings, towards *hupomnēmata*.

The systematic use of *hupomnēmata* in the culture of the self I am speaking about is another break with the Platonic tradition, a quite different use of memory.

AND NOW LET'S START WITH techniques which deal
    —not directly with assimilation,
    —but with the control of this assimilation.
And here's the place where we meet the knowledge of the self.

That's the main thing I'd like to stress in this lecture.

We can find in this culture of the self a lot of procedures and techniques which are supposed to give us the knowledge of ourselves.

This self-knowledge does not have as its aim the constitution of truth (of true discourses) about ourselves; its aim is to control the process of acquiring true discourses, of making them a part of ourselves, of transforming ourselves through them. And to control this process means to be aware of it, to measure it, and at the same time to reinforce it, to speed it up.

It is not a question of making the self appear in its reality in true discourses; it is a question of making the true discourses transform the self by a permanently controlled appropriation of truth.

Self-knowledge, in such a technology, must not be conceived as a hermeneutics of the self, deciphering a hidden reality under the apparent surface of representations. It must be conceived as the necessary trial of the process of truth appropriation, in its ethopoetic function.

Maybe, all this sounds rather banal or bizarre to you. I'd like only to remind you that such a notion of self-knowledge is not very current in our culture. You know very well that the two major forms of self-knowledge in our culture are:

1. the knowledge of ourselves as far as our reality is hidden to us → the hermeneutic knowledge of the self;

2. and the knowledge of the structural or transcendental conditions which make us able to know the truth → that's the critical knowledge of the self.

In the pagan culture of the self we have a kind of self-knowledge which does not deal with the general and permanent conditions of knowledge—as in the critical knowledge of the self—but with the actual, the active process of appropriation of truth; and it does not deal with a reality hidden inside ourselves; it deals with the distance which is still to be covered, to be crossed in order to become really subject of this truth. (That's the difference with the hermeneutic self-knowledge.)

The Greeks had a word for a true proposition when it was deeply rooted in mind and when it was not only an opinion but a matrix for behavior. This true discourse considered as a conviction, as a firm belief, as an effective rule of behavior, was called a *gnōmē*.[5]

I'd like to propose to call "gnomic knowledge of the self" this permanent trial of truth-assimilation and of its ethopoetic function. And to oppose this gnomic [knowledge] with

—hermeneutic self-knowledge;

—critical self-knowledge.[6]

I am afraid I have been much too abstract. And maybe you are a little confused with this pretentious Greek terminology. Before I give you a sketch of a clarification of these "gnomic exercises," I'd like to take a precise example. It is a passage of Marcus Aurelius which has been interpreted as a witness of a Platonic influence over Marcus Aurelius and a sign of a certain mystical trend in his philosophy.[7]

I think it is something quite different. It is, I think, a very precise exercise of gnomic self-knowledge. It is scarcely difficult to recognize its function and its goal:

—Put to the test the truths we think we have appropriated.

—[Recall] them as clearly and completely as we can.

—Confront them with a real and actual situation.

—Reinforce them by this complete inspection.

At first glance, we could imagine that this text of Marcus Aurelius is pure and passive "retreat into himself," or something like a Christian "examination of conscience."[8]

II[*]

MY THESIS IS

1. that the role of self-knowledge is really important in the culture of the self, even if it is more a consequence of the rule "take care of the self" than an autonomous principle;

---

[*] The manuscript of the lecture cuts off abruptly at the end of section 1. Two additional, unnumbered manuscript pages survive and are most likely the beginning of section 2 of the lecture (reproduced here), as they do not reference the analysis of Marcus Aurelius that Foucault announces where the paginated manuscript cuts off. The end of the lecture could not be recovered.

2. that this self-knowledge rests upon techniques which are, for the main part, tests, trials for the process of assimilation of the truth.

In order to give a brief survey of these exercises of truth asceticism, I think we can use a distinction which was current in this literature.

LECTURE V

INTRODUCTION

1. AS YOU KNOW, PHILOSOPHERS HAVE their own way of being interested in truth. A rather tricky way. I don't mean that they do not pretend to tell the truth; I don't mean that they do not succeed in saying, from time to time, something which happens to be true. Do they succeed more or less than other people? That's not my point. But like everybody else — no more, no less than other people — they use assertions; and in this way, they pretend to tell the truth.

But they pretend to tell the truth about truth itself:

— either about the criteria which are to be used in order to determine if a proposition is true or not;

— or about the necessary conditions which one has to accept in order to formulate a true proposition;

— or about the status of error (the epistemological or ontological status of error).

There is also a set of questions about truth, which, I think, deserve to be raised. These questions are of the following type:

— Why do we want to know the truth?

— Why do we prefer truth to error?

— Why are we obliged to tell the truth? What is the nature of this obligation?

These kind of questions are, I think, less familiar than the others. My assumption is not that nobody has never raised them. For instance:

You could find in Plato a theory of *Eros* as a desire for truth.

You could find in Aristotle a theory of curiosity.

Or in Schopenhauer or in Nietzsche you could find an elaboration of the notion of *Wille zum Wissen* (will to knowledge), *Wille zur Wahrheit.*

Or you could find in [William] James a theoretical development of the question, Why do we prefer truth to error?

And as you know, one could say that Heidegger moved from the question "Why being?" to the question "Why Truth?"

Pardon me if I refer to such fearful patronages. My intention is only to indicate this field of research which does not deal with the internal rules of true propositions, nor with the general conditions of true discourses, nor with the ideological or mythological factors of error, but with the will to truth, with the fact that we accept to be linked by the obligation of telling the truth.[1]

2. WHAT I AM TRYING TO do in this general domain is to analyze several historical forms of this "will to truth," about human being, human behavior, human conscience.

Why, for instance, and how madness has been introduced in a certain game of truth and error; and has moved from one game of truth and error to another.

Why a certain type of truth and error game has been inserted at a certain moment into our relationship to madness.[2]

Same question about crime,[3] same question about sex and sexual behavior.[4]

And asking this question about sex and sexual behavior, I have been led to analyze the games of truth and error in our relationship to ourselves.

ENOUGH FOR THE GENERAL PROJECT. I am not sure that this general outline is able to give a satisfactory answer to those who are surprised by all those silly little things about Seneca or Marcus Aurelius and so on. But what is interesting in the history of truth is that it is strange and bizarre, and sometimes looks silly. (I think we could say the same about the logical structure of true discourses.) Truth, I am afraid, would sometimes [appear] rather boring if it was not so bizarre.

Anyway, what I intended to show you in the previous lectures was a very specific form of truth-game about oneself in the Greco-Roman culture.

This truth-game had [five]* main characteristics:

1. It took place in the general framework of something which has been a really important theme, one of the main precepts in ancient ethics: the care of the self.

2. This precept "take care of yourself" gave rise during the Hellenistic and imperial periods to a rather large social practice and at the same time to a set of very precise techniques. And these techniques, you may find them in the works of the technicians of the care of the self, I mean the philosophers, since it is as such technicians that they present themselves.

3. To these techniques, the Greeks gave the name of *askēsis*; but we must be aware of the fact that this asceticism is deeply different from what we traditionally call "asceticism," which implies renunciation as one of its main features.

Asceticism has to be understood as a set of costly and regulated techniques for transforming the self.

4. The fourth point was that this asceticism had as its target the acquiring of truth:

— The reason why one had to exercise was that he had to acquire truth and, better, that he had to assimilate truth, to make of the *logos* the permanent matrix of his behavior.

— The way to assimilate truth was to learn it, to interiorize it, by procedures like

— the art of listening,

— the exercise of writing,

— a regular attempt to memorize what had been learnt.

5. The fifth point was that—rather surprisingly—this "truth-oriented asceticism" did not give [rise] to a specific development of self-knowledge.

---

* The manuscript reads "three" rather than "five."

—I don't intend to say that self-knowledge was of no importance in this culture of the self. It would be ridiculous to say such a thing about a culture which put such an importance on the precept *gnōthi seauton*.

—What I wanted to show is that self-knowledge was [primarily] a procedure of control on the acquisition, on the assimilation of truth.

Hence it has a permanent role to play, a permanent function to exercise.

But this self-knowledge does not constitute the self as a specific and autonomous object of true discourse.

Its task is not to uncover the hidden reality of what we are.

Its task is to assure the permanent control of the process through which we are becoming the *Logos* itself.

So we arrive at the conclusion—at this paradoxical conclusion that

—in a culture where the care of the self was so important,

—in a culture where the *gnōthi seauton* was so often quoted and so highly praised,

—and in an asceticism which had the acquisition of truth as its main objective, in such a culture, self-knowledge did not [have] the amplitude and the complexity it was to take later on.

And reversely, we can perceive the birth and the first developments of a specific and autonomous self-knowledge in Christian spirituality—in this Christian spirituality which has as one of its first precepts "Renounce yourself."

Paradoxically enough—but I think that most of you who are familiar with this kind of historical transformation won't be really surprised—the great hermeneutics of the self does not [have] its roots in a culture dominated by the care of the self, but in a spirituality dominated by the renunciation of the self.

TWO BRIEF REMARKS BEFORE WE START:

1. I think that here we have one of the reasons why we feel so familiar with the precept *gnōthi seauton*; and that on the contrary the

precept *epimele seautō* sounds for us either a little strange or at least egoistic.

It is rather difficult for us to accept as a foundation for our ethics the principle that we should give ourselves more importance than anything else in the world. We are rather more inclined to recognize in this the basis of an immorality which permits the individual to escape from all the rules.[5]

Through our Christian heritage, we easily recognize ourselves in the *gnōthi seauton*; we scarcely recognize our ethics in the *epimele seautō*. This principle of the care of the self is for us much more a principle of economic behavior, or a principle for aesthetic choices, or even a *mot d'ordre** for an ethical revolt.

2. The second remark I wanted to make deals with the difference between self-knowledge and the theory of soul:

—When I speak of self-knowledge I mean this kind of personal knowledge any individual is supposed to constitute about himself through appropriate techniques.

And it is not the same thing [as] the theory of soul, the theory of spirit, the analysis of mind, even if they are related . . .

— The techniques proposed or imposed to individuals in order to constitute and develop their self-knowledge are of course more or less dependent [on] the contemporary theories of the soul.

—And these theories most of the time rest on, rely upon, those techniques.

Let's think of Plato's conception of memory: it is both a technical element for self-knowledge, and a part of his theory of soul.

But I insist on the fact that in this research about the care and the knowledge of the self, I deal with something [other] than with theories or conceptions about soul, mind, body, and so on.

I

IN EARLY CHRISTIANITY, WE FIND some considerable changes in the culture of the self. As you know the problem of continuity

* In French in the original English manuscript.

between pagan and Christian culture in late antiquity is one of the most puzzling an historian of ideas can meet.

In the precise domain of the culture of the self and of self-knowledge it is possible to recognize strong continuities and very clear-cut discontinuities.

Very schematically, we can say that Christianity belongs to the large category of salvation religions. That means that Christianity is one of those religions which are supposed to lead the individual

—from one reality to another,

—from death to life,

—from time to eternity,

—from this world to this world beyond.

And in order to achieve this change, Christianity proposes or imposes a set of conditions, of rites, of procedures, of rules of behavior, and a certain kind of transformation of the self [which are characteristics of a reality-oriented asceticism].*

But Christianity is not only a salvation religion: it is a confession. That means that Christianity belongs to a much narrower category of religions: a religion which imposes on its adherents very strict obligations of truth. You know very well that in the Greek and the Roman religions, ritual obligations were very strict; ethical duties, rules of personal behavior, were rather vague; and the obligations to believe this or that were still much more imprecise. It is very difficult nowadays to imagine what exactly a Greek believed in; what he accepted as true in the religious field; which kind of incredulity was considered as impious and eventually condemned.

On the contrary the truth obligations in Christianity are numerous.

For instance: obligations to accept a set of propositions which constitute a dogma; obligations to hold certain texts or books as a permanent source of truth; obligations, also, not only to believe in certain things, but also to show that one believes in them. Every Christian is obliged to manifest his faith. At least in the Catholic branch of Christianity, everyone is supposed to accept the decisions of certain institutional authorities in matters of truth.

* This passage is in brackets in the manuscript.

But Christianity requires another form of truth obligation, quite different from those I have just mentioned. Each person has the duty to know who he is, to know what is happening inside him, to be aware of the faults he may have committed, to recognize the temptations to which he is exposed. Moreover, everyone is obliged to disclose these things either to God (in spite of the fact or because of the fact that God knows them much better than anyone does), or to other people, and hence to bear public or secret witness against himself. Of course the forms of this obligation are not the same in the Catholic Church and Protestant communities.

Anyway the main thing is the following: these two ensembles of truth obligations—those which deal with the faith, the Book, the dogma, and those regarding the self, the heart—are linked together.[6] A Christian is supposed to be supported by the light of faith, if he wants to explore himself, if he wants to be able to decipher what are the deep and dangerous movements of his heart. Conversely, access to truth of the faith cannot be conceived of without a purification of the soul: without this difficult attempt in order to dissipate the inner obscurity, it would be impossible to get access to light. Purity of the soul is a consequence of self-knowledge, and purity of the soul is a condition not only for the understanding of the text, of the Book, but for the strength of the faith.

Augustine has a very significant formula, *Qui facit veritatem venit ad lucem*:[7]

—*Facere veritatem*: that means to make truth in oneself.

—*Venire ad lucem*: to get access to light.

To make truth in oneself (*facere veritatem*) and get access to the light (*venire ad lucem*) are two very strongly connected concepts.

LET'S STOP HERE FOR A while; and look back briefly to the pagan culture of the self developed in the first centuries of philosophy.

1. First, you can see a very clear-cut difference. As a salvation religion, Christianity proposes or imposes a kind of asceticism (a regulated and costly transformation of the self) which is oriented towards a move from one reality to another (one type one level).

2. But this reality-oriented asceticism is linked in a very close relationship to a set of numerous truth obligations which present themselves as a necessary condition for this move from one reality to another.

— So that in the general framework of this reality-oriented asceticism, which is one of the main features of Christian religion, the place and the role of a *truth-oriented asceticism* has been very important since early Christianity.

— Christianity has integrated, or has tried to integrate into its reality-oriented asceticism, an asceticism oriented towards truth in order to make of the latter an element or a condition for the former.

DIAGRAM 3

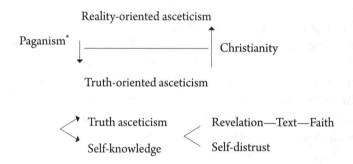

Reality-oriented asceticism

Paganism* | Christianity

Truth-oriented asceticism

Truth asceticism   Revelation—Text—Faith

Self-knowledge   Self-distrust

---

* In the manuscript, there is an upward-pointing arrow that has been crossed out; for this reason, we have only maintained the downward-pointing arrow in Foucault's diagram.

We have a lot of witnesses from Christian authors for this attempt to integrate a truth-oriented asceticism in the frame of a reality-oriented asceticism. And precisely to integrate the pagan form, the philosophical form of truth-oriented asceticism.

Christians could be at the same moment very hostile towards Greco-Roman religion and deeply respectful towards, or secretly dependent on, the philosophical ethics.

You remember the countless borrowings of Clement of Alexandria from the Stoic ethics. You remember how highly Augustine praised Seneca. You remember that during centuries and centuries Epictetus's *Enchiridion*[8] was considered a Christian text, written by Saint Nilus.

A large, or at least a certain, part of the "truth-oriented asceticism" which was characteristic of the pagan philosophical ethics has taken place in the general framework of the Christian reality-oriented asceticism.

3. But—and that's the third point—this truth-oriented asceticism has been deeply transformed, for some reasons I'll try to indicate later on.

Briefly, this transformation consists in the following:

—You remember that following Seneca, Plutarch, Epictetus, Marcus Aurelius, knowing oneself was nothing else than trying oneself in the process of assimilating the truth. One had to know oneself insofar as one had to know where he was on the path of a complete assimilation of truth. Did he know the necessary truths? Could he remember these truths as often it was necessary? Were those truths really at his disposal? Such was the general form of self-knowledge: the permanent control of the assimilation of truth; hence it could not be isolated from this assimilation neither in its form nor in its chronology.

—On the contrary what is characteristic of the Christian truth asceticism is

—not only that it has been inserted into the frame of a reality-oriented asceticism,

—but also that the two features of this truth asceticism (assimilation of truth and self-knowledge) split and became relatively independent of each other, each of them taking a specific form.

I don't mean that they became quite isolated, or two separate forms of activity. I told you—and this theme is constant in the Christian tradition—that the light of truth could not penetrate men's souls without a previous purification through self-knowledge, and that this purification could [not]* be completed without the light of truth.

But in spite of this reciprocal relationship, these two processes

---

* The manuscript reads: "could be completed"; but this is clearly a typo.

are different; they have their own forms, their own obligations, their own techniques, even if there are certain similitudes between them.

What I would like to show you today is that the Christian form of truth asceticism has broken the unity of the "gnomic knowledge of the self," and that it gave rise to two different types of relation:

—relation to the revealed truth, through the *Logos*, through the Word, through the Book;

—relation to the truth as it is revealed through the figures of the text.

And this relation has to take the form of faith.

—And there is another relation to our inner reality, to a reality which is hidden and buried in the depth of our heart, in the secret of our conscience, in the scarcely perceptible movements of our thought.

And this relation has to take the form of distrust (towards ourselves).

I'd like to insist on this distinction of the truth in the text and the reality of the self; on their difference, and on their deep and often obscure relation. I think that it is one of the main features of Western culture, and one of the main characteristics of our subjectivity. The equilibrium, the conflicts, the bringing together, the removal from each other of the truth in the text and of the truth in the self, have been, I think, one of the permanent challenges of Western culture.

The gap—the differences and relationships—between social sciences and natural sciences is a very familiar feature of our theoretical field—or at least of our academic life. The gap between those two relationships (the relationship to truth in the text and the relationship to truth in the self) has been for much more time a permanent challenge.

BUT BEFORE CONSIDERING SOME OF the consequences of this gap, I would like to make this distinction clear. And to show how aware early Christians were—at least some of them—of this distinction.

I'll be referring to one or two texts of Cassian in his *Conferences*.

Maybe I should say [a] few words about Cassian. He was a contemporary of Augustine. He was born in what is now Yugoslavia, a place where people spoke Latin or Greek; at the end of the fourth century, he visited Asia Minor, for the reason that he felt attracted by the spiritual life in Eastern monachism, and by those rather new institutions—the monasteries. At this date, there was a great tension among Christian ascetic practices between the anachoretic practice, which implied a personal retreat far from towns and a solitary life (or semisolitary), and the cenobitic institutions, which implied common life, common rules, strict hierarchical structure, and a disciplinary system. Very briefly, we could say that when Cassian visited Galilee and Egypt, the cenobitic institutions were overcoming the anachoretic tradition. That does not mean that that the *anachōrēsis* had disappeared; but there was a very strong reaction against some of the excesses linked to this type of solitary life, against certain prowesses which were highly praised by some of the anchorites.

The cenobitic rules of life were an attempt to give a disciplinary framework—for a certain part borrowed from the Roman army—to this asceticism considered as too individualistic.

Anyway, Cassian visited those cenobitic institutions, came back west, stayed for a while in Rome, [then] he settled in the South of France, where he wrote a kind of reportage about his visits in the most famous places of the Eastern spiritual life. And this reportage was supposed to be—and has been in fact—a kind of program for the foundation of monastic institutions of the West.

Cassian is not to be compared to Augustine. He is not original: his theological or philosophical conceptions are not far-reaching. But that's the reason why he can be accepted as a trustful witness for the most current topics of this spirituality. And he has been a "go-between" (between East and West), he has been not only a witness but also an important agent. He has written two books:

—One, the *Institutions*, is an exposé of the different rules of cenobitic life.[9] It is really a program for the foundation of the monastery in western Europe.

—The other book, the *Conferences*,[10] is a much more extensive and (from our point of view) much more interesting exposé of the spiritual doctrine which was most influential in those monastic institutions.

One of these conferences is devoted to the *scientia spiritualis*, to the spiritual knowledge and it shows how clear for Cassian, and with him, for the main figures of this spirituality, were the links, the proximity, and the differences between the interpretation of the text and knowledge of the self.

You find this analysis in the fourteenth [conference] (eighth paragraph).[11]

—Following a tradition which you know very well and which is rooted in the pagan culture, Cassian makes a distinction between two kinds of "science":

—*scientia pratikē*, which we'll put aside for the moment,

—and the *scientia theōrētikē*; [and] in the "theoretical science," he proposes as the first division the

— "historical interpretation,"

— "spiritual intelligence"; and in this spiritual intelligence he makes still a tripartition:

—allegorical knowledge

—anagogical knowledge

—tropological knowledge

Hence we have four types of knowledge [see diagram 4]. I'll put aside all the historical and technical problems which can be and which should be raised by this text and this theory of spiritual knowledge. What I am interested in is the relation between

—this spiritual science

—and "practical knowledge."

This practical knowledge is defined by Cassian as a knowledge which *emendatione morum* and *vitiorum purgatione perficitur*.[12]

Between this practical knowledge and the theoretical one, Cassian shows very close relationships. For instance:

—On [the] one hand, the tropological interpretation of the text consists in deciphering its practical meaning.

—On the other hand, Cassian insists on the reciprocal relations between theoretical knowledge and practical knowledge: it is impossible to acquire the theoretical science without the purification

DIAGRAM 4

—Historical knowledge It shows events as they really happened.	Jerusalem as the city of Jews	Doctrine
—Allegorical knowledge It consists in using those real events or things as figures for a mystery.	Jerusalem as the Church	Revelation
—Anagogical knowledge It consists in using those events or things as figures for a divine secret (heaven's secret).	Jerusalem as the celestial city	Prophecy
—Tropological knowledge It consists in reading those events as figures for rule of the ascetic life.	Jerusalem as our own soul	Science

of the soul; and impossible to get purified without the help of theoretical knowledge.

That's the general thesis, on which Cassian insists [in] several places of his text. But in fact, and at the same moment, Cassian shows the very specific features of this practical knowledge. He shows how different this knowledge of the self is from the spiritual intelligence of the text. And he shows this difference in three main points:

1. The basic importance of the purification in the process of theo-

retical knowledge. Purification is necessary; purification is primary; and—what's the main point—without purification, truth can't do anything by itself.

This has two consequences:

α. Some people could know everything about the interpretive techniques. If their heart is not purified, they cannot really understand the spiritual realities.

β. Purity of heart can be a substitute for the learning of interpretive techniques. Cassian gives an example for the capacity of purity to achieve what science could not do:

A very famous and saint anchorite, Abbot Johannes, could not perform an exorcism on a possessed person.

One day comes a man—a simple peasant—and he succeeded in carrying out the exorcism. And everybody wondered why he could achieve what Abbot Johannes couldn't do. He was very simple-minded, he knew nothing of spiritual science, his piety only consisted in praying to God every morning and every evening.

But he was of perfect purity; and in spite of the fact he was married, he never had any sexual relation with his wife.[13]

Such a privilege of purification, you could [not]* find in the philosophical culture of the self in antiquity.

2. There is a second idea you can find in Cassian and which seems to indicate the specificity of self-knowledge, with regard to knowledge of the text. This idea is that the purification of soul requires a very long and strict negative work on oneself. It will take twice as much work to expel vices as to acquire virtues.[14]

3. But what deserves to be underlined more than anything else is the nature of the work which has to be done in order to get purified.

For this work, Cassian used the Latin translation of the Greek term *diakrisis*: *discrimen* (operation) or *discretio* (attitude). What does this *discrimen* consist in? I'll come back to this point after the

* Foucault omits the word "not" in the manuscript, but this is clearly a typo. Indeed, on the bottom of manuscript sheet 51, he has written and crossed out the following statement: "This privilege of purification, you could not find it in the culture of the self I exposed in previous lectures."

pause and I'll give some more explanations, since it is one of the main features of the Christian hermeneutics of the self.[15]

Briefly: discrimination or "discernment" is an operation by which we test the real nature of an idea, of a thought, of a representation, of a desire.

What* does he mean by the nature? He makes a distinction between *logos* and *logismos*:

—*Logos* is the discourse insofar as it says the truth.

—*Logismos*[16] (reasoning […]).† For Evagrius and Cassian, it is the thought considered "materially" as a movement of the thought.

And what does the nature of an idea, of a thought, of a desire, depend upon?

—It does not depend upon its objective content; it does not depend upon the thing which is represented.‡

—The nature of an idea is determined by its origin; by the source where it comes from; the ontological status of its point of departure:

—flesh or spirit,

—Devil or God

—And this nature of an idea can be recognized by determining the point to which it leads us:

—spiritual life

—or material life.

The *discretio* is, in Christian spirituality, both a virtue and a technique. It is the art of determining, among all the movements of our soul, which are

—the movements which come from God;

—the movements which come from Satan.

It is not a question of determining what they mean; it is a question of determining their origin and their goal.

Cassian gives very numerous explanations about this *discretio* in several of his conferences; and mainly in the second one.[17]

---

* Before this "What," the manuscript includes a number, 1), but as there is no 2) that follows, we have omitted it here.

† Manuscript illegible; it is possible the term here is "action."

‡ The second clause was added in the margins.

But in the fourteenth conference, which I am now analyzing, he gives an example which we are familiar with, the example of silence.[18]

— You remember this rule about keeping silent, which is imposed on anybody who is a novice in the cultivation of himself.

— The reason given in pagan philosophy was that you had to keep your mind and your attention as free as possible, in order to let the true discourses penetrate our soul, and take root in it.

— Following Cassian or the spiritual master he quotes in this lecture, the main reason why a novice has to keep silent is that he has to be distrustful towards himself. Maybe, he is inclined to ask a question, because he is eager [to know] the truth. But this thought may be an illusion: he thinks he is eager for truth, and in fact this idea has been inspired in him by Satan, by the Seducer; and asking a question will lead him not to know something else, but to show how brilliant or witty he is.

And the discrimination is an attempt to recognize the real origin and the real finality of an idea, beyond its objective content.

LET'S STOP HERE. BUT BEFORE we take a break, I'd like to stress two or three things which seem to me rather important:

1. WE ARE FAR FROM THIS "gnomic" structure which is characteristic of the pagan ethics.

— On [the] one hand, truth does not have to be barely transmitted (taught and learnt), acquired, assimilated.

Truth needs to be deciphered by a specific hermeneutic procedure.

Truth is not given by *paideia* anymore, and it is not acquired by memorizing. It is given by revelation and has to be understood through the figures of discourse, through an interpretive technique.

— But on the other side, symmetrically to the interpretive hermeneutics of the text, another kind of hermeneutics is to be found in the Christian spirituality. This other type of hermeneutics is related to the first one. They are linked by a set of reciprocal relationships, but they are different in their structure.

The second one, the hermeneutics of the self, is both different from the gnomic knowledge of the self (which is mainly the permanent control of acquiring truth), and from the interpretive hermeneutics of the text. It is a discriminative hermeneutics of the self.

— The interpretive hermeneutics deals with the text, its meaning, its figures, and the truth which is revealed through them.

— The discriminative hermeneutics deals with the self, the movements of the soul, the illusions of conscience, and the reality where they come from.[19]

2. THE SECOND POINT I'D LIKE to insist on is the coexistence in Western culture of these two types of hermeneutics. Their relationships, their specificity, their equilibrium, have always been a great problem.

a. Inside Christianity itself.

— You feel very well, for instance, that one of the most important issues in the sixteenth [century], with the Reformation, was the relationships to be established between the hermeneutics of the self and the hermeneutics of the text.

— But I think that this problem was not specific to this period and this precise conflict. There were permanently in Christianity three major temptations:

— The "gnostic" temptation, which consists in bringing together, as if they were the same process, the revelation of truth and the discovery of our own reality. Inside of ourselves, we discover the sparkle of the divine light; in the revelation of truth through the text, we recognize the real and divine nature of our soul.[20]

— There is also the "textual" temptation, which gives the main importance to the relationship to the text, and to its interpretation not only as a way of acquiring truth, but also as a way of deciphering oneself and achieving the discrimination of the movements of the soul.

— There is also the "self-analysis" temptation, which gives the main importance to the relationship to oneself, and to the work of discrimination among thoughts. The role given in Catholicism to

penance, to confession, to the art of directing the consciences, belongs to this inner temptation of Christianity.

    b. But more generally the coexistence of those two kinds of herme-
neutics had a great influence upon our culture. And the attempt either to find a general form of hermeneutics or to establish between
the interpretive and the discriminative [hermeneutics] an explicit
and rational system of relationships is clearly visible in the history
of some of the so-called human or social sciences.[21]

THE SEMINAR,
JUNE 1982

FIRST MEETING

[...] THE LAST TEXT, AS YOU SEE, is a photocopy of a translation of the *Alcibiades*. We'll have a look at it first. Then the first texts are xeroxed from [...] and the third part is the *Correspondence* of Cornelius Fronto. That makes three different materials. And among the texts of Epictetus, there are still three different parts. The first one has three pages, the first three pages, that make this text. And those three pages will be the third part of what we have to study today. The three next pages, Chapter 16, "About Providence," are the second part and the last two pages [...] [The] last two pages will be the first part of what we have to study today. OK? Plato, *Alcibiades*, then Epictetus, Book 3; Epictetus, Book 1, Chapter 16; and Epictetus, Book 1, Chapter 1. And then, if we have time, a letter ... two ... three letters from Marcus Aurelius to Fronto. That's it. OK?

Really I would like to ask you several things [...]. I would really like you to take the initiative in this seminar for several reasons. The first one is that it is the first time in my life—in spite of the fact that I'm rather old—[this is] the first time that [I've] run such a seminar with foreign people, people I don't know ... [So] I don't know [...] if you are interested, what you have studied and so on. I'm ignorant of you, and that's a first difficulty. The second thing which makes things rather difficult is that my English, as you may have noticed, is not perfect. And I was told that I could run the seminar in French, and I prepared my stuff in French, but I am afraid that it couldn't be possible. First thing at least I would like to ask you is, Do you think that we could do this seminar in French or both in French and in English—you speak English if you like and I speak French—or do you prefer that I try to speak in my broken English rather than my childish French?

—*[Personally I can do both, French or English.]*

—*Are there people who don't understand any French?*

—And how many people could speak French? So, well, I'll try to do it in English. The third reason why I would like you to take the initiative is that during the lectures of course I am obliged to speak, and maybe I speak too much, too long, and so on, and I don't know exactly what are your reactions, how far you are responsive to what I have said, and if you are interested or not, if it's too technical or not . . . or insufficiently technical . . . and so on. So what I suggest would be for those two hours, first that you speak very freely and frankly about what you want concerning our meetings or the lectures or the seminars. Then, after that, we could read together. Or no, we could speak about the *Alcibiades* so far as some of you had the opportunity before the seminar to read the text of the *Alcibiades*, since it was this text, or part of it, that I have commented [on] in my last lecture.[1] So we could do that, react to this text, to the interpretation I have proposed to you. Then, after that, we could read together the texts of Epictetus, and I have prepared a kind of commentary about these three texts of Epictetus, and then, if we have time left, we could read together the letters of Marcus Aurelius and Fronto. How do you say that? First, free discussion, reactions, then discussion about the *Alcibiades*, then discussion about Epictetus, and then Marcus Aurelius and Fronto. Is it OK? So who wants to speak first?

—*[. . .] if you could elaborate on that a bit more, and talk about what the distinctions between different classes of citizens might mean for what you've been talking about.*

—Yes, yes, that's a good question. But maybe, first of all, I would like, is there any question or critiques or anything to say about the formal aspect of the things about the lectures? I have heard, for instance,

that you couldn't understand exactly that I have said or at least—
it's the fault of my bad pronunciation—that you couldn't catch the
names I told. That's true? No?

The second question I would like to ask is, Do you think that
what I am telling you, what I have tried to tell you about the *epimeleia heautou* and the taking care of oneself and so on is that . . . isn't it
too far from what you are supposed to study in a seminar on semiotics and things like that? I'm afraid to disappoint you!

—[. . .]*

—[. . .] *In a cafeteria discussion today, some people were [wonder-
ing] why you decided to go back to late antiquity, Greco-Roman philosophy, and early Christianity. [. . .] We have people on a lot of different
levels taking part here: some people who have been studying this themselves, some people who have been keeping up with your own studies,
and we have heard different explanations in the past. [. . .] But I think
it would be helpful if there was more of an explanation for this choice of
material . . . I think you covered this to some extent in your first lecture,
in the explanation of the four different technologies, but I think that a lot
of people are still out in the cold on that.*

—Yes, well, you see, the reason why I went back to this stuff, late
antiquity or postclassical, Hellenistic period, Greco-Roman period,
and so on, the reason is that what I have tried to do from the beginning is not exactly a history of sciences or a history of institutions like
asylums, prisons, and things like that. Of course I was interested in
this field, but when I had studied those things, those institutions, and
so on, the reason was that the deep problem I wanted to treat was the
history of our subjectivity. It is not a history of sciences, it is a history
of subjectivity. And I think that our subjectivity—and that's for me
the main difference with what we could call the phenomenological

* The recording is partially inaudible here; Foucault can be heard to say,
"Yeah, sure," then an auditor seems to mention Foucault's name, and says
something about how people are crowding to be at the seminar because
they heard that Foucault is there. Foucault can be heard to say, "No, I am
not sure, I hope he is not. I am deeply hoping," though it is unclear what he
is referring to or responding to.

experience ... no, the phenomenological theory—subjectivity is not a kind of radical, of immediate experience of oneself, but there are a lot of social, of historical, of technical mediations between ourselves and ourselves. And the field of those mediations, the structure, the effects of those mediations, that's exactly the theme of my research from the beginning.

For instance, each of us has a certain relationship to his own madness. He has conscience and experience of [...] the part of himself which is supposed to be mad. He has, to madness in general and to himself as possibly mad, a certain experience. And I think that this experience of oneself as possibly mad is of course historically, socially, culturally, determined. And I will make an exaggeration saying that all of us have a kind of asylum inside of himself, but it is a way to exemplify what I want to say. Each of us has a kind of prison inside himself, and his relation to law, his relation to transgression, his relation to crime, to sin, and so on has not only a historical background, but there is a part of history, of historical structure, of this inside relation, in each of us, you see. And that was the reason why I have studied madness, why I have studied the prison and so on, and now when I am studying sex and sexuality, I put the question in the same light. I don't think that the relation we have to our own sex is something so immediate as people could think. There is not only a historical framework, but a historical structure of our sexual subjectivity. And I have tried to study that from the sixteenth century on to now.

But I became quickly aware that it was nearly impossible to take the sixteenth century, or the end of the Middle Ages, or the Reformation and Counter-Reformation, as a point of departure. And reading all those texts, quickly I came to the conviction, I became convinced that I had to come back, go back to late antiquity, the Hellenistic and Greco-Roman period as the real historical point of departure of this kind of subjectivity, this kind of consciousness, and so on. And the relationships between asceticism and truth in late antiquity and early Christianity seem to me to be [...] a historical point of departure [...].

—*Part of what I was suggesting is that if that fact could work its way into the lecture a little bit it could be helpful . . . A lot of people are coming not having studied this period, so it's dry material in some senses.*

—Well, maybe I'll try in the beginning of the next lecture to explain that a little.[2] That's your suggestion?

—*I don't know what other people feel about it, but that's what I picked up from . . .*

—Yeah, sure. I'm grateful that you tell me that.

—*I heard both sides: classicists feeling that you were giving short shrift to the ancients and people who aren't interested in that [. . .] [You need a] good middle ground.*

—Yeah, certainly.

—*I think part of the problem is that it's very difficult for someone to pick up certain threads to which they might object, or to snipe at particular remarks, when they're not sure just how you're knitting these threads together. [In some cases, it is even more difficult, because you may] pick up the thread again later on, and weave it more deeply into the structure of where you're going. So without a clearer understanding of just why you're putting certain structures in place, it is difficult for participants to make certain objections or pose certain questions, especially because the lectures are in a sense already concluded in your presentations. I for one would like you to elaborate a little bit on the careful distinction that you initially made between individualism and a technology of the self.*

—Well, that's a very good question. My purpose was to speak about it in the last lecture. So maybe we can start [with] that, but it will be the historical and social background of all that. The problem is why those technologies of the self have been so important in this period—I mean the beginning of the empire—and the explanation which most of the historians of ideas at least would give would be "Well, it is the rise of individualism in the Greco-Roman societies." But I don't think that is [a] good explanation, for a lot of reasons. Among them, the fact that the people who practiced this care of oneself, or the people who were the theoricians of the care of oneself, these people were not at all individualistic figures, they were not at all people retiring from social or political life, they were not at all people who were not interested or were not active in the political field. People like Plutarch, in his small town, [were] very active; he was involved in all the social and political life of the province. And of course somebody like Seneca, who was the minister, the prime minister of Nero, has during the last years of his life been involved in a very intense political life, political activity. So I think that the rise of individualism and the decay of the collective life of the city is not, cannot be considered as, the reason of the development of those technologies of the self.

The second great reason is that those technologies of the self are very archaic, and you can see the development from the elder documents we have about Greek life. So individualism cannot be the reason of the development of those technologies of the self.[3] The problem is to analyze the reason why at a certain moment people [who] were really involved in social and political life have presented, developed, new forms of techniques of the self. That could be the theme of the last lecture. [But] I don't know if I catch exactly the question you were asking.

—[...] I had understood you to make a distinction in the first lecture between a technology of the self as an apparatus of power engaging the personality which is related to, for example, the [linguistic-sociality mode]* of man, and an individualism which didn't seem to be attached to that technology, which seemed to be simply a hinge that everyone ... that functions as a hinge that belongs to everyone including the body and the society at large.

—Hinge?

—Gond.

—Gond.

—[Charnière.]

—For example, the body and the social personality, the hinge by which the body is related to the social personality. [It] seems to me that we're distinguishing first a level which you termed individualism insofar as everybody must [acknowledge the difference] between the body and the social personality, our own habits ...

—But I won't make a difference between, or at least this kind of difference, between body and social personality. We don't need any

---

* Conjecture; the sentence is partially inaudible.

hinge to relate body to social personality. Our body is a part of society, our body is a part of our social personality, and . . .

— *It's OK, but then is there a distinction, or am I misunderstanding you, between this unity described as, in quotes, "individualism," and this unity as enclosed by technologies of the self?*

—Well, I would say . . . I would rather say that individualism is a result of certain kind of techniques of the self. And I would say the reverse: I think that most other people would say that, if the techniques of the self have developed, the reason is the [rise] of individualism. I should say that in the history of those very numerous techniques of the self, at certain moment, for certain reasons, and of course we have to explain, to elaborate those reasons, at certain moment those techniques of the self take the shape and have as a result the form of an individualism. I don't know if that is exactly an answer to your question. No?

— *I had thought you had made that clear . . .*

—Between individualism and techniques of the self?

— *I'm not sure I understand the question either. Perhaps someone else could elaborate . . .*

—Maybe I think that . . . I have the feeling that you touch an important point, but I can't catch exactly what is your question. Maybe we could do: one, to write in a few words your question, or a few pages if you want, give me the paper, I'll read it and try to give an answer either in a lecture or in the seminar or in a conversation with you. Because I think it's a very fundamental question. So there is no reason to treat this question, to answer this question now or later on or at the end. I think that I have to answer this question, I'm sure that I have to answer. But it is a deep and general question, and I think maybe that is not exactly the moment now.

Anyway I would like to understand quite well what is your question. So, please, you could do . . . You agree to do that? Thanks.

So. There is one question more, the question you ask about . . . yeah, it was about the different social categories of individuals concerned with those technologies. So there are two very great differences, and of course it's not at all for me a question of saying that everybody in late antiquity or in this Greco-Roman period is obliged or [. . .] published a few years ago in 1975 or 1976 a book, *Roman Social Relations*,[4] a very short book, an overview, by a very serious historian. He says that Roman society was characterized, first, by its verticality, the fact that the scale of social differences was very, very large and that everybody in this society—that's the second point— was very conscious, very aware of this verticality, everybody knew exactly [his] own place on the scale. And the third thing is that this verticality was accepted as, not exactly a destiny, but as something quite necessary and nothing revolting about it. And in this society, it's quite sure that the care of the self—as I suggest you from the anecdote of the king of Sparta saying: "We don't farm by ourselves because we have to take care of ourselves"[5]—taking care of oneself is the privilege of the upper class, this upper class which is of course the main cultural vehicle—you say that?—the main vehicle of culture. So we cannot imagine of course that small people, peasants of course or even small merchants, shopkeepers, and so on, those people are not at first glance concerned with this kind of problem. It is an aristocratic practice.

But this must be corrected by several things. First, the problem of the slaves. The slaves live in the house, in the house of the master, and directly or indirectly they—some of them at least, the more clever or the more beautiful, who are the lovers of the mistress or of the master of the house—take part in the culture of the family and—even by themselves or at the second generation—really they are members of this culture, and when they are freed and become freed men, then they are, some of them are, most representative of this aristocratic culture. That's the first important point.

The second point is that this culture was of course owned by the upper classes, but we must remember that, for instance, in the Greek cities, it's not only in the classical period but even in the Hellenistic period and in the Roman period, because in the Roman period there was a political life in the cities, in Greece or Asia Minor or Egypt there was a political life in the cities, well, small people, shopkeepers and so on, were . . . as far as they were members of the city, took part in this political activity, and political activity and cultural activity were deeply linked.

The third reason is that all the religious movements that developed so quickly and so largely and so deeply in the Hellenistic world and in the Roman world from the third or second century before Christ, [before the advent of Christianity],* well, all those religious movements had as one of their main objectives and targets to help people to take care of themselves. So those religious movements were popular movements and most of them had this kind of preoccupation.

And, I should say, the fourth thing is that several philosophical movements, the Epicureans at the beginning, Epicureanism in the beginning, third . . . third century, was a democratic movement, politically hostile to the local aristocracy, and Epicureanism, as a philosophical movement, was directly related to the democratic movement in the Hellenistic world, this democratic movement which was very often the main support of tyranny or monarchy. So, you see, that this . . . that was the case for Epicureans in the beginning . . . and Epicureanism in the third century. And after that the Cynical movement, or the Stoico-Cynical movement from the second century before Christ, this Stoico-Cynical movement was also a democratic movement, very often related, in Rome, for instance, to republican ideas. After that this Stoico-Cynical, Cynico-Stoical movement, Stoic movement was related to . . . well, it was, with Dio of Prusa, [who] was a partisan of monarchy, and absolute monarchy, but always against the aristocratic power and the aristocratic class. So, you see, you can't say exactly that those themes I spoke about, the theme of the care of oneself and so on, you can't say that it was only something typical of a small aristocratic group. It has been much larger in all . . . during all the history of ancient society.

The problem of women. It's true that all the culture, or nearly all the culture, Greek culture, was a man culture—you can say that?

—*Male culture.*

—A male culture—and that females never appear at least, never appear at least as active agents in this culture. That does not mean that women did not take any part or were excluded from this culture. But

* Conjecture; the sentence is partially inaudible.

there are no female great authors, for instance, with the exception, of course, very well known, of Sappho and later on in the first/second century after Christ, [but we'll come back to that]. And that's another point, that during the Hellenistic period and during the Roman period, for a lot of reasons, the role of women in society, in economics, never in politics . . . no, no, at least in economic life and in social life, the role of the women increased very quickly and in a very perceptible way. There is a rather good book, the title is *Goddesses, Whores, Wives, and Slaves*, written by Sarah Pomeroy.[6] Well, she very clearly shows that the role of women increased in the Hellenistic period. And in Roman society, we mustn't forget that the political role of women was great, much greater than in Greece, much greater than in Athens, where the political role of women in Athens was zero. In Roman society, the role of women was rather great and that had a great influence in the imperial [era].[7] And you can find in the second century, for instance, several books about the art of life, the art of living, about family life, about the relationship between men and women inside the family, or relation between parents and children, and those books are attributed to women. It's difficult to know if the real authors were men or women. Most of those books [were] written in Pythagorean circles, and it was a habit in those circles to use pseudonyms. So it is difficult to know if those books [were] written by women. But the fact that they have been attributed to women, the fact that the people who wrote those books used women's names proves that it was not a scandal, it was quite natural, it was accepted that those kinds of books were written by women. OK on this point? Please.

    —I want to clarify a point that has come up in these lectures that you referred to. If I understand you correctly, you're saying that the imperative to know oneself is rooted in a more fundamental imperative to take care of oneself. Now, would it be correct to say that the desire to take care of oneself, for the Greeks at this period of Socrates, is rooted in a more fundamental desire, which is the desire to take care of the city? And, my specific question is: I'm a little confused as to whether the Socratic dialogue represents a tension with that traditional Greek conception of taking care of the city, in which the self derives its importance because of the service it gives to the city, while it seems to me that the dialogues suggest the pos-

*sibility that the good that the city receives is a result of the good that the
self comes to create for itself. Is there a real tension there?*
—A tension? Well, this is a very important problem. There is a
text which is very . . . well, very enigmatic, or very significative, if you
like, it is in the *Apology*, where Socrates says: [instead of punishing
me, you] should give me a reward for what I have done since, as far I
teach people to take care, not of their possessions, but of themselves,
I teach them at the same time to take care of the city and not take
care of the *pragmata* [their material affairs].[8] [In the *Republic*, Plato]
grounds the assertion, the thesis, that if one cares, as he has to do, if he
cares for his soul, he will care in the same way for the city. So I think
that the *Republic* shows very clearly in which way the care of oneself
may be at the same time the care of the city.[9] [But the tension between
the care of the self and the care of the city becomes]* more acute in
the Roman period. Well, people like Seneca ask, if not in each letter,
very often: "What should we do? Should we take care of ourselves
or should we take care of the city?" And it is very difficult for him
to take care of both at the same time. I think that for Socrates, or for
the Socratic period, it was not so difficult to make, to [see] the unity.
   There are two questions, I think. Do you [want to] ask first . . .
   —[. . . *You might have overlooked something important . . . about
Aristotle . . .*]†
   —Yes, I'm quite aware I am overlooking all that, you see . . .
   —*Of course* [. . .].
   —Yes, you see, the main target, the main field of those lectures
and those seminars is this period of the two first centuries after Christ.
So I'm obliged to take as a point of departure a very schematic draw-
ing of Plato, Aristotle, and so on . . .
   —[*What is the place of the* Alcibiades *in the dialogues of Plato?*]‡
   —What I'd like to say about this is that, for instance, for the
Neoplatonists—I mean Neoplatonists [like] Albinus, second cen-

---

* Conjecture; the sentence is partially inaudible.
† Conjecture; the sentence is extremely distorted and barely audible.
‡ The sentence is again barely audible, so the question has been recon-
structed based on Foucault's response.

tury after Christ, Proclus, Olympiodorus, Iamblichus, Porphyrus—it was quite clear that [two different lines issued] from the *Alcibiades*: the political line and the mystical line. The political line from the *Alcibiades* to the *Laws* through the *Republic* and the *Statesman*: that was the political Platonic line. And there was the mystical Platonic line from the same *Alcibiades* to the *Phaedo*, *Phaedrus*, and so on. And of course the Neoplatonists, Albinus and so on, have chosen for themselves the second one. But they saw Platonism as this tension for this bifurcation in two lines, with the *Alcibiades* [as a point of departure].* They were quite aware of this tension. One question more?

—[...]†

—Has anybody here read the *Alcibiades* and has anybody a question to ask about it? [...] Is there any question? No? Or maybe we could come back to it later on in other seminars. Yes?

—[*In the* Alcibiades, *Socrates says that one must care for oneself when one is young, because after that it will be too late. On the contrary, in the* Apology, *he declares that he is addressing everyone, young and old. Why, in that case, have you chosen to focus on the* Alcibiades *in your lectures?*]‡

—Yes, yes, that's different. Anyway I [will] speak about this point because Epictetus[10] [says] something about it. It's quite true that— this affirmation, that you need to be young to take care of yourself— you find it in the *Alcibiades*, you could find it also in other Socratic dialogues. But, for instance, in the *Apology*, Socrates says [...] that he addresses himself to anybody walking in the street, citizen or non-citizen, young or old.[11] So that's two different things and, if my purpose were to explain what the *epimeleia heautou* is for the theory of the soul in the Platonic doctrine, well, I think I could give an account of what it is. But if I have chosen this text, it is because a relation between education, pedagogy, the efficiency of Athenian pedagogy, and the obligation of taking care of oneself is very clear. And the second

---

* Conjecture; the sentence is partially inaudible.

† The exchange with the auditor is completely inaudible.

‡ The exchange with the auditor and the questions posed are inaudible; the question has been reconstructed based on Foucault's response.

reason is that this problem of the relationship between pedagogy and care of oneself, this problem has been elaborated and transformed. And at the period which I have chosen, the early empire, it is quite clear that the care of the self comes after education and is not a substitute for education, but a criticism of education. That is the reason why I have privileged this text, but in the Platonic doctrine the *epimeleia heautou* is not the privilege of young people or even [...].

—[*Weren't some techniques of the self in Greece influenced by other cultures?*]*

—Yes, sure. Well, in one of my lectures, I don't remember which one,[12] I have mentioned those practices which came, following Dodds or Vernant,[13] which came from shamanic [or Eastern cultures].† I mentioned those techniques like abstinence, fasting, sexual abstinence, holding your breath, and so on. Those techniques [appeared in Greece in the seventh / sixth century]‡ and they [were taken up] in the Pythagorean and Orphic circles. Orphism and Pythagoreanism [were] the first religious, mystical, and at a certain point philosophical elaboration of those techniques and [...] as those movements have [...].

—[...]§

—I think I do not understand. Could you speak a little louder?

—[*What can the* Alcibiades *teach us about the culture of the self in the Hellenistic and Roman periods that is so different from Greek philosophy in the classical period?*]¶

—What I would like you to pay attention to, if you read this text of the *Alcibiades*, is the fact that, in the [...] text, the theory of soul is quite central. For Plato you can't take care of yourself without know-

---

* The exchange with the auditor and the questions posed are inaudible; the question has been reconstructed based on Foucault's response.

† Conjecture; the sentence is partially inaudible.

‡ Conjecture; the sentence is partially inaudible.

§ The next exchange is extremely difficult to make out because of an interruption in the recording.

¶ The question is partially inaudible and has been reconstructed from Foucault's response.

ing exactly what the metaphysical status of your soul is. The care of
the self and the metaphysics of soul are strictly related. And what is
very striking in the Stoics, or even, I would say, in all of the culture of
the self in the beginning of the Roman Empire, is that people show
that this metaphysics of soul is not at all relevant for the culture of
the self. You can, you have to take care of yourself without having to
know what your soul is, what its structure is, and so on. The problem
of medical knowledge, for instance, is much more important, or the
problem of the passions, the problem of the movements of the passions, the developments, the [...] the development of the passions,
that's a real problem, for instance.

But what is the soul? Is it different from the body or not? It's not
at all a problem. I don't know if I answered the question. That's very
striking. And, I should say, very original, if you compare it both to
the Greek, to the Platonistic tradition, and to the modern philosophical problem. The problem is the self. But they never give any definition of the self.

Please read a very, very important passage in this text of *Alcibiades*. I'll find it. I don't know what ... what the English translation is.
Well, tell me please and I'll find it in the text. Voilà. Ah, it is in 129b
[...] Well, then let's see in what way the true nature of the self can
be discovered:*

SOC. Well, and is it an easy thing to know oneself, and was it a mere
    scamp who inscribed these words on the temple at Delphi; or is it a
    hard thing, and not a task for anybody?
ALC. I have often thought, Socrates, that it was for anybody; but often,
    too, that it was very hard.
SOC. But, Alcibiades, whether it is easy or not, here is the fact for us
    all the same: if we have that knowledge, we are likely to know what
    pains to take over ourselves; but if we have it not, we never can.
ALC. That is so.

* The next few sentences are partially inaudible; Foucault can be heard
to say, "Just before. Socrates: 'And if self-knowledge can be such an easy
thing and what ... and was to be like [...].'"

SOC. Come then, in what way can the same-in-itself be discovered. For thus we may discover what we are ourselves; whereas if we remain in ignorance of it we must surely fail.

ALC. Rightly spoken.

SOC. Steady, then, in Heaven's name! To whom are you talking now? To me, are you not?

ALC. Yes.

SOC. And I in turn to you?

ALC. Yes.

SOC. Then the talker is Socrates?

ALC. To be sure.

SOC. And the hearer, Alcibiades?

ALC. Yes.

SOC. And Socrates uses speech in talking?

ALC. Of course.

SOC. And you call talking and using speech the same thing, I suppose.

ALC. To be sure.

SOC. But the user and the thing he uses are different, are they not?

ALC. How do you mean?

SOC. For instance, I suppose a shoemaker uses a round tool, and a square one, and others, when he cuts.

ALC. Yes.

SOC. And the cutter and user is quite different from what he uses in cutting?

ALC. Of course.

SOC. And in the same way what the harper uses in harping will be different from the harper himself?

ALC. Yes.

SOC. Well then, that is what I was asking just now—whether the user and what he uses are always, in your opinion, two different things.

ALC. They are.

SOC. Then what are we to say of the shoemaker? Does he cut with his tools only, or with his hands as well?

ALC. With his hands as well.

SOC. So he uses these also.

ALC. Yes.

SOC. Does he use his eyes, too, in his shoe-making?

ALC. Yes.

SOC. And we admit that the user and what he uses are different things?

ALC. Yes.

SOC. Then the shoemaker and the harper are different from the hands and eyes that they use for their work?

ALC. Apparently.

SOC. And man uses his whole body too?

ALC. To be sure.

SOC. And we said that the user and what he uses are different?

ALC. Yes.

SOC. So man is different from his own body?

ALC. It seems so.

SOC. Then whatever is man?

ALC. I cannot say.

SOC. Oh, but you can—that he is the user of the body.

ALC. Yes.

SOC. And the user of it must be the soul?[14]

So. All this passage. Socrates has been explaining just before that Alcibiades had to take care of himself and what does that mean, take care of oneself, and then comes the answer: you cannot take care of yourself without knowing what you are—so the reference to the Delphic precept comes here—and this self-knowledge is something important and difficult. You have to know the true nature of the self. And the Greek text is very, very explicit, the English translation is quite good. It is: *"Phere dē, tin'an tropon heuretheiē auto tauto." "De quelle…"* "Which way could you find what is the self?" And it is very [significant] that, from this question on to the end of the text, you do not at all find a definition of the self, not at all a definition or a description of reflexivity, of subjectivity, but a theory of soul, as in opposition to the body. When you have to take care of yourself, you don't have to take care of your body, or you don't have to take care of your riches or your clothes or your shoes and so on and so on—you know the Socratic way of running a discussion—you have to take care of your soul. And what is the soul?

What is very interesting in this text, it is that the soul is not defined in this passage as it is defined, for instance, in the *Phaedo* or in the *Phaedrus*. The soul in this text is not the prisoner of the body, it's not something, a substance [which] is present in the body. It is not something like the carriage, *l'attelage,* carriage of the *Phaedrus, vous savez* . . . you know, two horses, the white one and the black one.[15] It's not this kind of soul that is analyzed in this passage. The soul is defined in this passage as the *dunamis,* the power, the capacity of using the body. That's very important because we'll find this notion of using the body as something quite central in the Epictetus doctrine, the *chrēsis,* use. First point.

The second reason why it's very important is that in early Socratic dialogues you never find this notion; you find it only in Aristotle's texts. It's an Aristotelian definition, not a Platonic one. And that is one of the reasons why the status of this text is very enigmatic. Well, anyway, you see that there [are] interesting things, but I'm not sure it's possible to discuss them, since you didn't have the opportunity to read the text. So, if you want, if you are interested, read it and, next time or in one of the following seminars, we could have a discussion about this very strange text.

There is also a passage—I don't know if it is mentioned in the English translation—about the soul, no, it's not. There is a passage which seems to be interpolated. Anyway it is a text you find only in a Christian author. It's about the fact that the divine substance is a much clearer mirror than anything else to look [at one's soul].* Ah, yeah, 133, and this text, yeah. It is on page . . .

—65.

—No, no. Anyway it's on 133c: "May we say then that, as mirrors are purer and clearer and brighter than the mirror [. . .] in the eyes, so also God is by his nature a clearer and brighter mirror than the most excellent part of our own soul?"[16] You can't find this text in most of the manuscripts of this dialogue, but you find it as a quotation of this dialogue in Eusèbe de Césarée [Eusebius of Caesarea], a Christian author of the fourth century. So some people think that this passage

---

* Conjecture; Foucault does not finish the sentence.

is an interpolation, that Eusèbe de Césarée has invented this text, or brought it from a Neoplatonic text.

— *Then could you speak on the thematic importance of the mirror and the soul? Why is it important, a specular relationship between the soul and . . .*

— Really, I couldn't do it now. If you want, we could put aside certain important questions, but I cannot elaborate *en improvisant . . .*

— *Improvising.*

— Improvising. First because I do not know exactly the answer, because the question is very important, because my English is for me much more [. . .] and so on and so on. Anyway, I think that this metaphor of the mirror is quite typical of Platonism and Neoplatonic movements. I think you never find it in other texts even about the care of the self or the [. . .] and so on and so on. Anyway in Seneca, even in Epictetus, which is very Socratic. Maybe once, maybe once in Epictetus. Anyway, I think that's a good question. Let's see. If you are interested in this question, I would be happy to do something about it.[17] But not now, but later on in another seminar we could do something on that. Yes? That would be OK?

— *[It seems to me that the idea that the body serves the soul can be found in other texts of Plato.]**

— Ah, yes, sure, the fact that the soul uses the body is not at all an *apax†* in the Platonic world. But the fact that soul is only defined as the power which can use the body, that's something quite strange. Sure.

— *[Don't we find the idea that the soul is the actor elsewhere in Plato?]‡*

— Yes, you see, I don't mean that [. . .] in other texts of Plato you couldn't find the idea that soul is the actor, but the definition of soul as something which is the principle of action, [. . .], use, the using power of the body . . .

---

* The question is inaudible and has been reconstructed based on Foucault's response.

† English: "hapax legomenon."

‡ The question is inaudible and has been reconstructed based on Foucault's response.

—*[What is the Greek word used here to say that the soul directs the body?]** —It's *chraomai,* it's *chresthai.* Anyway that's a problem we could also elaborate more ... But anyway, what strikes me in this text is the fact that, that there is not ... you see, this text is strange because, first, it is a dogmatic text. The difference between the early Socratic dialogues and this one is that this one gives answers, and a lot of answers. He says what is the soul, what is the knowledge of oneself, what is contemplation, and so on and so on. A lot of dogmatic solutions but not at all the traditional dogmatic solutions you could find in dialogues like *Phaedo* and *Phaedrus* about the metaphysical status of [the soul]. All that is strange. So. There are any more questions about Plato's *Alcibiades?*

WE ARE LATE. WELL, DO you want us to read Epictetus, those three texts of Epictetus? Because I think that Epictetus has been the theoretician of the concern of the self, the concern of the self at this period. I would like to comment on those three texts. Maybe the best would be, first, to read what I would like to comment on first, that is the last one, the text from the third book. The page begins with "Like but you will say it ..." You have got it? Maybe you could read it in English because your English, I think, is better than mine.

—*How much? Where?*

—"If you bring this charge against me ..." Stop ... well, stop at "... maybe different from the rest."

[A participant reads the first text of Epictetus:]

If you bring this charge against me some day, what shall I be able to say in my own defense? Yes; but suppose I speak and he does not obey. And did Laius obey Apollo? Did he not go away and get drunk and say good-bye to the oracle? What then? Did that keep Apollo from telling him the truth? Whereas I do not know whether you will obey

---

* The question is inaudible and has been reconstructed based on Foucault's response.

me or not. Apollo knew perfectly well that Laius would not obey, and yet he spoke. But why did he speak? And why is he Apollo? And why does he give out oracles? And why has he placed himself in this position, to be a prophet and a fountain of truth, and for the inhabitants of the civilized world to come to him? And why are the words "Know thyself" carved on the front of his temple, although no one pays attention to them?

Did Socrates succeed in prevailing upon all his visitors to keep watch over their own characters? No, not one in a thousand. Nevertheless, once he had been assigned this post, as he himself says, by the ordinance of the Deity, he never abandoned it. Nay, what does he say even to his judges? "If you acquit me," he says, "on these conditions, namely, that I no longer engage in my present practices, I will not accept your offer, neither will I give up my practices, but I will go up to young and old, and, in a word, to everyone that I meet, and put to him the same question that I put now, and beyond all others I will especially interrogate you," he says, "who are my fellow-citizens, inasmuch as you are nearer akin to me." Are you so inquisitive, O Socrates, and meddlesome? And why do you care what we are about? "Why, what is that you are saying? You are my partner and kinsman, and yet you neglect yourself and provide the State with a bad citizen, and your kin with a bad kinsman, and your neighbors with a bad neighbor." "Well, who are you?" Here it is a bold thing to say, "I am he who must needs take interest in men." For no ordinary ox dares to withstand the lion himself; but if the bull comes up and withstands him, say to the bull, if you think fit, "But who are you?" and "What do you care?" Man, in every species nature produces some superior individual, among cattle, dogs, bees, horses. Pray do not say to the superior individual, "Well, then, who are you?" Or if you do, it will get a voice from somewhere and reply to you, "I am the same sort of thing as red in a mantle; do not expect me to resemble the rest, and do not blame my nature because it has made me different from the rest."[18]

— Thanks. Well, of course I have chosen this text because, as you see, there is a very explicit reference to the theme of the concern for oneself, the expression *epimeleia heautou* is to be found in this text, and the *Alcibiades* indirectly and the *Apology* directly are quoted by it.

First thing, I think, is to, of course, remember what we could call the Socratic renaissance which this text is a witness of. The Socratic renaissance in the second century, in the beginning of the second century, was a part of the great Greek Renaissance of those two first centuries, but you must keep in mind that the Socratic renaissance was a part of this Greek Renaissance, but also a kind of counterpart, it was a critique against the great renewal, revival of classic studies, of classic pedagogy, of Greek studies, and so on, in the Roman Empire. To come back to Socrates was to come back, sure, to Greek culture, but also to a kind of Greek culture which was the opposite of rhetorical pedagogy, of rhetoric, literature, and so on. This Socratic revival was not the property of Epictetus. You can find it among certain Stoics and among the Cynics, most of them. But—and Epictetus considers himself as a kind of Socratic figure—he has Socrates as a model and he wants to be the Socrates of this new period. What Socrates has been against the Sophists, he wants to be the same against the new Sophists, the new bearers, the new representatives . . . the people who were representative of this new Greek culture. But of course there is one main difference between Socrates, the historical figure of Socrates, and the situation of Epictetus. Epictetus was a schoolmaster. I mean that great difference is, from the technical point of view of the care of the self, the fact that Epictetus ruled a school, he ruled a school in Nicopolis and at this moment [Epictetus's objective] was to use those scholastic forms, these [. . .] pedagogical institutions and turn them towards this Neo-Socratic theme of the *epimeleia heautou*, the care of the self. How is it possible to learn [teach] people in the frame of a school, of a very traditional school, of an ordinary school, towards this activity of taking care of oneself?

And I think that most of the *Discourses* of Epictetus have to be read like that: it is in a form of normal scholarity, teaching, education, which intends to teach people how to take care of themselves. And there are several discourses, several discussions in the *Discourses* which are devoted not only to the teaching of the taking care of oneself, but which are devoted to the teaching of teaching. That means that the school of Epictetus was not only a school for young people or older people who wanted to take care of themselves, but Epictetus wanted to form teachers for taking care . . . it was a kind of *faculté de médecine* where doctors were formed for this taking care of the self.

—*It's interesting simply in the form of the discourse that there's an attempt to place a dialogue like a Socratic dialogue inside of this discourse . . .*

—Yes, we could, we could in fact discuss about these things. Yes. This *Discourse*, as most of the *Discourses* of Epictetus, has a very typical form, which is the form of the diatribe. It's very amusing, very interesting to compare it to the Socratic dialogue, because Epictetus wants, of course, to use the Socratic form. But he uses the Socratic form inside a form which is traditional in the schools, in the Hellenistic and Greco-Roman schools of philosophy, that is diatribe. In the Socratic dialogue, who ask the questions? The master. Who gives the answers? The disciple, the pupil. And why is that? Because of the theory of the reminiscence. The fact that the truth lies inside the mind of the pupil is the reason why it is the master who asks the questions.

In the diatribe, it's something else. First, the diatribe was a kind of discussion which took place after a lecture, exactly as we are doing now. Most of the pedagogical forms we use now in our universities, we can find them in the Hellenistic and in the Greco-Roman schools. In the Alexandrian schools, it was quite clear. So the diatribe is a kind of seminar after the lecture. And in the diatribe, the pupil asks a question. He asks a question to the master about the theme which has been the theme of the lecture. And the master answers to the disciple, and the answer most of the time has two or three separate phases. In the first phase, the master turns the question back to the pupil. The pupil asks the question, the master asks the question in reverse [. . .] And that's the Socratic moment of the discussion. Then after that . . . No, excuse me, excuse me, I have told you that there were three phases. In the first phase, the master gives a certain answer to the disciple. Then in a second phase he turns back the question to the pupil, and that's the Socratic moment, and after that he starts a new elaboration, a new comment, without dialogue, without asking questions or answering questions, and it is the dogmatic formulation of the thesis. And we have something like that in this dialogue. So there is the Socratic method inside the diatribal scholarly pedagogical form.

As you see, in this text there is a very explicit reference to the *Apologia*, and not to the *Alcibiades*. And the reference to *Apologia* is nearly quotations about [four] important features of the *epimeleia heautou*. First, the fact that Socrates has been assigned to his post by the divinity—a theme we find in the *Apology*. The fact that if he had to choose between his activity and to be acquitted by the judges, he would choose to pursue his activity. Third point, Socrates addresses himself both to citizen and to noncitizen. And, fourth point, he addresses himself both to young and to old people. Those two last points are to be found in the *Apology*, and we can't find them in the *Alcibiades*.

In the *Alcibiades*, on the contrary, Socrates addresses himself to a young boy so far as he is interested in politics, so far as he wants to become the leader of the city, and not to other people. He addresses himself to Alcibiades so far as he is young and not as he is old. It is very interesting to notice that in the *Apology* you find the thesis that Socrates addresses himself to anybody who is walking in the street, young or old, citizen or noncitizen. In this text, in the text of the *Apology*, Socrates presents himself as somebody who makes no political choices, no age choices, no erotic choices, but in the *Alcibiades* and in most of the early dialogues you find very clearly that Socrates addresses himself only to young people, and young people who have political projects. Of course Epictetus chooses the model of the *Apology* and not the model of the *Alcibiades*. As Epictetus is a schoolmaster, he addresses himself to every [pupil] who is registered in school, everybody who comes into school and his vocation as a Stoic, and that's the second feature, that's the second reason to be interested in everybody, as a Stoic he is a cosmopolitan, he has every man in the world as *concitoyen* . . .
    —*Fellow citizen.*
    — . . . as a fellow citizen, and so he has no choice between citizen or noncitizen, old and young. So. That's the reason, I think, why you

have this quotation and this reference to the *Apology* and to the universal role of Socrates as the master of the care of the self.

I think we could also underline something else. It is the fact that in the first part of the text, in the first paragraph, you can see a reference to the Delphic precept and to Apollo and to the *gnōthi seauton*. All [of the] first paragraph is devoted to this. There is a development about the *gnōthi seauton* and after that, and after that only, you have the reference to the Socratic precept of the *epimeleia heautou*. So. It is very interesting to see that the two precepts, the Delphic precept *gnōthi seauton*, the Socratic precept *epimele seautō*, those two precepts are effectively related, linked together, in this text. You may also notice, if you are interested in psychoanalysis and things like that, that there is also a very clear reference to Oedipus and to Laius, Laius who is the father of Oedipus. So you have Oedipus, "know yourself," "take care of oneself": some of the main features of our culture are present in this text.

But what I would like to underline is the fact that the relation between the Delphic precept and the Socratic precept—you know what I mean by those two words—the relation is not a relation of implication. Epictetus [doesn't] say: "You have to obey the Delphic precept 'know yourself,' and in order to apply this precept, you have to take care of yourself." He [doesn't] say that. [...] It's not what the text says. He doesn't say that, on the contrary, that in order to take care of yourself you have to know yourself. The Delphic precept is *neither* the larger one which implies the second one as a part of it, [*nor is it*] on the contrary the second one, the Socratic precept, which implies as a condition the Delphic one. There is *only* a relation of analogy between the two. And the analogy does not concern the content of the precepts, but something else. Look at the text. What does Epictetus say? Epictetus says: the Delphic precept is something that [...] has been inscribed, carved, on the stone, on a stone of a temple which is in the middle of the civilized world. So that anybody in the world could see and should know the Delphic precept. But, says Epictetus, in spite of the fact that anybody . . . that everybody could and should know this precept, very few have noticed this precept or at least very few have understood this precept and very few apply this precept. In the same way, says Epictetus, Socrates has addressed himself to everybody in the street or to anybody in the street, and in fact very few have observed what Socrates has said. It is an analogy in the structure of the appeal which leads to the comparison of the *gnōthi seauton* and the *epimele seautō*.

And this structure, the fact that everybody is called, but very few hear the call, you know very well what it is: it is the structure of salvation ideology or salvation religion. The idea that there is something which is valuable for everybody, that there is something which has been a message, which has been addressed to everybody in the world, but that very few have really caught, that is something which is very particular. We know it through the Christianism, but of course Christianism is [in no way] the single religion which knows this structure. But it is very interesting to see this structure in this text, since it is not at all a Socratic or a Platonistic structure. For Plato, for Socrates, very often it happens that somebody has been called by the philosopher, but the philosopher has not the been heard or understood. The fact that the crowd does not understand philosophy, the fact that philosophy is not *destinée* . . . [destined to be] addressed to the crowd, it's a very Greek idea. But philosophy is not really addressed to everybody. Philosophy is addressed only to people who are able to understand, to people who deserve it, to people who have the culture to catch and to understand philosophy. It's not at all a universal, a universal appeal. And I think that one of the most characteristic structures of this text is that you find this change between Socrates addressing himself to those young boys whom he had chosen, because they were beautiful, because they were powerful, because they had good status, good birth, and so on, and because they were ambitious; well, Socrates has made his choice.

And now you see another structure in which the philosophic call, the philosophical precept *epimele seautō* is addressed to everybody in the world, and it is only the blindness and the deafness of people which makes [it such] that very few are able to understand. We are not yet in a religious climate, in a religious tonality, but you see very well that the structure of the thought has been deeply changed. And that is something very important, the fact that the philosophical appeal is something for everybody; it is one of the main features of this kind of philosophy, of the Stoicism and Stoico-Cynicism to which Epictetus belonged, and it is one of the cultural conditions by which Christianity, very few years after that, took the extension you know. It is . . . In this way, the philosophical work has been a very important preparation for the development of Christianity. That was the second point I wanted to underline.

[Here is] the third [point]. [I did not xerox the text.] I thought it was a little too long, but it is very interesting, this passage I [want to] comment [on] now. This passage is a part of a larger discourse in which Epictetus answers a question, or not exactly a question, a claim of one of his young pupils. And this young pupil is described this way. Could you read just the first sentences?

[A participant reads the second text of Epictetus:]

> Once, when he was visited by a young student of rhetoric whose hair was somewhat too elaborately dressed, and whose attire in general was highly embellished, Epictetus said: "Tell me if you do not think that some dogs are beautiful, and some horses, and so every other creature." "I do," said the young man. "Is not the same true also of men, some of them are handsome, and some ugly?" "Of course." "Do we, then, on the same grounds, pronounce each of these creatures in its own kind beautiful, or do we pronounce each beautiful on special grounds?"[19]

—[You find] this kind of young pupil several times in Epictetus's *Discourses*, I think three times, [. . .] this kind of young guy. Young, beautiful—or thinking that they are beautiful—with perfumes, wearing several ornaments, and so on and so on. Of course that is the typical portraiture of the *débauché* . . . how do you say that in English?

—*Decadent.*

—Decadent, no, no, *débauché*. Somebody who is sexually *débauché*, licentious?

—*Debauched.*

—Debauched, debauched. It's not the portraiture of a homosexual. First, because homosexuality did not exist at this moment as a category, and the second reason is that the same portraiture is valuable both for the young prostitutes for men and for those young boys who were too much interested in women. To be debauched and to have this kind of behavior, this kind of body, this kind of coquetry, was typical of what is for us two different categories of people: those who were prostitutes to men and those who were too much interested in women. But it was the same category for the Greeks, and they had exactly the same type of description for those two types of behavior. That's the type of boys we see here. Those boys are in the three dialogues where we see this category, are always students in rhetoric. The reason is quite clear: the reason is that rhetoric is an art, a science, a technique of ornament. To transform the life in truth, to let appear beautiful what is not beautiful, and so on and so on, that is the reason, that is the target of rhetoric. So to have this kind of behavior and to be students of rhetoric belong to the same ethical category.

And the third feature of this kind of young boys is, their trait is that they want to hear, they want to listen at Epictetus's lessons and Epictetus does not want [them to], he rebuffs them. There is another dialogue, much more explicit on this point, where one of those young boys comes and says: "I have been spending months and months with you, and you never addressed me a single word, I'm obliged to leave without taking any profit, having taken any profit of your lessons."[20] Of course, this kind of personage and this kind of situation are to be related to the Socratic situation, where the boys are also beautiful, but they are not feminine, they have no ornaments, they are beautiful because they do sports, because they are active, and so on and so on. The second difference is that those boys of course are very anxious to listen at Socrates' lessons, but Socrates desires those boys and accepts the discussion with them and asks them questions, pays attention to them. I think that these figures of young boys, these negative figures of young boys who are excluded from Epictetus's lessons, are a way for Epictetus to make a difference between this ambiguous Socratic pederasty which was related to the Greek culture, to this kind of philosophy or of philosophical behavior, and so on. It is also a way to turn the . . . well, to change, to change some of the principal features of the Socratic *epimeleia heautou.*

In this . . . with this kind of guy, what's going on? It is the fact that, if they behave like that, if they have ornaments on them, if they are so proud of their beauty, supposed beauty, it is the fact . . . it is the proof that they take care of themselves, but they take care of themselves in the bad way. They take care of their body, they take care of their reputation, they take care of their own money, they are prostitutes, and so on and so on, and they are excluded by Epictetus so far as they don't take care of themselves as they should do. The objection comes very quickly: if the school of Epictetus is devoted to teaching [one] how to take care of oneself, this kind of [person] should not be excluded. On the contrary. And that's the reason why they complain. They come, taking care of themselves, believing that they are taking care of themselves as they should, and nothing happens, Epictetus does not [. . .] pay attention to them. From their point of view, they have done everything to be the best pupils possible in such a school and they are rebuffed. Why? Because they don't take care of themselves in a good way.

That means that to learn to take care of oneself in the good way, you have first to take care of yourself in the good way. There is a circular . . . circularity of the care of the self: the care of the self is not something that you can learn from the beginning, you have first to have the good attitude, the good care of yourself, to be able to learn how to take care of yourself. You see that it is exactly the situation of the reverse structure from the structure of the reminiscence of Plato. In Plato, or in Socrates, Socrates could address himself to any young boy since he was beautiful, since he was of good birth, and since he had political ambition, and through a good Socratic question-and-answer game he could let them remember what they had always known from the beginning, from the moment where in the *supracéleste* world they have seen the truth. So, the Socratic interrogation took place in this circularity of reminiscence: you knew what you did not know. In the Epictetus structure of *epimeleia heautou*, the circularity is quite different. You have to first give proof of your goodwill, you have to give proof that . . . your choice, your explicit choice—what in the Stoic vocabulary is called the *proairesis*—you have to prove that your choice is good, and then, after the fact, after this proof, then the master can intervene and help you to go on with this good choice. But this good choice, this good choice of the way you take care of yourself, must be the first thing to be chosen ... to be shown to the master, and then the master can intervene.

And there is something interesting in another dialogue[21] where [...] a young rhetorician who is perfumed and comes and complains that Epictetus didn't pay attention to him. Epictetus answers: "Well, I couldn't pay attention to you because I am like a goat. A philosopher is like a goat. A goat is excited by the grass when the grass is green, and you were not green enough as a grass for me, you didn't excite me. And since you didn't excite me, I had no reason to speak to you and to be your master."[22] And the Greek word is very interesting. The Greek word is *erethizein*, "excite." And this word is—it is interesting—just close to the erotic meaning, but it is not the ordinary erotic word. To be excited, from an erotic point of view, to say that, the Greek had another word. *Erethizein* only means ["to be] stimulated." It is much larger ... it has a much larger meaning [than the erotic meaning], but of course the erotic meaning is very close to it. It is impossible not to think of this erotic meaning when you read this text: "You did not excite me." But [...] it is another word, the erotic one, and I think that [...] the situation of Epictetus, close to the Socratic position, to the Socratic attitude, but with a lot of different things, [becomes] very clear from this kind of text. Anyway I think that this one I wanted to comment on before you is very explicit for the proximity of the theme, take care of oneself, and some of the major differences ...

Well, it's too late now and I have two texts. So. Maybe you have something to do now, or do you have still a few minutes, one or two minutes? Because I would like to ask you several questions about this seminar, about what we could or should do in the next one, and so on. Do you want us to continue with those kind of commentaries or do you think it's not ... or would you like something else? Because there are several possibilities. Of course we can mix together those possibilities. [One] possibility is that some of you do some exposés,

sometimes it will be either a formal exposé or a brief informal inter-
vention. We could read together texts [on] the condition, of course,
that you have read the texts before. This time it was . . . you were
short of time to do it. But next time you could do. Or any other formula, if you want?

— *This seems like a good method* . . .

— But I would like really that you read the texts before, and that
will help me because really it's for me very hard. The first time I nearly
improvise a seminar in English. So if several of you could intervene
[with] some interesting things . . . Would you like us to read the
two other texts of Epictetus, "On Providence," and Chapter 1. The
first . . . well, the text about Providence, Chapter 16, first book. It is
very interesting, this text, because it is the . . . well, the theoretical
background, the theoretical principle of the care of the self. It is the
analysis of [the] human being as the single living being who has to
take care of himself. From the strictly philosophical point of view,
it's very interesting. And the first chapter of the first book which I
would like you to read after the sixteenth one. Anyway you know
that Arrian has published those discourses in an order which seems
to be arbitrary, which has no [. . .] dogmatic or theoretical importance. So after that you could read the first chapter of the first book,
in which you find the—how could I say?—the technical application of the philosophical principles you find in the sixteenth chapter, Chapter 16. See it? And in this first chapter—I can understand
why Arrian put this text there—you have what that consists in to
take care of oneself, which was of course the program of the school.
So we could read that next time.

Well, and after that we could read the Fronto and Marcus Aurelius
correspondence. The principal letter, the most significative, I think,
would be the letter you find on pages 181 and 183. That's a short letter, but very, very interesting from the point of view of everyday life,
everyday experience, everyday self-experience.

— *When will we be going into early Christianity in the main lectures?*

— Well, in the next main lecture, I'll speak about the technical aspect of this care of the self in pagan society and in the two next lectures I'll speak of Christianity. When is the next seminar?

—*Wednesday.*

—Wednesday. Anyway, maybe I'll choose another text, because I have a . . . I don't know . . .

—*If you choose another text, just look at the bulletin board in Emmanuel College, right in the lobby there . . .*

SECOND MEETING

HAS EVERYBODY READ THOSE TEXTS? Yes? No? Nobody? Yes, you'll be punished, for sure! I won't tell you how . . . that's a surprise for the last day. So. If there any, before we start, because we have to wait a few minutes for the last course to . . . If there's any specific or general question you would ask either about the lectures or about the seminar or about anything else or about semiotics or about non-semiotic . . . ?

— *How about the circus atmosphere . . .*

— The circus atmosphere . . .

— *TV cameras, . . .*

— That's not my fault!

— *Well, some people have an interest in circus and carnivals here,*[1] *but I'm not one of them . . .*

— And you feel uncomfortable because of this camera? Well, I think, it's not a problem of theater or spectacle or things like that, that's the problem, there are . . . there were a lot of people registered in this seminar and the room was too small. But maybe we won't have to use this camera . . .

— *It's not broadcast channel — it's a closed circuit [. . .]*

— *You are more comfortable, you are [. . .]*

— Yeah, last time it was really overcrowded and warm.

—*Several people have mentioned or asked that there be no smoking...*

—*In your first class you spoke about the hermeneutics of the self. What is the importance of the term "hermeneutics"?*

—In this one? Not the tiniest importance! I think that what we could call hermeneutics of the self does not begin, is not to appear, before Christian spirituality. And what I would like to show you is that the same or nearly the same techniques, the same technology of the self, was used during this pagan era, during the beginning of the imperial culture, without any reference to something like the hermeneutics of the self, and I'll show you that in the next lecture, tomorrow. And what is the hermeneutics of the self, the deciphering of oneself, starts, I think, later on, in Christianity and in the monastic institutions. And that, I'll show you in the next Monday lecture. Yes?

—*At some point I could use a little historical background on what exactly the relationship of Socrates would be or would have been to Alcibiades after he had entered public life. I'd like to know something about where the discourse is leading in an everyday-life sense, in a material sense, and in their relationship to institutions. What would have been typical at the time after the student passed into public life? How would he relate to the teacher? Because to me that would influence to some degree how I would read the narrative, or the text...*

—I don't know if I catch exactly your question. You mean that, for instance, Alcibiades, what he is supposed to do when he enters the political life?

—*In part, but on one page towards the middle it says... "Practice yourself, sweet friend, in learning what you ought to know before you enter on politics." You talked about this as well, but I just wanted to know what kind of divergence would occur where Alcibiades would then go into public life. What kind of typical relationship would then be established [between Alcibiades and Socrates]? Because [I think] that would color our reading. [...]*

—Yes, sure. That's a very difficult question, a good one, and a very difficult one. The first thing to say is, you must remember that the relationship between Alcibiades and Socrates in this dialogue is not a definitive relationship. When Socrates promised Alcibiades in the beginning of the dialogue that through his teaching Alcibiades will be able to become the first in the city, that means to exercise a kind of tyrannical power; you must understand that Socrates is not sincere, of course. It is a promise to induce Alcibiades to take care of himself, but if [Alcibiades]* takes care of himself in a real philosophical way, then he will understand that he mustn't exercise this kind of power over the city, but that he has to exercise a reasonable type of power, and this reasonable type of power will be explained ... is to be explained in the *Republic*, in the *Laws*, and so on. So there is, I told you, a kind of trap. That's the first point.

—*I want you to go on, if you will, but also there's this little phrase* ...

—At the end?

—*Second page from the end, "I will be the security for your happiness ..."*[2] *And I don't know quite what that referred to* ...

—134e. [*"Socrates: For you and the state, if you act justly and temperately, will act so as to please God.—Alcibiades: Naturally.—Socrates: And, as we were saying in what went before, you will act with your eyes turned on what is divine and bright.—Alcibiades: Apparently.—Socrates: Well, and looking thereon you will behold and know both yourselves and your good.—Alcibiades: Yes.—Socrates: And so you will act aright and well?—Alcibiades: Yes.—Socrates: Well now, if you act in this way, I am ready to warrant that you must be happy."*][3] I can't explain it, I should have the Greek text to understand, and unfortunately ... Nobody has the Greek text? Because ...

—*Are you asking what sort of economic relationship* ... ?

—Because anyway I would like to say something about this, not to give you an explanation, but to refer to a very particular problem. It is exactly at the end. So the first thing is that this Alcibiades is not, does not give any solution to the ambition ... well, what Alcibiades promises ... what Socrates promises to Alcibiades does not fit really with what Alcibiades wishes.

—*I have the Greek.*

—Ah, thanks. And at the end of this dialogue, there is something very, very enigmatic, and I cannot explain it, only give a few references to it. It is when, in 135c: "Socrates: And do you know how

---

* Foucault says "Socrates," but clearly means Alcibiades.

to escape out of your present state—you see that?—which I do
not even like to name when imputing it to beauty?—Alcibiades:
Yes I do.—Socrates: How?—Alcibiades: By your help, Socrates.—
Socrates: That is not well said, Alcibiades. What you ought to have
answered is by the help of God.—Alcibiades: I agree. And I further
say that our relations are likely to be reversed [That's in praise of Alcibiades: to be reversed—MF]. From this day forward, I must and
will follow you as you have followed me. I will be the attendant and
you shall be my master."⁴

So that's quite clear, in the beginning of the dialogue, Socrates
was a follower of Alcibiades, and now Alcibiades has accepted to
have a master, and he will follow Socrates as Socrates followed him
as a lover: "—Socrates: That is rare! My love breeds another love:
and so like the stork I shall be cherished by the wind creature whom
I have hatched.—Alcibiades: Strange, but true; and henceforward
I shall begin to think about justice.—Socrates: And I hope that you
will persist; although I have fears, not because I doubt you; because
I see the power of the state which may be too much for both of us."⁵
Well, the Greek text doesn't say, I think, exactly that . . . yes it says,
excuse me, I thought that it was the demos. Yes, well, that . . . this sentence about the state, the city refers of course to what was to happen
after Alcibiades took over the power of Athens and what happened
and so on, but really I don't know exactly what means this sentence,
this expression *tēn tēs poleōs horōn rōmēn,* saying the force, the energy,
the violence of the city.

—*In other words, Alcibiades would be in the court, and Socrates
would be in the court as well, with the ruler? Where will Socrates end
up being, and what will their relationship end up being within the institutional . . .*

—That I do not understand.

—*Is Socrates independently wealthy, or is he peddling his wares, so to
speak. What will be the relationship between Alcibiades and Socrates . . .*

—Yes, well, there is, I think, something to say also . . . I couldn't
find it here . . . In the traditional love relation between a man and
a young boy, this relation was supposed to be a reciprocal relation
but throughout life. That means that, when the boy was young, the

elder was supposed to give him good examples, lessons to help him, to [teach]* him to become a good citizen, to become a good soldier, to become a good . . . hunter? *chasseur*, hunter, and so on and so on. He was supposed also to give him some very traditional gifts, which were different [according to] the social and economic status of the man. For instance, if he was rich, he was supposed to give to the young boy a horse and an equipment of horseman. If he was not rich, he was supposed to give him only a sword or something like that. He was also supposed to give him as the first gift un *lièvre* . . .

—*A rabbit.*

—Yes, a kind of rabbit. And the boy was supposed to give him his favors. But, after that, after this phase of their relations, when the boy grows up, if there is not a very great difference of age between them, they become friends, they have a relation of *philia*, which was also something very traditional, very statutory—statutory, you say that?—with reciprocal obligations and when the elder became really old, when he couldn't afford his own life, then the younger was supposed to help him, or even to help him if he became crippled, or if he became ill and so on and so on. You see there were a lot of reciprocal relationships which were very important in the social and the political life of the town, very important in the personal life of people also, but there it was not a kind of professionalized status, you see. Is that enough?

— *Yes, that's much clearer, but after Alcibiades went into the public life, I wonder . . . yes, I guess that's included.*

—Yes, yes, for instance, suppose, suppose everything would happen as Socrates would like [for it to] happen, well, Alcibiades would have been a good ruler in Athens and then he [would] help Socrates when Socrates [became] old and so on and so on. And they would have been friends, statutory friends, during all their life. OK?

— *I wonder if that reply takes sufficient account of Socrates' ironic attitude towards the state in general. That what you're saying is that eventually there would be just a normal social relationship that would emerge, but that shanks and completely overlooks the . . .*

* Foucault says "learn" where he clearly means "teach."

—No, no, my answer was only at the level of the social institutions. It's not at all an answer about what is the Socratic figure. Of course with the real Socrates or with the Platonic Socrates things wouldn't happen like that. But I thought that the question was at the most ordinary social level. [...] But of course, I quite agree that with the real Socrates, the irony of Socrates, the role of Socrates is to do something else with ... with Alcibiades or with his lovers. Sure.

Is there something else? Questions about the *Alcibiades*? No? Yes?

—*I have another question. What would be the relationship of this mirror-reflection of the truth which is stated in the* Alcibiades *to the pedagogical techniques that you ...*

—Pedagogical, yes.

— *... techniques that Philo describes as taking place in* Therapeutae[6] *...*

—I don't see any ... relationship ...

—*You keep ascribing a whole apparatus of techniques that are slowly emerging here in the juncture between care of the self and know thyself, and you used as an example Philo's instruction in the* Therapeutae: *sitting rigidly at attention, interjecting with their finger—a famous gesture—and the ears pricked at attention like so many indoctrinated rabbits ... but I'm a little bit confused as to the levels at which your analysis takes place. It's very famous, for example, that there were two levels of initiation ...*

—Where, two levels of initiation?

—*Right through the entire mysteries of late antiquity ...*

—No, that has nothing to do with mysteries, not at all.

—*The* Therapeutae, *I know ...*

—No, no. Well, as far ... you see, about the Therapeutes, we know only what Philo has written. We have not a single other source about it. And it's the description of an ascetic community, that's sure. A certain number of the rules are derived of course from Jewish culture, others seem to be much more related to Greek communities; the most likely is that it is one of those Hellenistic Jewish communities, but we have no signs that it is something related to mysteries.

—*The reason I'm asking this question is that I want to, I'm not quite sure what methodology you used, or how you are employing your examples. You make certain distinctions, you say, for example, that the Stoics*

don't have a conception of [Platonic eros], and you make other distinctions as you go along, but I'm not sure where it is that you make a distinction between a social character like [Aristides],† for example, and the
kind of more serious techniques of the self that were employed by Neoplatonists, and how it is that people . . . Why are you choosing these examples? Which distinctions are you employing? You're using Epicurus
here, who has no doctrine of immortality at all, or Epictetus, or Stoics.
Are you drawing distinctions between these techniques and say the techniques employed by the Neoplatonists? Am I making myself at all clear?
Why are you choosing these specific examples?*

—No, I don't . . . I would like to know if somebody else has the
same type of question or interrogation, because I don't catch exactly
[your meaning].‡

—*I think the trend that I see is that Socrates is looking into himself,
looking into mirrors, looking into eyes, examining the self with the self,
and you move along to Seneca especially, and Epictetus is more oriented
towards knowing the self in relation to others or other people rather than
the self itself. Is that one of the trends we should be looking for?*

—*I don't know that I have the same question, I don't know if I understand it fully, but I understood the question to be, What is the criteria for
choosing people who are affected by and have a lot of different ideas and
a lot of different practices that would be considered dissimilar with other
figures who you're comparing them at within this train of techniques of the
self. Is that what you were saying? What is the intelligibility behind that,
of making these kind of categorizations within the techniques of the self?*

—*Yes, I want to know, to have a clearer idea of why you've chosen
this lineage of examples.*

—Well, I have made a choice. It is my choice. And this choice is
the techniques of the self, that means I have chosen to study the way
[that] in this period, people tried to use for themselves, to [teach]
other people the way of transforming themselves in order to arrive at
a certain state which is commonly described as a state of sovereignty

---

* Conjecture; the sentence is partially inaudible.
† Conjecture; the sentence is partially inaudible.
‡ Conjecture; Foucault does not finish the sentence.

over oneself and of tranquility of soul [...]. That's my choice. But
after that, we know that the sources about this are not very numerous, and when you have read Seneca, Epictetus, Marcus Aurelius,
Aelius Aristides, and several others, well, you have all the sources,
so I have ... I didn't make any choice, I have read what is left, what
has been preserved as sources. So ... but maybe I don't understand
exactly your question ...

— *Well, what bothers me is that, in choosing these sources which you
claim are the only ones, but in using these examples, and we're talking
about you're building a way of reaching finally Augustine in the course,
Augustine who was described by [Mullany]*[7] *as the first modern man ...
In doing this it seems to me you're overlooking a psychology of the self [that
is] employed in Neoplatonism which can't be subsumed theoretically in
the way in which I see you eventually subsuming them ... It stands in a
critical relation to everything you've done actually, which is why, I don't
want to take up any more time in the seminar [...], but I guess I'll submit [...], but in overlooking this ...*

— In overlooking what, exactly?

— *The type of psychology that underlies Neoplatonism.*

— What are ... what are the texts, the sources you have in mind
when you speak of the, of the Neoplatonic mysticism?

— *Rather than take up any more of everybody else's valuable time,
I'll give you a written ...*

— Well, because my answer is this one: that the sources we have
about Neoplatonic mysticism are later than the period I am studying. You have no Neoplatonic sources in the first century, or nearly
nothing. The great Neoplatonic movement, at least sources you have,
you have them from the second century to the fourth–fifth and so
on. You mean Porphyrus, Jamblique [Iamblichus] ...

— *Well, there's the Neoplatonist claim that there's a direct line from
Plato that comes ...*

— That's sure!

— *... which raises the possibility of bridging that gap, that they themselves claim that there was a direct historical ...*

— Sure. Well, my thesis is exactly this one: that you find in the
end of the Hellenistic period, in the beginning of the imperial period,

first and second century [after Christ], a lot of techniques of the self which are . . . which have been built, developed, and so on in Epicurean schools, in Stoic schools, in Cynic schools; that those techniques of the self are deeply, not entirely, but for the large part quite independent from this very enigmatic Neoplatonic movement or this post-Platonic movement between Plato and the known Neoplatonism of the third–fourth century and, it's not my hypothesis, but what we can see, what we can know and prove is that, among the so-called Neo-Christian Platonists like Clement of Alexandria, you find a lot of those techniques which were rooted not in the Platonic tradition, at least as far as we can know about this tradition through our sources, but from the Stoic, Epicurean, and so on, traditions. I am not over-looking this [Platonic] tradition, I am trying to show the existence of this specific Stoic, and so on, tradition and its real effects, and its real succession in the Christian tradition. We'll see, for instance, next time the use of the control of the thoughts, which has nothing to do with Platonism and which is a technique you can find very precisely in Marcus Aurelius and in Epictetus, and you find it in Cassian and in Evagrius. That's something typically Stoic.

—*I have a question that I think might take us back to the first question, which is that in one of your early lectures, you made a distinction, you said that one of the changes that takes place between the time of Plato and the later period [. . .] is that in the earlier period the care of the self has to do with the formation of the self, the later period has to do with the purging of bad influences and so on. But in the* Alcibiades *text, it seems to me there's a definition of the self by negation and detaching . . . Socrates is detaching Alcibiades from his belongings and so on. This is why I think it relates to the first question, because we get to that point and there is the occasion or the assertion that the care of the self will relate us back to the city, as it were, but it seems to me that isn't there an element, even here in* Alcibiades, *of the purging, the detachment from the belongings, from the body and so forth?*

—No, but you see, in Socrates . . . in the *Alcibiades* this problem of detachment was a methodological *démarche* . . . you say that, *démarche*?

—*Technique . . . strategy.*

— ... strategy, because the problem was to give a definition of the self, and looking for the self, [Socrates] says, we cannot find the self in such and such thing, but only in the soul. So. In Seneca or in Epictetus, the problem of detachment is an ethical problem, it's not a theoretical one. I mean that for them the problem [of] the care of the self had to be such that people could be deprived, for instance, of their wealth, of their house, of their relatives, of their family, of their parents, children and so on, without suffering. And, you see, that's something rather different. There are of course relations between ... and in one of the texts we will explain now, you see that there is something ... some relations with this Platonic problem. But it's not ... it's not exactly the same.

— *This might be more a request, but I'm a little confused between the lectures and the seminar. In the third lecture, in the last one, you were talking about* askēsis, *and I believe you had explained what is this type of preparation, what does it mean to get prepared, and you had begun to explain how truth is acquired through listening and through writing. I was wondering ... I felt there was probably more that you wanted to say about that, both in terms of how truth is acquired and then what kind of truth we're talking about and what is the place of self-knowledge. Those were all questions that I was interested in, and I didn't know if they're going to be continued in the next lecture ...*

— No, well, I think in the next lecture, that means tomorrow, I'll explain something about this acquisition of truth. Of course I am obliged to put aside a lot of problems, of theoretical problems, and maybe we can discuss about that in the next seminar. But I don't think that it would be useful to discuss about this topic just now, since I'll try to explain some things about it tomorrow. OK?

SHALL WE NOW START READING the texts which we could explain today? So we have three texts, two texts from Epictetus and a text from Marcus Aurelius or, more precisely, two letters from Marcus Aurelius and a letter from Fronto to Marcus Aurelius.

I would suggest [that we] begin with Chapter 16, "Of Providence," [in Book I of the *Discourses*] by Epictetus. You remember that last time we explained another chapter of Epictetus, from the third book, because it was, I think, the best introduction to the relation between the Socratic theme of the care of the self and Epictetus, or the Neo-Stoic form of this care. Well, in Chapter 16, "Of Providence," I think that we have there the theoretical elaboration . . . well, one of the most clear, the clearest theoretical explanation of what is the care of the self and the relationship between reason and care of the self. Do you want us to read it together first, before we start explaining it? In this case I will ask you to read it. No? I think it would be better. Yes, the first paragraph, 16, the first paragraph, and then we'll explain it, and after, the following paragraph, and so on.

[*A participant reads the selection from Epictetus:*]

Marvel not that the animals other than man have furnished them, ready prepared by nature, what pertains to their bodily needs—not merely food and drink, but also a bed to lie on,—and that they have no need of shoes, or bedding, or clothing, while we are in need of all these things. For in the case of animals, born not for their own sake, but for service, to have created them in need of other things was not beneficial. Why, consider what it would be for us to have to take thought not for merely ourselves, but also for our sheep and our asses, how they are to be clothed and shod, how they are to find food and drink. But just as soldiers appear before their general, all ready for service, shod, clothed and armed, and it would be shocking if the colonel had to go around and equip his regiment with shoes or uniforms; so also nature has made animals, which are born for service, ready for use, equipped, and in need of no further attention. Consequently one small child with a rod can drive a flock of sheep.[8]

—Fine, thank you. So I think that one thing which is to be underlined in this paragraph is the fact that this theme, this comparison between men and animals, as you know, is a very traditional theme in philosophical thought: comparison between men and animals and the fact that, compared to men, animals are much more furnished, equipped, than men, much more . . . provided in a lot of things. You know very well that this theme, you find it throughout Greek philosophy from the Sophists to the Stoics, of course, but what is interesting is that, most of the time, I think, the fact that men are not so well equipped, not so well provided [as] animals in order to get their food or to protect themselves from the cold and so on, this fact, the inferiority of men compared to animals, was and is traditionally attributed to a deficiency, to a lack of human nature. For instance, remember what it was in Plato, in *Protagoras*, the myth of Epiméthée. You'll remember that Epiméthée was in charge of giving to every living being a gift and ability and in this distribution Epiméthée forgot men, and, since there were nothing left to give to men, then Prométhée decided to rob fire from the gods and to give it to men with reason.[9] I think that in this tradition or in this kind of analysis, there is a strict relationship between the deficiency of men, the lack of several things in human nature, the fact that reason comes to substitute [for] this deficiency and that *technē* is the result or the main expression of human reason as a substitute, or a complement to this deficiency, to this lack.

As you see, the analysis of Epictetus is quite different, and that, I think, is very interesting and important. As you see, the animals are given everything they need, not because they are superior to men, not because there is something which is deficient in human nature, but they are given everything they need in order to let man first exercise his own superiority on them, and to let man [be] free [to take] care of himself. And the fact that there is no lack, no deficiency, in human nature, that the so-called superiority of animals from this technical point of view, this so-called superiority of animals for satisfying their own needs [is in reality an inferiority] ... and the so-called inferiority [of man] is in fact his superiority, or it is a means by which nature or God has established the superiority of men over animals.

And then comes the metaphor of the soldiers, which is, as you know, a very important metaphor in Plato and in other philosophies, and among the Stoics. You know that this metaphor of soldiers in [an] army is traditionally used to explain what is the position of men towards God: God is like a general of an army and he has given to everyone a certain position in the army, with certain duties, certain obligations, and so on and so on, and men have to occupy their post—*non, on dit ça?*—to play their role following the place they have received in the army. Well, as you see, this metaphor is displaced: the animals are the soldiers, and the man is in the same position as God was in the reverse use of this metaphor. Man is the general, and the general, of course, as Epictetus explains it, [does not have] the same equipment as the soldiers, and he [does not have to] provide the soldiers with their equipment. They must arrive with their own equipment, and that, not because they are superior to the general, but because they have to obey the general and because the general has other things to do than to provide. And something more must be said, I think, about it. As you see, the animals can provide their own food, they can protect themselves against cold, and so on and so on. But Epictetus never says that in doing that, they are taking care of themselves. Providing one's own food is something, but it is not taking care of oneself. And taking care of the self will be something that man will be free to do, since the animals are doing that for themselves. Men have time left for something which is the care of the self, but the animals were provided with all that, not in order to take care by themselves of themselves, but to let man free [to do] something which is the care of the self. So. That's the first part. Is there any question about it? No? Shall we go on?

[*A participant reads the second passage from Epictetus:*]

But as it is, we first forbear to give thanks for these beasts, because we do not have to bestow upon them the same care as we require for ourselves, and then proceed to complain against God on our own account! Yet, by Zeus and the gods, one single gift of nature would suffice to make a man who is reverent and grateful perceive the providence of God. Do not talk to me now of great matters: take the mere fact that milk is produced from grass, and cheese from milk, and that wool grows from skin—who is it that has created or devised these things? "No one," somebody says. Oh, the depth of man's stupidity and shamelessness![10]

—Fine, thanks. Well, I think that this paragraph is a little more enigmatic than the first one, which was, I think, quite clear. As far as

I understand this paragraph correctly, I think that . . . well, we can find . . . there is something quite clear in the beginning of the paragraph: it's the fact that we are free, since the animals are furnished with what they need, we are free to take care of ourselves; you see the expression *tēn isēn epimeleian epimeloumetha.* What is much more enigmatic is what Epictetus says about the milk, the grass, cheese, and so on and so on . . . wool . . . As far as I understand this paragraph, I think that Epictetus means this: in the traditional analysis of the so-called superiority of animals, men were furnished with reason in order to realize certain things, certain technical things like cheese, cloth, and so on. The use of reason was a technical use. And the first and the principal use of reason was this one. And what Epictetus says, I think, is that in fact to do milk, to do cheese with milk, or to do cloth with wool, that is nothing very difficult and important, since God or nature has given us grass, cloth—or I don't know [about] cloth—well, and wool and so on. Doing, making cheese or making cloth is not something really important, and nature has done nearly all the work. And since nature has done nearly all the work in preparing all these things, we understand that reason had not been given to men in order to do those things, but for something much more important. I think that this idea is rather important, since, as you see, the relation between *technē* and *logos*, technique and reason, was something very important and fundamental in the traditional analysis of this superiority-inferiority of men and animals. Now *technē* is moved from the human sphere, the human domain of activity, to the natural Providence, the natural Providence as care for everything, even for those technical things. And then reason, human reason, or the use by men of reason, will have another field of application than those material things. That's, I think, the meaning of this paragraph. Is there any question, objection?

— [. . .] *What was the state of this belief in gods in this time?*

—What was the, excuse me, the . . . ?

— *His belief, or I would say that he is scolding someone who is not grateful to the gods. What would be more or less [the view of] most people regarding gods?*

—Well, I think it's really difficult to answer. I think that in this paragraph and in this last line, he doesn't curse people who do not believe in God. I think that he curses people who say that all those things which are done by men . . . that all those things that men use are not due to divine Providence, that they are only natural things and that men have invented the techniques to use them. Maybe he refers to the Epicureans, maybe he refers only to people who attribute too much to the human technique, and not enough to gods. I think that this . . . he tries to extend, as far as possible, the domain of nature, of natural Providence, of natural reason *englobing* in this way what was attributed most of the time to men, to human invention, human innovation, and so on. And that is the signification of this paragraph. No other questions?

[A participant reads the third passage from Epictetus:]

Come, let us leave the chief works of nature, and consider merely what she does in passing. Can anything be more useless than the hairs on a chin? Well, what then? Has not nature used even these in the most suitable way possible? Has she not by these means distinguished between the male and the female? Does not the nature of each one among us cry aloud forthwith from afar, "I am a man; on this understanding approach me, on this understanding talk with me; ask for nothing further; behold the signs?" Again, in the case of women, just as nature has mingled in their voice a certain softer note, so likewise she has taken the hair from their chins. Not so, you say; on the contrary the human animal ought to have been left without distinguishing features, and each of us ought to proclaim by word of mouth, "I am a man." Nay, but how fair and becoming and dignified the sign is! How much more fair than the cock's comb, how much more magnificent than the lion's mane! Wherefore, we ought to preserve the signs which God has given; we ought not to throw them away; we ought not, so far as in us lies, to confuse the sexes which have been distinguished in this fashion.[11]

— Thanks. Well, what do you think about this paragraph? I have the feeling that it's not much clearer than the previous one. As far as I understand this paragraph, I think that it is devoted [to] what is called in the translation—I don't know how it is in this translation—the *parerga* of nature. No, we don't have this word ... Well, anyway ... Yes, the things ... yes, the *parerga* it is in, excuse me, the Greek text ... the *parerga* which is translated in English by "what nature does in passing." That is the *parerga*. Well, I think that for Epictetus it is possible to make the following distinction.

First, there are the things which have been provided to animals in order to get them able to get what they need. That's a first level of nature. I would say that it is what has been effectively, actually, built up by Providence, from the beginning to the end. Then there is a second level which is the level of those technical objects which Epictetus spoke about few sentences before when he spoke about cheese, about clothes, and so on, wool and so on. That is those things which have been prepared by nature in order for men to have clothes and so on, and which are for the most of part due to nature and only for a small part to men.

Then there is, I think, a third level, and it is this third level to which Epictetus refers in this passage. This level is the level of natural objects [that] have apparently no usefulness, they are useful to nothing, neither to animals nor to men, but they are signs. They are signs for something. And, for instance, the beard on a chin has no usefulness for anybody, but it is a sign. And people ... have to pay attention to those signs. And the care of the self which is free to develop ... which we are free to develop, since Providence has provided animals and us with a lot of things, we have to take in account those signs, because those apparently un-useful signs refer to our nature, or refer to what we are. And as far as taking care of ourselves, we have to take care of what we are, of course, we have to take into account those signs which refer to what really we are.

And what is significant, I think, in this passage is the fact that, among the signs of what we are, Epictetus quotes as an example the beard, which is a sign of what we are as men. Well, as we are as men, as we are both or either as men and as philosophers. As you know, wearing a beard was a sign of the philosophical existence. And among the different signs of the philosophical existence, the poorness of the clothes and so on and so on, there was the wearing of a beard. But wearing the beard, the philosopher, at least following Epictetus, did nothing else than using explicitly a sign of what we are, and what we are as men versus women. It is our own nature as men, as males, which is signified by the beard. So we could be surprised that the care of the self starts with taking into account those signs of what we are, and that those signs quoted by Epictetus are precisely the signs of the male existence, the male being. Maybe we have to refer . . . to compare this text to another text written by Marcus Aurelius, and I'll speak of this text in my lecture tomorrow,[12] where Marcus Aurelius says that when we are retreating in ourselves, doing our *anachōrēsis* in ourselves, we have to consider ourselves [. . .] after that [. . .].* The fact that we have to take into account what we are first of all as men, I think, is something rather important. At least, I think, that's the signification of this passage. Is there anybody who wants to comment?

—*[What is the relationship between utility and the care of the self?]*†

—[. . .] the usefulness is quite constitutive of that.‡ Of course, when we take care of ourselves as we are supposed to do, of course [we find there are many obligations to these same] things which in fact are useful either for us or for the others, for our relatives, for our fellow citizens, and so on and so on. But that will only be a consequence of the fact that we are taking care of ourselves; it is not because we are trying to do useful things, either for us or for the other, that we take care of ourselves correctly. We take care correctly of ourselves and then, as a natural consequence, as a logical consequence, then it is useful for the other. That is quite clear, for instance, in Marcus Aurelius when he speaks about his profession of emperor. There is one text which is very interesting where he says that every morning he does, as a good Stoic had to do, he does the prospect—you can say that?—of his day, what he had to do during the day, and it is . . . and it's very characteristic that Marcus Aurelius does not say that he has

* Interruption in the recording.

† The question is inaudible and has been reconstructed based on Foucault's response.

‡ The beginning of Foucault's response is inaudible.

to do his métier ... his profession of emperor well. He says that he has to behave as an *honestum* ... *honestus vir*, an honest man. And it will be when he will apply the rules inherent to this kind of existence that then he will do naturally his profession of emperor [well]. There is no specific duty for the emperor besides or other than human obligations, human duties.

—*We could characterize it as the exchange value rather than the use value ...*

—Well, I'm not sure.

—*It's also interesting that he's willing to use a natural phenomenon in this sign, he's willing to use the beard to go back to the self, as opposed to having chosen a sign that in fact isn't natural, that in fact isn't suggesting that the self is somehow ... can naturally be signified.*

—Yes, the problem of nature is of course very important. That refers to this portrait of the philosopher, with a beard and so on, of course refers to the Cynical tradition. Since Diogenes, it was a sign, a manifestation, an expression, of the philosophical existence to be as close as possible to nature.[13] And everything which could be considered as an artifice has to be banished from the philosophical existence, and to shave, for instance, is something artificial. Well, all this ... that's of course another problem, but what the Greeks called the *paraphusis*, contrary or outside nature, is a very open field in which, a very large field in which, you find a lot, a lot of things. For instance, for Seneca, to bath in warm water is something contrary to nature. The nature of water is to be cold, and so on and so on. It was one of the themes, one of the imperatives of the philosophical existence to relate as close as possible to ... and of course a beard is a natural sign.

But that does not exactly mean that the self is given by nature. Self is the reason, or at least self is a kind of use of reason, it is a reasonable use of reason. We will see that in the next text. But the self has to ... the philosophical self, this philosophical use of reason, has to stay as close as possible to nature.

—*It's because of that reasonable use of reason that the sign then can be more magnificent than the lion's mane, or whatever.*

—Yes, yes.

—*In the doctrine of saving the symbols at the end is the idea that God first preserves kinds, and is there not some similarity to the doctrine in Genesis of a Jewish dietary rule, where God lays down for the Jewish people that they ought not to mix certain kinds of animals, or eat animals who have mixed forms, and the injunction being that you ought to preserve kinds as God himself does, and this is a sign of God's holiness, because he makes kinds. It seems there's a strong doctrine at the end of that paragraph that we ought not to mix sexes . . .*

—That has nothing to do, I think, with the food prohibitions. In the Pythagorean tradition, there were food prohibitions. Somebody like Seneca, for instance, had, during the time he was young, had a master who was a Pythagorean and who imposed on him some food prohibitions. He [talks about] that in some of his letters. But that has nothing to do with this problem of confusing the sexes. Of course, I agree with you, I was wrong not to comment further on this last sentence. This confusion of sex relates exactly to this kind of figure we met last time with the young rhetorician, you know, who arrived at Epictetus's lectures, lessons, with perfumes, jewels, and so on and so on. And this kind of thing, this kind of behavior, in which people confused sex, behave as women, and behave as women in this perspective is not being homosexual, it is changing one's own appearance, using perfumes, using ornaments, and so on and so on, and that is this confusing of sex which is in all this literature deeply, sharply, permanently despised. I think that this has nothing to do with the food or the food prohibition, but to this strict separation, not of the sex, but of self-identification. We have to identify ourselves first by our sex, or by the fact we are male or female. And the debauchery, the sex debauchery, was always perceived as a confusion of the sexual identity. And that, I think, is something very important in this text and in all this sexual ethics, much more than the violation of a prohibition or a law. There were very few laws about sex in antiquity. What was the great debauchery, what was the great sexual sin, if you want to use this word, this expression, was that you didn't identify your sexual role, and by sexual role I don't mean only the fact that as a male you have to have sex only with females, but as a male you don't have to behave like a woman, that means perfume yourself, wear ornaments, and so on and so on. I think that's the . . . Is there anything else you should ask? Well, read the last paragraph.

[*A participant reads the final passage from Epictetus:*]

Are these the only works of Providence in us? Nay, what language is adequate to praise them all or bring them home to our minds as they deserve? Why, if we had sense, ought we to be doing anything else, publicly and privately, than hymning and praising the Deity, and rehearsing His benefits? Ought we not, as we dig and plough and eat, to sing the hymn of praise to God? "Great is God, that He hath furnished us these instruments wherewith we shall till the earth. Great is God, that He hath given us hands, and power to swallow, and a belly, and power to grow unconsciously, and to breathe while asleep." This is what we ought to sing on every occasion, and above all to sing the greatest and divinest hymn, that God has given us the faculty to comprehend these things and to follow the path of reason. What then? Since most of you have become blind, ought there not to be someone to fulfil this office for you, and in behalf of all sing the hymn of praise to God? Why, what else can I, a lame old man, do but sing hymns to God? If, indeed, I were a nightingale, I should be singing as a nightingale; if a swan, as a swan. But as it is, I am a rational being, therefore I must be singing hymns of praise to God. This is my task; I do it, and will not desert this post, as long as it may be given me to fill it; and I exhort you to join me in this same song.[14]

—Thanks. So, what is your impression about this text? Well, I think, as you may notice, in the last sentence, "This is my task and I do it, I will not desert this post as long as it may be given me to fill it," it is exactly the replication of what Socrates said when, before his judges, he said: "I have been put in this post by God and I won't leave it from my own *volonté.*"[15] You find the same thing. But, as you remember, the . . . Socrates spoke about this post . . . when he spoke about this post, he meant the fact that his function was to incite or to invite people, everybody, anyone who went through the street, to take care of himself. Now, his function, his post consists in singing in honor of God, in singing a hymn of gratitude to God.

Of course we may understand that this supposes or assumes that there is a huge difference between the two. But we have to remember this last paragraph takes place in a chapter where it is a question of the *epimeleia heautou*, the fact that we have to take care of ourselves and that God has done everything in order to let us free to take care of ourselves. Nature has been organized, animals have been furnished, the things have been prepared around men, even signs have been put in the human being, in the human body, in order to let men and women, everybody, be free to take care of oneself. So it is this which is the reason why we have to be grateful to God. Being grateful to God because he has . . . he has organized everything in order to let us be free to take care of ourselves, and taking care of ourselves is a sign of gratitude to God; it is the same thing.

And I think that's the idea and the reason why this paragraph, which sounds so mystical and so different from the traditional problematic of the care of the self, is in fact really directly related to this theme of the care of the self. For instance, you'll find in Christian spirituality [. . .] signs of gratitude to God, in nearly the same style, but [. . .] those things [are not] the care of the self. [Instead] the fact that we can forget ourselves and that we have to forget ourselves, that we have to renounce ourselves and turn entirely towards God, [the reason for this is that] we don't care for ourselves anymore.

Here it is this exact adequation of taking care of ourselves and singing hymns to God which is one of the most remarkable things in this last paragraph, and in all [of] this chapter, which begins with the traditional theme of the animals compared to men. It starts with the traditional idea that apparently animals are superior to men, but it finishes with that very Platonic or Socratic or Sophistic theme. It is rooted in the oldest tradition of Greek philosophy and, as you see, the last paragraph, the last sentences sound very near what you can find in the Christian spirituality of the fourth–fifth century and after. So this chapter, from the beginning to the end, embraces nearly one thousand years of Greek culture, if you look only at the things on the surface. But the use of this, the first idea, the comparison of men and animals, is quite particular to Epictetus, and I think that the reference, well, the allusion to this hymn to God has another signification than the Christian one. So we have to restrain this large horizon to something which is quite typical either of Epictetus or at least of the Stoic movement, Stoic philosophy of this period.

—*Do you think an argument might be made that the notion of office in this last paragraph represents a kind of mediation that the philosopher in this case is not only someone who praises God because others have gone blind, but also is responsible for the comprehension, for the continuation of a task for the comprehension of these things because people are blind? It seemed to me that you limited the understanding of the office . . .*

—Maybe . . . do you find something in the text which could confirm what you say?

—*Yes. In the middle sentence: this is what we would sing on every occasion, and above all to sing the greatest hymn, that God has given us the faculty to comprehend these things and to follow the path of reason. What then? Because mostly you have become blind—not just blind to the duty to sing praise, but also that you no longer can understand these things, ought there not to be someone to fulfill this office for you, on behalf of all . . .*

—Yeah, yeah, but that's quite . . . you are quite right, and that's something quite different from the [Socratic] office, which was to invite other people to take [care of themselves].* [Here, the philosopher]† is in the place of the other. You're quite right, that's something very specific and very different. Maybe we can refer to what was written in another . . . in the other discourse we commented [on] last week, where Epictetus said that he was the red thread in the garment. He compared humanity to the senators gown—you say that, gown?—with red part of it, and he says: "I am among humanity as the red part of the gown and I am an ornament."[16] And in this case . . . well, you see, you have . . . maybe we can say that there are three possibilities of understanding the philosopher's office. Either as somebody who is necessary to invite the others to do their duty, that means to take care of themselves, and that is the use of the philosopher for humanity. There is an aesthetic role of the philosopher, insofar he is the red part of the gown, and which he is insofar as he

* Conjecture; the phrase is inaudible.
† Conjecture; the phrase is inaudible.

[brings] honor to humanity. And there is a third role: he is the substitute [for] the people, who are blind and cannot by themselves, are not able to do what they have to do, say, to sing a hymn of gratitude in honor of God. Quite right. And those [three]* roles are ... I think you could find them in Socrates, the figure of Socrates.

— *One small question about what you were saying about the hymn itself. When you spoke yesterday about the problem, later, the problem of needing certain discourses upon which to rely [...], this hymn would not be linked to that tradition at all ...*

—To the tradition of?

— *You spoke of needing specific discourses or the generation of certain discourses in* askēsis, *which ... does that make sense?*

—I am not sure. You ask me what is the meaning of this hymn, the philosophical hymn? That's ... that's a very important and difficult question, and I must confess that I am not able to answer. Well, you know that the philosophical hymn since early Greek philosophy is something very traditional. It's a fact that during the classical period it's rather difficult to find such a philosophical *genre*† in Greek culture, but you know very well that one of the first Stoic philosophers, Cléanthe, has written a hymn.[17] And the hymn as a manifestation of philosophical piety towards God, is something which is important among the Stoics. So I think that is the reactualization of this practice which is [referred to in this text].‡ Is there anything else you want to know about it? What shall we do? Do you want us to read another text of Epictetus, or do you want us to jump to Marcus Aurelius and his letters with Fronto, his correspondence with Fronto? What do you prefer?

—*Jump.*

—Jump. I think it would be best, because it's much [...] easier, and, you see, as far as I have ... I am right, I think that it's rather difficult to comment on those rather difficult philosophical texts together. I have relied—you can say that?—on you, but I thought that

---

* Foucault mistakenly says "two."

† Foucault uses the term in the French sense here.

‡ Conjecture; the phrase is inaudible.

you would have prepared a lot of things to say about those texts. Well, eventually we can come back Monday to other texts of Epictetus . . .
—Can I just [ask] a question about the other one, the other text?
—Which one?
—The beginning of the other text, chapter 1.[18]
—Chapter 1.
—He says in the fourth sentence: "How far does the art of grammar possess the power of contemplation?" He answers: "Only so far as to pass judgment on what is written."[19] I was not concerned so much with the answer as with actually how did all this taking care of [oneself] did or did not affect the lexicon of that time? Did it affect the words that they would have used to describe . . . many words very specifically to explain the steps, the techniques, and all that, which happened, for example, with the Indians, with Sanskrit and all that, I don't know . . .
—Vous avez compris?
—Oui, est-ce qu'il y a un vocabulaire spécial, particulier pour [le souci] de soi?*
—Well, sure, there is a vocabulary, but most of the time this vocabulary [. . .] uses rather common words, and if you don't know the technical meaning of these words, then you risk . . . there is the risk that you do not understand. I'll show you tomorrow by two texts of Marcus Aurelius how he uses the word anachōrēsis.[20] Anachōrēsis is a military word, and he uses it in a very technical sense. And if you don't know this technical use, I think you [will] misunderstand all the text. So there are a lot of those words, for instance, epimeleia. Epimeleia is a rather common word which means "care." But epimeleia heautou is something very precise.
[. . .]† Anyway, the translation of theōrētikē as "contemplation"

* "Yes, is there a special, particular vocabulary for the [care] of the self?"
† Foucault is remarking on the beginning of the passage from Epictetus that the auditor is referencing, specifically the sentences preceding those the auditor cites. "Among the arts and faculties in general you will find none that is self-contemplative, and therefore none that is either self-approving or self-disapproving (oudemian heurēste autēn hautēs theōrētikēn)." Book I, Chapter I, "Of the Things Which Are Under Our Control and Not Under

is rather problematic. What he means . . . what Epictetus means by *theōrētikē* is the possibility for a faculty to know, not what it is as a faculty, but to know when, in which condition, it is good or bad to use this faculty. That's the meaning of *theōrētikē*. It's not at all that this faculty is able to make its own theory, it's not at all the meaning that the mind could look at itself as in a mirror. *Theōrētikē* here, *autēn hautēs theōrētikēn*, means possibility for a faculty, for example, for grammar or for the art of writing, to determine when it is good and when it is not good to use this faculty, to write or to play flute and so on. So. And ordinary faculties, all the faculties that we have, give us the possibility, the ability of, for instance, writing or playing flute, things like that. But none of them can say if we have to write to a friend now or not, if it is good or not. And this faculty of telling us if it's good or not to do something in such and such circumstances, that's only reason, *logos*. And reason says, is able to say that, to determine that, for any faculty, for the use of any faculty, and also for itself.

That's the reason why reason has to be the sovereign over all the faculties, and the reason why reason is free, because it determines its own. This notion is very important, since, as I said when commenting on the previous text, reason has nothing to do with the technical aptitudes of man. The technical aptitudes are given by other faculties, other abilities, that's something else. Reason begins with the appearance of the problem: "Shall I use or not this faculty? Is it a good moment to use it?" And, as you see, reason they have . . . there are two fundamental notions to understand what is reason, the notion of using the other faculties, and the Greek word is *chrēsis, chraōmai, chresthai*. And maybe you remember that in the *Alcibiades* Socrates says: "What have you . . . what is the self which we have to take care of?" And the answer was that you have to take care of what? Of the faculty which uses—*chresthai*—your body, your feet, your hands, and so on.[21] The second thing is that the office of reason is to deter-

Our Control," in Epictetus, *Discourses, Books I and II*, §§1–3 (p. 7). The seminar participants had copies of the full text in front of them, so Foucault does not read the full passage aloud before commenting on the English translation of the term *theōrētikē*.

mine the use of a faculty in certain circumstances: Is the circumstance good or not? Is it good or not to use this faculty in such and such circumstances? And then you have the notion of *kairos*.[22] *Kairos* is the occasion, the occasion when you can use it. And that also refers to Aristotle and Plato.

Anyway, you have a definition, technical definition of the reason as the faculty which can determine the use *(chrēsis)* of the other faculties in a certain *kairos*, occasion. And that is why reason is *the* faculty by which we can take care of ourselves. Taking care of ourselves is to be able to determine exactly in which circumstances, in which *kairos* we have to use, *chresthai*, the other faculties. Then in this chapter we have the positive definition of what is reason as the faculty specific to the care of the self. And then you can see that, when God [gave] us reason, he didn't give us reason in order to furnish us with all the technical things we need, he gives us reason as a supplemental gift. It's not a [vicarious]* gift, it's not a substitute for a lack or deficiency, he gives us this as a supplementary gift which makes us free [to use it] in a good or in a bad sense [with] our other faculties. The reason is really the faculty of the care of the self. In this way, we can say that human being as a rational being is a being who has to take care of himself. But *not* to take care of himself insofar as he has something deficient in his being. [Instead] he has to take care of himself [in] so far as he is free, because he has been furnished with reason, with reason as a faculty which is *autē theōrētikē*, which can use the others and [itself].†

Well, of course there is also the problem of deficiency we've seen‡ at the end of this chapter, [or] not exactly deficiency, the problem of material mastership over the world, but that's something else. Well, anyway, what I wanted to show you in asking you to read those texts, it was the fact that, in Epictetus, you have really a philosophy of the

* Foucault uses the French *vicariant*.

† Conjecture; Foucault does not finish the sentence.

‡ Although Foucault says "which we have seen at the end of the chapter," he only comments on the beginning of the chapter here. The auditors would have had copies of the complete text of the chapter, however, and would have read the material before the seminar.

care of the self. You have a definition of human being which implies [that] reason [is] a specific gift from God, not as a substitute or a complement because human being is deficient, but a definition of reason which is the faculty given by God to men in order to do nothing else with this reason than taking care of themselves. OK?

I'LL STOP NOW THAT AND ... well, we have few minutes to read Marcus Aurelius. Everybody, I hope, has read it, so maybe we don't have to read anymore. Well, maybe we'll read the second one, but before, I would like to say few words about those three letters and specially the first and the third one. Well, as you see ... who didn't read these letters? Nobody? Nobody, well. Excuse me, but we have a very short time.

Well, first thing, I think, worthwhile to note is of course the importance of writing, of letters, of correspondence in this culture of the self.[23] As you have seen and read, Fronto and Marcus Aurelius write each day a letter to the other. And more ... not each day, every day, and more than every day, because there is, I don't know if you remember, a remark about the word *quotidie*.[24] *Quotidie* is not sufficient to express the number of letters they [write to each other]. This fact that two persons were writing each other every day is of course something both rather strange and maybe rather characteristic. This exchange is specific of course [to] very wealthy people, the top level of society, and so on and so on, and you cannot imagine that everybody was writing each other in Roman society. But I think that, in spite of the fact that it is typical of a certain social level, in this art of the self, say, in this culture of the self, which was in any case something which took place only in certain social classes, the importance of writing is proved by that.

I think that we could say that in the evolution from *homo civicus*— you know what I mean: the man as citizen in Greek society—the evolution from *homo civicus* to *homo interior*, well, this evolution went through a stage, a phase, that we could call the *homo litteratus* or *homo epistolaris*, the fact that writing has been a very important technique in this evolution from *homo civicus* to *homo interior* is important. I would like also to underline a fact that at this moment in history, the social and political history of the Roman Empire, writing was important both from a personal point of view and from the political point of view. I refer to the third letter you have read, this third letter written by Fronto. Fronto said to Marcus Aurelius: "I would like to write to you much more than I do," and in fact they . . . they send letters to each other nearly every day, "I would like to do it much more often, but I know that you have a lot of other letters to write" because—he was not emperor at this moment, but he had political responsibilities—Marcus Antonius had a lot of letters to write. At this moment, during the second century, during the dynasty of the Antonins . . . the Antonine dynasty, during the Antonine dynasty, the imperial bureaucracy was developing, and Hadrian, for instance, has led a reorganization of all this imperial bureaucracy with several . . . with a lot of people who were, who have as their job, profession, to write letters to people in the empire: proconsuls, procurators, and so on and so on. So that I think we can say that writing, both as a bureaucratic technique and as a personal technique, were both developing at the same moment. At least . . . anyway, I think that this concurrence between bureaucratic writing and personal writing is quite perceptible in the last letter which has been xeroxed.

And, as you see also, those letters show the importance of the relation, the personal relation, the relation to another, in the culture of the self. This culture of the self is not at all something egoistic, something solipsistic; the culture of the self needs and goes always through the relation to somebody else. You know that the great English historian Dodds has said that in the ancient culture there were a trend, an evolution, from the shame culture to a guilt culture.[25] [A "shame culture" is a] culture in which shame, that means the pressure of the group, [plays a determining role in] ethics. And the guilt is the relation to God. I think that, if we can accept this hypothesis—and I am not sure that we have to keep it[26]—but if we keep this hypothesis, I think that we should add a step between the shame culture and the guilt culture.

I should call that the "scruple culture," in which the problem is not the pressure of the group, the pressure of opinion over somebody, it is not yet the problem of the guilt towards God, but it is the problem of the psychological, ethical scruple between two people. Look at the way [Marcus] Aurelius and Fronto express their scruples. For instance, Fronto doesn't dare to write too often to Marcus Aurelius, who has so many things to do and so on and so on. Marcus Aurelius doesn't know if he uses the good word or not and, since Fronto is a professor of rhetoric, Marcus Aurelius shows all the scruples he has to use this word or that word. Anyway, I don't know if we have to use or to keep this word, "scruple," anyway [to identify a culture that is] between a culture in which the opinion of the group, the opinion of the city, the opinion of the statutory group, is determinant for the ethical consciousness, and another culture in which the religious relation to God will be determinant for this ethical consciousness. [But] I think that there is a stage, a phase, which is represented by these [...] documents in which the relation of two people to one another is determinant for this formation of the ethical consciousness. That was the reason why I wanted you to read those letters.

A second thing I would like to underline, of course, is the role, the huge role, of medical notations in those texts. I don't know if you have been struck by the fact that they are always writing each other that they have caught a cold, [...] and so on and so on. That's also very characteristic of the fact that in this kind of the care of the self the body has a very important role, very different from the gymnastic, nothing to do with the gymnastic, this body culture which was so important in classical ages, but it is the body as a cradle, a nest for a lot of small troubles, either body troubles or psychological troubles. And that, I think, is quite important, quite clear in that, in those letters.

Well, of course the third great problem is the problem of love, and that really I can't say anything about. You have read this strange last letter, a letter from Fronto to Marcus Aurelius.[27] I don't know what we could say about it. That's nothing of course to do with Socratic love, erotic love, pederastic love; I think that it has nothing to do with what we call homosexuality or things like that; it is passionate love, with physical relations, physical, I don't say sexual, with physical relations, they kiss each other and so on. Well, anyway I think that's a

very interesting document. I am afraid that those very numerous letters of this correspondence are one of the reasons why this very interesting correspondence has never . . . is, I guess, rarely edited there
in France . . . Anyway, they are very interesting . . . Well, I would like
now to read or to let Tim read the second letter: "Because it is my
sweetest of masters"; I et II-1.
—*All of it?*
—Yes, please. You can go quick, but it is necessary to read.
[*A participant reads the letter from Marcus Aurelius to Fronto:*]

Hail, my sweetest of masters.
    1. We are well. I slept somewhat late owing to my slight cold, which
seems now to have subsided. So from five a.m. till nine I spent the
time partly in reading some of Cato's *Agriculture* and partly in writing not quite such wretched stuff, by heavens, as yesterday. Then, after paying my respects to my father, I relieved my throat, I will not
say by gargling—though the word *gargarisso* is, I believe, found in
Novius and elsewhere—but by swallowing honey water as far as the
gullet and ejecting it again. After easing my throat I went off to my father and attended him at a sacrifice. Then we went to luncheon. What
do you think I ate? A wee bit of bread, though I saw others devour-
ing beans, onions, and herrings full of roe. We then worked hard at
grape-gathering, and had a good sweat, and were merry and, as the
poet says, *still left some clusters hanging high as gleanings of the vintage.*
After six o'clock we came home.
    2. I did but little work and that to no purpose. Then I had a long
chat with my little mother as she sat on the bed. My talk was this: *What
do you think my Fronto is now doing?* Then she: *And what do you think
my Gratia is doing?* Then I: *And what do you think our little sparrow, the
wee Gratia, is doing?* While we were chattering in this way and disput-
ing which of us two loved the one or other of you two the better, the
gong sounded, an intimation that my father had gone to his bath. So
we had supper after we had bathed in the oil-press room; I do not mean
bathed in the oil-press room, but when we had bathed, had supper
there, and we enjoyed hearing the yokels chaffing one another. After

coming back, before I turn over and snore, get my task done and give my dearest of masters an account of the day's doings, and if I could miss him more, I would not grudge wasting away a little more. Fare-well, my Fronto, wherever you are, most honey-sweet, my love, my delight. How is it between you and me? I love you and you are away.[28]

— Thanks. Well, this letter is something very interesting. The first reason is that it is the description of a day during one of these famous retreats in the country which was a tradition, a habit in this kind of self-culture. You find that from the end of the Roman republic at least to very . . . late in antiquity. To retreat in the country was a way to, first, come closer to nature, then to have time and leisure to take care of yourself, and to have also to go through a good regime for the body and for the soul. A lot of people have villas, as you know, in the country and make retreat there. Pliny writes letters in which he explains all the profits made from this kind of retreat, he gives advice to friends to do that sometimes. Musonius Rufus in one of his texts says that it is a very good thing for everybody, and specially for young people—I think he says that, I'm not quite sure—it is a very good thing to go sometimes in country and to live the same kind of life, have the same kind of regime as the farmers because there you work, there you have a healthy regime, there this way you can take care of yourself. The problem between country and self, life in the country and care of the self, is something very important, very cur-rent at this period, and you know the long history of those relation-ships between the self and the country.

This letter is written from the country and the letter is [an] ex-posé of what a day in the country [is like]. And all the elements you see mentioned in these letters are the elements of what was called in the techniques of the self and in the medical techniques the *régime*— how do you pronounce?

— *A regime.*

— It is a regime. A regime implies following Hippocrates and the Hippocratic tradition: sleep—the letter begins when he awakes and finishes when he goes to sleep—sleep, eating, and drinking—you have a description of it—exercising, there is something which [is lacking, which is]* sex, and [...] the bath. So all of that is ... it is a letter about the regime. All of that is interesting. The strange discussion with the mother is also interesting ... Excuse me, you see that the regime is typically a country regime, in which the food is the food of the farmers—and Marcus Aurelius is very proud to say that his father, his mother, and so on and so on ate something else, but he had exactly the same food as the [peasants]. We'll see tomorrow a letter of Seneca about the same things. You see also that the exercise that he does is farmers' work. He does the *vendanges* ...

—*Grape harvest.*

— ... as an exercise for his own health. The thing which is strange also is the ... no, that's not strange—what is much stranger is the conversation with the mother. Following a good regime, a conversation, a philosophical or important conversation must take place after dinner. Plutarch gives the same advice. After—not during the meal, but after the meal—then you can have a serious conversation. They have a serious conversation, and the theme of the conversation is love. That's, as you know, a very traditional idea, [there's] a tradition [of discussing] love, but, as you know, the classical tradition about love is about love of men or women, or about the difficult question "Was Patroclus the lover or the beloved of Achilles or ... ?" and so on and so on.

But here, this discussion is, as far as I know, quite maybe new or at least strange, since it is a discussion about the feelings of Marcus Aurelius towards Fronto and the feelings of the mother of Marcus Aurelius for the daughter of Fronto (Gratia is the daughter of Fronto). Of course that has ... is different from the erotic discussions, or from the discussions about the nature of love which was traditional in [...] Xenophon, Plato, and so on. It is something also different from what will happen and what you can find in the medieval period when the discussions about love were beginning. That's love as an affective intense relationship which is, as far as we can guess, which has, as far as

* Conjecture; the recording is inaudible.

we can guess, nothing sexual in it. And it is the theme of discussion. The idea that this kind of affective intense relation is the theme of discussion, of serious discussion, it is quite characteristic.

And there is a last point I would like to evoke because it is of course the most important. It is the sentence "After coming back…" You see? End of the letter: "After coming back, before I turn over and snore, I get my task done"—I don't know what that means—"and give my dearest of masters an account of this day […]." If you refer to the Latin text, he says not "I get my task done," but *pensum explico, meum pensum explico.* That is the roll where things … all the things he has done were written. *Explico,* that means *dérouler,* unroll. It is an examination of conscience. At the end of the day, when he goes to bed—we will see that tomorrow in Seneca—when he goes to bed, he reviews in his thought, his *pensum,* the things he had to do and the things he has done in the day, he, and that's a metaphor, a metaphor of the book, of the notebook, I think—maybe here it has really the sense of a real book, but I think it is a metaphorical notebook he has said—he looks at what he has done during the day and this examination of conscience he gives, he writes to Fronto what he has discovered or what he remembers in this examination of conscience. So that this letter is [either] an explanation or an exposé of what the regime is in [the country].*

* Conjecture; the recording ends abruptly here.

THIRD MEETING

I THINK THAT WHAT WE decided last time was today we'll try to make several short exposés about the notion of *parrēsia*, reading several texts from Galen and Seneca,[1] and tomorrow we are supposed to have a free discussion with free questions, and maybe free answers... Anyway today it will be, the theme will be "free speech," and as far as it is about "free speech," I hope it will be a good incitation for what we have to say tomorrow.

Well, I don't remember if it was in the last lecture or in the previous one, I don't remember exactly, I spoke about this notion of *parrēsia*, which means, which is translated traditionally in English by the expression "free speech," and we have in French the expression *franc parler*. It's not from a chauvinistic point of view, but I think that the expression *franc parler* has some connotations which fit much better than the expression "free speech" to translate *parrēsia* [...] because there is in the expression of *franc parler* some ethical connotations which are quite clear, and I don't think that in the expression "free speech" you have anything like that. Anyway, etymologically, *parrēsia* is *pan-rhesia*, that means the possibility, the freedom to say whatever one thinks.

Well, the reasons why I chose this theme for this seminar, the reasons why I have chosen the theme of *parrēsia* are the following:

First. This notion of *parrēsia* . . . *parrēsia*, how do you pronounce
that in English?
—*Parrēsia*.
— . . . this notion is a complex, many-sided notion. Anyway, I
think it's impossible to understand and to analyze the notion of *parrēsia* from the point of view of [the] binary schema [of] freedom-
prohibition. I think that with *parrēsia* we escape this kind of schema
and we have to find another form of analysis than the analysis in terms
of what is permitted, what is allowed and what is prohibited. *Parrēsia*
is both a freedom and an obligation. First point. The second point
is that *parrēsia* implies always certain circumstances in the situation
of the interlocutors. It refers also to the personal situation, the personal status, the ethical qualities of the interlocutors, and it implies
that one is obliged to speak and the other is obliged to listen. Well, all
those conditions which are implied by the notion of *parrēsia* show,
I think, that the notion of *parrēsia* is much closer to an implicit, or
eventually to an explicit, pact between the speaker and the listener
than to the freedom, the pure and bare freedom, of speaking. From
that point of view, I think that this notion is very important and, I
should say, a very good example for a historical analysis of discourse
from the point of view of the pragmatic of discourse. That's the first
reason: the complexity of the notion.
    The second reason why I am interested in this notion and why I
propose to analyze it today, the second reason is that this notion is
linked to the notion of true discourse, to the notion of truth. *Parrēsia*
is not only the freedom or the obligation [. . .] to say something; it
is also the freedom and the obligation of telling the truth. But which
truth? For instance, it's quite clear and obvious that the Greeks won't
say, for instance, that a naturalist or that a historian or that an ar-
chitect, for instance, uses *parrēsia* when they say, when they tell the
truth about the living beings or about a historical event or about their
technē, their art as architects. The truth which is put in question in
parrēsia, this truth, first, belongs always to a specific field, or to two
specific fields: the field of ethics and the field of politics. A scientific
truth does not need to be . . . *véhiculée*, to be transported by *parrēsia*.
But, in several cases, several important cases, ethical and political
truth needs *parrēsia*. And the second character of this truth is that

173

this truth is dangerous or, more precisely, that it may be dangerous for the speaker to tell this truth and unpleasant or wounding—we can say that "wounding?"—wounding for the hearer to hear it. It is an ethical or political truth which has by itself a kind of danger, which implies a kind of danger, different . . . this danger is not the same, of course, for the speaker and for the listener, but there is a danger in this truth which has to be told through *parrēsia*. *Parrēsia* refers to the dangerous game of telling the truth in the political and ethical field.

The third reason why I have chosen to study this notion is that it is both an ethical and a technical notion. I mean that *parrēsia*, or to be a *parrēsiastēs* (that means somebody who uses *parrēsia*), to be a *parrēsiastēs* is a virtue. But to be a *parrēsiastēs* is also a *technē*, it is an art, it implies a know-how. And this art or this mixture of art and virtues plays an important role in ethical and in political life.

The fourth reason [for] the importance of this notion, from my point of view, is that the meaning of this notion changed considerably during ancient civilization. From the classical period to early Christianity, it [took] several different meanings, and this transformation has something to do with both the political structure of ancient societies and with self-knowledge and the techniques for the [. . .] disclosure of oneself through discourses.[2]

[These] are several [of the] reasons why I have proposed [to] study this notion of *parrēsia* with you today. For a history of self-knowledge, for a history of avowal, and from the point of view of a pragmatic analysis of discourses, I think that this notion of *parrēsia* is a very good example and a very good point of departure. Of course, my intention today is not to follow this evolution throughout antiquity. I will insist only, as in my lectures, on the two first centuries of our era, and I'll only sketch out the classical meaning and the Christian meaning of the word. And the reason why I have chosen those two first centuries is that *parrēsia* at this moment is very closely linked to the technique of the care of the self.

WELL, FIRST A FEW WORDS about the classical meaning of the word. The word *parrēsia* in the classical Greek, this word is used with three different references.

First, it is used in reference [to the] constitution, the constitution of the city, with the *politeia*, more precisely with the democratic *politeia*, the democratic constitution, and still more precisely with the Athenian democratic constitution. You find, for instance, in Polybe, second book, paragraph 38, the characterization of the Achaean constitution with three terms, three [characteristics], *dēmokratia, isēgoria, parrēsia*.[3] *Dēmokratia*, well, [...] *isonomia*, excuse me, *isēgoria* [...]. In fact those three or four words, *dēmokratia, isēgoria, isonomia, parrēsia*, are traditionally linked together. *Dēmokratia* is the general term; it is the fact that the *dēmos*, means not everybody, but the citizens, those who have the status of citizen exercise the power in the city. That's *dēmokratia*. *Isonomia* means that ... well, the meaning of the word has changed from the archaic period to the classical period, well, at the classical period, *isonomia* means that the *nomos*, the law, is the same for everybody and that there is no privilege for some citizens compared to the other citizens. *Isēgoria* is something else. It is the fact that everyone has the same right to speak, to speak in public, to intervene on the political scene, to ... *prendre la parole* ...

— *To take the floor.*

— ... to take the floor in a political assembly. That's *isēgoria*, the equality of the right to speak. And *parrēsia* is the freedom to speak and to say in the political assemblies anything or whatever you think, and whatever you think is true or useful for the city or just and so on, without being victim of the aftereffects of what you have said if people do not agree with you. That's *parrēsia*. This ... is there any question? No? So. Those four notions, *dēmokratia, isonomia, isēgoria, parrēsia*, are characteristic of the Athenian constitution and they are regularly quoted as the glory of Athens, anyway as something quite characteristic of its constitution. The freedom of Athens, the fact that Athens is free, and that Athens gives the freedom to its citizens, is characterized ... is analyzed by those four notions: *dēmokratia, isonomia, isēgoria, parrēsia*.

In order to understand this notion of *parrēsia* a little better, I think we can refer to Euripides, Euripides who in the fourth century has given in his tragedies several very different ... several very interesting aspects of the political life and the political notions and concepts in Athens. There are four occurrences of the word *parrēsia* in Euripides. First in *The Phoenicians, Les Phéniciennes* ... Phoenicians, let me ... there is a quotation in Plutarch, and I use this translation.[4] It is in the lines 388–393. It is a discussion between Jocaste, who is supposed to have lived after the discovery of her marriage with Œdipe, and Polynice, his son ... her son, excuse me, Polynice. And Polynice has been exiled, and Jocaste also arrives in the same town. And Jocaste still does not know what it is to be exiled, what is exile, why exiled people are considered as the most unfortunate people in the world, why is it such a misfortune to be exiled. That's the theme of the dialogue. And if you'll read it for the class, with your perfect accent ...

[*A participant reads the brief dialogue between Jocasta and Polynices:*]

JOCASTA. What is the loss of country? A great ill?
POLYNICES. Surpassing great; no words can do it justice.
JOCASTA. What is it like? What ills beset the banished?
POLYNICES. One greater than the rest: speech is not free.
JOCASTA. That is a slave's part—not to speak one's mind.
POLYNICES. The folly of the mighty must be borne.[5]

—So. You see in this text where the word *parrēsia* occurs: first, as you see, *parrēsia* belongs to citizens, and only to citizens. If you are not a citizen in a city, you don't enjoy *parrēsia*. First point. Second point is the lack of *parrēsia* is a common point to people who are exiled, who are not citizens, and to slaves. The slave doesn't enjoy *parrēsia*. The lack of *parrēsia* is characteristic of the slave's life. Third point: when you don't enjoy *parrēsia*, and you don't have *parrēsia*, then you have to accept the follies of the master, [...] that was the translation I have found, and he says "the folly of the mighty." That is, as a noncitizen, or as a slave, you are under the dependence of the citizen or of your master, and when your master said silly things, says silly things, silly things or follies or things like that, you cannot answer, you have to accept what he says, and you cannot either criticize him or refute him or rebuke him and so on and so on. You have to accept his follies. And that's one of the worst things in the lack of *parrēsia*:

to be obliged to accept and to bear the stupidity or the follies of your master, of the mighty. That means that *parrēsia* is, on the contrary, the freedom to criticize even the master, even the mighty, when they say stupid things, when they say [the worst things].* Well, I think this text is the most characteristic of the notion of *parrēsia* in the classical period. But you [can] also find in Euripides other occurrences where some aspects of *parrēsia* are [brought to]† light.

You find this in the . . . *Les Bacchantes*, how do you say?

— *Bacchae.*

— *The Bacchae.* I can give you the reference. It is the moment where a slave comes to Penthée in order to tell him what awful disorders the Bacchae were doing. And the slave, the slave arrives in front of Penthée and is afraid to say [the] bad news, because, as you know, it was a tradition that when . . . an archaic tradition that when a slave comes with bad news, he was punished for the bad news. [. . .] Also in *The Bacchae* . . . ah yes, it's line 420. The messenger says, comes and says . . . — I'll — read it because it is my awful *écriture*: "I am . . ." — and it is a very bad translation, I found here only an old translation, I was not able to find a better one, so excuse me — : "I am come to tell thee and the city the wondrous deeds they [the Bacchae] do, deeds passing strange. But I fain would hear, whether I am freely to tell all I saw there [*parrēsia*], or shorten my story; for I fear thy hasty temper, thy sudden bursts of wrath and more than princely rage." And then Penthée answers: "Say on, for thou shalt go unpunished by me in all respects."[6]

So. You see a very interesting aspect of *parrēsia*. The slave is exposed by the fact that [when] he comes with bad news he is exposed, naturally exposed to the anger of the prince, and he won't tell the bad news without this kind of pact, which is the parrhesiastic pact[7], that is, "I'll tell all the truth if you promise me that I won't be punished." And Penthée accepts this parrhesiastic pact: "Well, tell me the truth, tell me all the truth, and you'll go unpunished." That, I think, is very characteristic of the fact that, in *parrēsia*, the truth you say is danger-

---

* Conjecture; the end of the sentence is inaudible.
† Foucault says "put in light."

ous: dangerous for the other and dangerous for you. Well, the content of what you say is dangerous for the other and the fact that you tell it is dangerous for you. Those two things, those two dangers, the danger from the content and the danger from the act of speaking, those two dangers constitute, I think, *parrēsia* . . . well, the game of *parrēsia*, the risk and the danger of *parrēsia*.

The third occurrence of *parrēsia* in Euripides, it's in *Ion*, line 668. That's the aspect of *parrēsia* . . . an aspect of *parrēsia* that we met previously. He says that, when a foreigner comes in the town, the mouth, his mouth, will be slave, *kai ouk echei parrēsian*, and he can't have *parrēsia*. A noncitizen does not have *parrēsia*.[8]

And fourth occurrence, it is in *Hippolyte* . . .

—*Hippolytus*.

—*Hippolytus*, line 422. It is when Phaedra reveals her love for Hippolytus. And it's very interesting because it is a very important part of the tragedy, of course. Phaedra reveals her love and after having revealed her love, she evokes her own children and she says that she is afraid that her shame, her own shame, the fact that she is in love and the shame to be in love and so on and so on, [. . .] she is afraid that this shame will prevent her children from being complete and honorable citizens enjoying *parrēsia*.[9]

So. You see that it is not, it is not here a question of legal status, as, for instance, with slaves or free people, or citizens or noncitizens. The mere fact that somebody has done shameful things is sufficient to deprive him of *parrēsia*. And in this case, the mere fact that the parents, or one of the parents has done something shameful is enough to deprive the children of having, of enjoying, from enjoying the *parrēsia*. And that refers, of course, to the fact that one could be deprived [of] *parrēsia* by an infamous condemnation, but that also certain shameful dishonorable behaviors could deprive people from the right, the political and the ethical right of speaking, speaking in assemblies.

You have on this theme a lot of witnesses, in Demosthenes, for example, or also in Aeschines, and there is the well-known plea *Against Timarchus*[10] from Aeschines, all the plea—you say the plea?—all the plea has for theme is this one: Timarchus was a friend of Demosthenes, has been an ambassador to Philip and he came back, and then

Aeschines sued him because he was, Timarchus, a prostitute when he was young and, as he has been a prostitute—it was no legal condemnation, nothing like that—but it was an infamous situation, it was an infamous, dishonorable behavior, and he couldn't then enjoy the political right, well, not exactly the political rights, but the political . . . he couldn't have the political responsibility of speaking for the other citizens, and so he couldn't be an ambassador for Athens, such as he wanted. He was deprived of this *parrēsia*, of the right of speaking.

Well, as you see, *parrēsia*, enjoying *parrēsia* is something which depends upon certain oppositions between freedom and slavery, citizenship and the fact of being a foreigner, of honorable behavior or shameful behavior, and so on. That's the first point and the first aspect of *parrēsia*. It is one of the main features of Athenian democracy, but, as you see, it depended on a lot of things, and certain characteristics of the person who could have or not have the *parrēsia*.

Second important reference to this notion of *parrēsia* in the classical Greek, after the reference to the democratic constitution, it is the reference to monarchy. The reference to monarchy . . . and that, and those references, you find them in Isocrates and also in Plato.

In Isocrates, you find two kinds of references to *parrēsia*. First, a criticism of *parrēsia* in the Athenian democracy—because, as you know, Isocrates was a fervent monarchist—and a positive evaluation of *parrēsia* in the monarchy. For the first point, the critique of *parrēsia* in the Athenian constitution, in the Athenian city, you have two texts, one is in the discourse *On the Peace*, paragraph 14. It is a criticism [of] the way the Athenians choose their advisers. And the text is the following. Isocrates says: "I know that it is hazardous to oppose your views and that although . . . although it is a free government, although it is *dēmokratia*, [that's the text], there exists no *parrēsia*."[11] So, as you see, it's not a criticism against the notion of *parrēsia*, but it is a criticism against the way the Athenians were supposed to enjoy democracy, but do not really accept *parrēsia*, the freedom of speech.

In another text of Isocrates, you find a real criticism [of] *parrēsia*. It is in the *Areopagiticus*, paragraph 20. Isocrates says: "Solon and Clisthenes did not establish a policy, which in name merely was hailed as the most impartial government, while in practice they looked upon insolence (*akolasia*) as democracy, lawlessness (*paranomia*) as liberty (*eleutheria*), impudence of speech (*parrēsia*) as equality, and license as happiness."[12] So, as you see, that's a criticism of Athenian democracy itself. The laws which have been proposed by Solon and Clisthenes should have established in Athens a real democracy, a real liberty, a real equality, a real happiness, and in fact they established what? Insolence, lawlessness, *parrēsia* with the meaning of impudence of speech, and *exousia*, or license.

But in another text, where he speaks about monarchy, and which shows all the merits and advantages of the monarchic constitution, monarchic constitution, in the Discourse to *Nicocles*, then you find a very interesting use of this notion of *parrēsia*. In this text, he quotes *parrēsia*, he refers to *parrēsia* two different times. First, when he speaks about *paideia*, the education of the young prince, he says that a young prince cannot enjoy the *parrēsia* . . . well, that, when during the education of a young prince he cannot have friends who are bold enough to speak to him with *parrēsia*. And that's a difference between a private young man, a private person, and a prince. In private education, every young boy has friends who are willing to tell him the truth and eventually to rebuke him, since it's not very dangerous for them to tell him the truth. But, among the people who are around a young prince, it's very difficult to find people who are courageous enough to use *parrēsia* with him. That's the first occurrence of the word in this discourse.[13]

Then, a little later on, when he gives the portrait of the good monarch, he says that the good monarch needs advisers [who] are able to tell him the truth. But he cannot have such friends if he does not behave in such a way that his friends are not afraid to tell him the truth. So one of the first duties of the prince will be to allow his advisers to use *parrēsia* with him. And that is what he says to Nicocles, as advice he gives him: "Regard as your . . ." —Nicocles was a young . . . the son of . . . of . . . *comment on dit "tyran?"*

—Tyrant.

—Tyrant. No, not tyrant, I do not remember . . . in Asia Minor . . . I do not remember which one.[14] Anyway, so he addresses himself to Nicocles and he says: "Regard as your most faithful friends, not those who praise everything you say or do, but those who criticize your mistakes. Grant *parrēsia*, grant freedom of speech, to those who have a good judgment in order that, when you are in doubt, you may have friends who will help you to decide."[15] That is the positive definition of *parrēsia*.

Something very close to this text is to be found in Plato's *Laws*, in the third book, 694c. It is precisely a description, a positive description of Persia, when Persia was under the domination, under the reign of Cyrus, and Plato explains that under Cyrus's reign, the Persian monarch not only allowed his advisers to use *parrēsia*, but he gave great honors to those who were able to give him true, sincere, and good advice.[16] And as a result of this good monarchy, this good government, where the king of Persia allowed his advisers to use *parrēsia*, as a result, everything, says Plato, worked very well in Persia at this moment, and during this period, everything worked very well through *eleutheria* (*eleutheria* means "freedom"), through *philia* (friendship), *koinōnia* (community, you can say? Community of view, maybe, of feeling?). So, *parrēsia*, as used by the advisers towards the prince, is the principal cause, the principal element which induces in the city or in the state, in Persia, freedom, friendship, *koinōnia*, community. So, that's the meaning of *parrēsia* in the classical Greek in reference to the monarchic system.

And there is also in the classical Greek a reference of the word *parrēsia* . . . the word *parrēsia* is used in reference to . . . with the meaning of this kind of frankness and freedom of speech which is useful and necessary in order to help a friend in his ethical choices or for the improvement of his soul. And that is the private meaning of *parrēsia* [the ethical meaning of *parrēsia*, which you find, for example, in the *Gorgias*].* It is in a very ironic moment, but it doesn't matter for the specific meaning of *parrēsia*. Socrates says to Callicles that anyone has . . . when somebody has to try (*basanizein*), to try his own soul, he needs the help of somebody else, and . . . that's quite serious. What is ironic is that Socrates says to Callicles that he will be the good *basanos*, the good proof for his own soul. That of course is

* Conjecture; the passage is mostly inaudible.

quite false. But anyway, [each person] has to try his own soul with the help, through the help of somebody else. And this other person who is necessary for the truth of the soul needs to have three things to be a good *basanos*, a good *pierre de touche* . . .

— *Touchstone*.

— . . . touchstone, to be a good touchstone he needs to have *epistēmē*, knowledge or science. He needs to have *eunoia*. *Eunoia*, that means to have good feelings, something which is close to friendship. In the Greek friendship, in the Greek *philia*, there were two main elements, *eunoia* and *koinōnia ou homonoia, eunoia* . . . there are three things, *eunoia, homonoia, koinōnia*. *Eunoia*, that means good feelings towards somebody, *homonoia* is to think and to feel the same things as your friend, and *koinōnia* is you share everything in your life. So, to be a good touchstone for the other, for somebody, one needs to have *epistēmē, eunoia*, good feelings and so on, and *parrēsia*, that means he must be frank enough to say whatever he thinks about his friend and so on.[17]

So. Those are the three main uses, three main meanings, of *parrēsia* in the classical Greek.

Well, as you can imagine very easily, for some historical reasons you know very well, *parrēsia*, the notion of *parrēsia* as one of the main features of the democratic city, that means the first meaning, this notion of *parrēsia* disappeared in the literature of the two first centuries. And in the literature of the two first centuries you find only the two other meanings of the word, that means *parrēsia* related to the monarchic constitution, monarchic government, or *parrēsia* in the ethical meaning.

First, *parrēsia*—you find the word mainly among the historians, but also among the philosophers who were interested in political questions, for instance, in Dio of Prusa—*parrēsia* is characterized as a kind of speech relation between the prince, the monarch, and his advisers. On one side, the monarch has to allow his advisers to use *parrēsia*, and he must restrain himself from punishing his advisers when they use *parrēsia* towards him even if this *parrēsia* has something wounding for him. That's the *parrēsia* on the side of the monarch. And the advisers are also obliged to use *parrēsia*, they are linked by the obligation to tell the truth [. . .] but at the same moment, they are protected against the anger of the prince, of the monarch, by the freedom which has been granted to them, the freedom of using *parrēsia*. And this parrhesiastic pact between the monarch and the advisers is one of the conditions, the main conditions, for a good monarchic government. And this problem, this theme of *parrēsia* as one of the conditions for a good government, good monarchic government, I think, is to be found, of course, throughout the imperial Roman government, but also you can find it throughout all the monarchic governments in the history of absolute monarchy to the end of the eighteenth century.

I think that the problem of *parrēsia* disappeared when two institutions, new institutions at least for Europe, and I put England aside, appeared at the end of the eighteenth century [and the] beginning of the nineteenth century: the parliament and the press. You do say "freedom of press"?

—*Yes.*

—I think that the parliament and the freedom of press are the real inheritors of the problem of *parrēsia*. So I don't think you have to, from this point of view at least, to interpret *parrēsia* only as a private virtue or something like that. It has been in the political thinking, in political reflection, in political discussions as important as the problem of parliament, of the freedom of the press, in our societies. And I think that we could analyze a lot of things in the monarchic institutions from this point of view. The problem, for instance, of what is a favorite, what is a minister, the role of the preachers, the problem also of what is a court, or what is the role of people in the court, who will tell the truth to the king and so on and so on. All that is a very technical, very well-known political problem: who is the *parrēsiastēs*? And how the king respects, or does not respect, the parrhesiastic pact? How the court-man respects or does not respect the parrhesiastic pact? I think that that is something very important. So you find *parrēsia*, in this meaning, in the literature of the imperial period.

[Second,] you find also and during the same period the notion of *parrēsia* used in the technical field of the care of the self. And *parrēsia* was something as necessary in the relation between the director and the directed, was something as necessary in this kind of relationship as between the monarch and his advisers. But what I would like to underline is the fact that those two meanings of *parrēsia*, the political one in the monarchic government and the ethical one, the relationship between the director and the directed, those two meanings are in fact very close to one another. In both cases, it is a question of governing, of governing somebody's soul. In one case, it is the problem of governing the king's soul, and in the other case, it is governing somebody, a private person's soul. And on the one hand it is of course much more important to govern the soul of a king who has to govern other people, so that governing the monarch's, the king's, soul is a task of much greater responsibility and of much greater influence than governing [just] anybody's soul.

But on the other hand there is no real difference between the rules of behavior which the prince has to acquire and the rules of behavior a private person has to apply, so that there is no real technical or philosophical difference between governing a king's soul and governing a private person's soul. The virtue of the prince is the common virtue. And one has to govern the prince's soul as if he was a private person. So if governing the king's soul is much more important, the basis of this kind of soul's government, the government of the king's soul, this kind of government has exactly the same roots and the same forms, and must have the same forms and the same roots, as the governing of anybody's soul. There is no difference in the rational principles of the behavior of the monarch and of a citizen. And that, I think, is one of the main things about this technique.

And the second point is that it is a fact that most of the people who presented themselves as technicians of the soul in the everyday life pretended also to become advisers for the prince. To be a good director for the soul, to be a good physician for the passions of everybody ... of everybody, enables one to become a good adviser for the prince. Seneca, Musonius Rufus, Dio of Prusa, even Plutarch, who wrote to Menemachos a treatise about governing a city,[18] all those people were both, and at the same time, directors of conscience and advisers for the prince. And the rules they wanted to apply to the prince were exactly the same [rules] they proposed to their correspondents. And it's very clear in Marcus Aurelius. In Marcus Aurelius, well, Marcus Aurelius speaks in the same terms of his human duties and of his professional obligations as an emperor. And . . . and so on, you have also other examples, Apollonius following Philostrate, Apollonius and Euphrates gave . . . who were directors of conscience, gave advice to Vespasianus when he was about to take over the imperial power.[19]

The proximity between the cure of the self and the political rationality, I think, is something very important in our history. And it is important, I think, for two reasons. As you see, there is a notion which is common to those two domains, the domain of the political rationality and the domain of the cure of the self. The notion which is common to those two domains is the notion of government, of governing. Governing oneself . . . governing oneself, governing other people, governing the behavior of somebody else, governing the world, governing mankind, all that constitutes one continuous field. So that I think we could say that there is in our political thought two different roots. One which has been always privileged, it is the problem of the constitution, of *politeia*. That was the problem of Aristotle, that was the problem of Plato.

And there is also another problem which is the problem of government, of governing people. And the problem of governing people, I think, is radically different from the problem of the constitution. It is not a question to know how the city is constituted, which are the permanent laws of the city, what is the equilibrium between the different parts of the city. The problem of government deals with the general rationality of the decisions, the general rationality of the choices, of the goals, of the means you use; it is the problem of the rationality of the behavior of people who govern us, who govern other people.

And I think that those two problems, the problem of *politeia*, constitution, which is the problem of Plato and Aristotle, and the problem of governing people, which is the problem of Tacitus, which is the problem of Seneca, which is the problem of all those people of the first century, those two problems, the problem of government and the problem of constitutions . . . are two different problems. And I think that in our political thought, since at least the seventeenth or eighteenth century, the problem of constitution has always been over-rated, compared to the problem of government. And that's a point I would like to study in the future, [. . .]* the problem of those two kinds of political thought, the one oriented towards the *politeia* and the one oriented towards the government.

And my hypothesis, but I have no evidence to give just now, is that the theory of soul is related to the political problem of *politeia* and the problem of self is related to the problem of government. *Politeia* and soul, the theory of *politeia*, and the . . . of constitution, and the theory of soul, [are] quite clearly related in Plato and Aristotle. And the problem of government and the problem of soul which are clearly related in this kind of thought I'm speaking about just now. Well, that's only an hypothesis.

Anyway I think that the continuity and the . . . well, maybe it's a little late now and we should jump to what I was supposed to tell you and put aside all those things about the historical destiny of *parrēsia*. Well, is there any question about what I have said just now? Either about the classical meaning of *parrēsia* or about the problem of government as the link between the political and the ethical meaning of the word in the first two centuries . . . two first centuries. No?

—*I would have one, and I don't know if it's relevant. I would go to other cultures, to the East, if these also stand [in philosophy] that does not grant so much importance to government of the self, maybe, I am just wondering, if this difference would still appear [. . .]?*

—No, no, no, I think it's quite relevant. Well, I think that the problem of the self, not the governing of the self, the problem of the self as a problem, the central problem of ethics is of course quite . . . it's one of the main features of the Buddhist . . . the Buddhist way of living, the Buddhist religion, if you call it a religion, but it is not one. It is an ethics. So. And I think that we have to compare this, our ethics of the self from the Greco-Roman period, with this ethics of the self in the East, in Eastern civilization.[20] What is interesting is that, when Western civilization in the beginning of the nineteenth century "discovered" Eastern civilization, they met the problem of the

* Foucault says "next future" here.

self. And in Schopenhauer, for instance, I think that you can find exactly what the counter-effect of this discovery was inside the Western philosophical theory of this ethics of the self which was something so strange for us, so far from the Christian experience of the self, and very far also from what we could call the Greco-Roman experience of the self. And I think that Schopenhauer has been maybe the single one among the great philosophers to react to this other . . . or to try to integrate this other experience of the self, this other ethics of the self, in Western thinking.

And what is also very significative is the fact that the Schopenhauerian influence [was] enormous in the nineteenth century, and it has completely disappeared now. I don't know if you are interested in Schopenhauer in the States, but I think that I never hear his name either in France or in the States. Or I think that, if you are interested in this field of research about the self, the technologies of the self, liberation of the self, and so on, you have to meet Schopenhauer, which is a central point, he is at the cross point, or he has tried to be at the cross point, if it is possible, in those two different traditions.

— I have the intuition — and I don't know if this is [correct] — that in the East, they stressed government much more than politeia, than the constitution.

— Yes, I think perhaps. But I cannot give you an answer or evidence about that. Anyway this relation between the self and government or soul and politeia maybe is quite a delirium.

SO LET'S TURN BACK, IF you like, to parrēsia now, parrēsia in the strictly ethical meaning of the word in the beginning of our era. A first thing I would like to underline is that we have of course a lot of indications about the importance, the primordial, primary, role of parrēsia in the culture of the self. In the culture of the self, parrēsia is one of the most explicit requirements in the relationship between the director and the directed. All the texts, all the texts which refer to this kind of relationships between the director and the directed, all those texts show very clearly that parrēsia is an obligation, but that parrēsia is an obligation on the side of the director. The parrēsia as an obligation or as a freedom to say whatever you think [...]* in a certain way and that of course is clear, you can see that in several texts.

I have chosen, only because it is a very good sociological document even if it is rather aggressive, the different texts of Lucianus about philosophy. He shows [...] what *parrēsia* is, insofar as *parrēsia* is not only a way of speaking, not only a way of directing people, but also a way of living. Or at least it is a way of directing other people linked to a certain specific way of living. And he gives two portraits... among all the portraits he gives of philosophers, one is the most aggressive, it is about Peregrinus, Peregrinus who ... really Lucianus hated this Peregrinus. Peregrinus was a very strange guy who [had] been a Cynic philosopher, he [had] converted himself to Christianity and then after he came back to Cynicism, and he burned himself, he burned himself maybe from a tradition which comes from the East, he burned himself publicly [at] the Olympic games [at] the end of the second century.[21]

And Lucianus hated this Peregrinus, and he explains that Peregrinus, when he went [to] Rome, behaved in such a way that the emperor was really obliged to exile him. And Lucianus explains that, of course, Peregrinus [did] that on purpose [...] to let people believe that he was a real philosopher. He was on everybody's lips as the philosopher who had been banished for his *parrēsia* and excessive freedom (*parrēsia* and *agan eleutheria*), so that in this respect he approached Musonius, Dio, Epictetus, and anyone else who has been ... anyone else who [had] been [treated similarly].[22] And he gives a positive portrait of another Cynic, Demonax, about whom he says: "From his boyhood, he felt an inborn love for philosophy and, committing himself unreservedly to liberty and free speech (*eleutheria* and *parrēsia*), he was steadfast in leading a straight, sane, irreproachable life and in setting an example to all who saw and heard him by his good judgment and the honesty of his philosophy."[23]

You see that in those two texts, the text against Peregrinus and the text in favor of Demonax, *parrēsia* and *eleutheria* are [...] *parrēsia* is *eleutheria* in the domain of discourse, and *eleutheria* is, if I could

---

* Interruption in the recording.

say, *parrēsia* in the domain of the everyday life, it is the way by which people, good philosophers show in their everyday life, in their way of living, that they are *parrēsiastēs*, that means that they hide nothing, that they live as they think and . . . yes, as they think. There is a deep continuity between their behavior and their way of thinking.

Well, I think that those are the principal aspects of *parrēsia* in this kind of literature and I would like now to turn to several texts. I have xeroxed a few of them, two, I think, of them, one of Lucian . . . no, one of Galenus and one written by Seneca. I think that the four great texts which have been preserved and which speak about *parrēsia* are, first, a treatise written by Philodemus, Philodemus who was an Epicurean, the great Epicurean of the first century B.C. and who has written a treatise, *Peri parrēsias*.[24] It is the only text precisely devoted to *parrēsia* which has been preserved. Unfortunately the preservation was not very good [. . .] and we have only fragments of this text, and those fragments themselves are rather corrupted, and there is no translation, neither in English nor in French nor in German nor in Italian nor in Spanish nor in Latin, of this text by Philodemus and . . . well, very competent people are struggling just now to give meanings to these fragments,[25] but I am not competent and I put this text aside, unfortunately, because it is the single document about *parrēsia* in [. . .] Epicurean philosophy.

The second great text, much more explicit, much more . . . you say "loud speaking," *bavard*?

— *Chattering.*

— . . . chattering has been written, of course, by Plutarch, who is, as you know, a very big chatterbox. The text is "How to Tell a Flatterer from a Friend."[26] The third text, or third texts are several of Seneca's letters,[27] and the fourth, which is rarely, I must say, ever quoted by people who study *parrēsia*, is the text of Galenus which I have had xeroxed.

About the theme of *parrēsia*, there is . . . the best study has been written in, I think, '64–'65 by Scarpat, an Italian author.[28] You have the book in the library here. It's about the notion of *parrēsia*, it's a very valuable book, very good for the classical references, very good for the Christian literature because […] Scarpat is a priest,* and he knows certain books very well. He has written a book about Seneca also,[29] but it is a fact that his book is quite insufficient about the relations between *parrēsia* and the care of the self, and all this aspect of the question is literally omitted by Scarpat. For instance, he does not quote Galenus, and there is also this strange habit in this book … not strange, this habit of the good philologist, you see, if the word *parrēsia* is not to be found in the text, so it [isn't there].[†] I think it is impossible to read this text of Galenus without having the notion of *parrēsia* in mind, but the word *parrēsia* does not [appear].[‡] So Scarpat does not quote Galenus.

Well, I would like now to say [a] few words about Plutarch, and after we'll turn to Galenus. And if we don't have time today to finish with Galen, we'll go on tomorrow. We can do that? Sure? Well. Yes, because I would like to start with Plutarch, for the reason [that] I'll be rather brief about him. So, [Plutarch wrote] in the beginning of the second century. Galen [wrote] at the end of the second century. Plutarch, in the beginning of the second century, [wrote] a text which very clearly appears as a theory of *parrēsia*. It is this treatise about flattery. Why [is] the treatise about flattery [also] a theory of *parrēsia*? For the very simple reason that flattery is the opposite of *parrēsia*. Of course, you know all the reasons why flattery could be in such a type of society, of the Greco-Roman society, something so important. In such a hierarchical society, in which personal influence, in which clientelism was so important, of course, you see, the hierarchical structure and the personal links between people and the dependence of people were of course in the social background of the importance of flattery. What is flattery from this […] philosophical point of view, from the ethical point of view? Who are the flatterers? Following Plutarch, the flatterer is somebody who tells lies in order to please his interlocutor and to give his interlocutor a deceptive, misleading

---

* Foucault is mistaken here; Scarpat was not a priest.
† Conjecture; the sentence is partially inaudible.
‡ Conjecture; Foucault does not finish the sentence.

image of himself. And of course since flattery […] gives someone this misleading image of himself, it is of course the most dangerous thing for the care of the self. And Plutarch has a very strong, very clear formula: the worst enemy of the *gnōthi seauton* is the flatterer. Either a flatterer or *gnōthi seauton*. That's the opposition. And that's the reason why we have to rely upon a *parrēsiastēs* and not upon a flatterer.

But the problem is how to recognize a real *parrēsiastēs* or how to recognize a real flatterer. Because of course, such … following Plutarch, of course the good flatterer is not somebody who shows himself as a flatterer. The flatterer who shows that he is a flatterer is not dangerous. The flatterer who is dangerous is the one who … who hides himself, who hides that he is flattering and who imitates the *parrēsiastēs*. So the problem is how to recognize a real *parrēsiastēs* from a flatterer who imitates the *parrēsiastēs*? So that the treatise, Plutarch's treatise, deals with the problem of the semiotics of flattery. And I am glad to use for the first time, at last, the word "semiotics."*

Anyway, if some of you are semioticians, they can read this text as semiotics of flattery and of the *parrēsiastēs*. But I am afraid they won't find this thing very interesting because Plutarch goes very directly [into a] philosophical theme, that is, you recognize a flatterer in the fact that, not that he says flattering things to you, because a good flatterer is somebody, of course, who will give you reproaches, who will rebuke you, and so on and so on, in order to let you think that he is not a flatterer but a *parrēsiastēs*. So he will tell you very nasty things. And so it's not the sign. The sign is the fact that the flatterer is changing in his opinion, in his behavior, in his way of life, according either to your own changes or to the situation in which he is and you are, or to which people … according to the people [he is with]. You can be sure that he who rebukes you is not a flatterer if his own choices for himself, in his own life, are the same, the same as the choices that [he will counsel you for yourself. The conformity of what he says and what he is,]† is the sign that he is really a *parrēsiastēs* and not a

* A joke on Foucault's part, in reference to the fact that the seminar and lectures took place in the context of a conference on semiotics.
† Conjecture; the passage is inaudible.

flatterer. This conformity of what he is … of what he says and what he is, and the conformity of what he is throughout [his own life],* those two conformities are the real signs of *parrēsia*. Conformity of what he says to what he is, conformity of his behavior to a sort of permanent schema.

And I would like to ask Tim to read one or two pages about that and then we jump to […] here and maybe … *là*. With "Alcibiades … ," yes. Just stop here and read […].

[A participant reads the text of Plutarch:]

What, then, is the method of exposing him, and by what differences is it possible to detect that he is not really like-minded, or even in a fair way to become like-minded, but is merely imitating such a character? In the first place, it is necessary to observe the uniformity and permanence of his tastes, whether he always takes delight in the same things, and commends always the same things, and whether he directs and ordains his own life according to one pattern, as becomes a free-born man and a lover of congenial friendship and intimacy; for such is the conduct of a friend. But the flatterer, since he has no abiding-place of character to dwell in, and since he leads a life not of his own choosing but another's, molding and adapting himself to suit another, is not simple, not one, but variable and many in one, and, like water that is poured into one receptacle after another, he is constantly on the move from place to place, and changes his shape to fit his receiver.

The capture of the ape, as it seems, is effected while he is trying to imitate man by moving and dancing as the man does: but the flatterer himself leads on and entices others, not imitating all persons alike, but with one he joins in dancing and singing, and with another in wrestling and getting covered with dust; if he gets hold of a huntsman fond of the chase, he follows on, all but shouting out the words of Phaedra:

"Ye gods, but I yearn to encourage the hounds,
As I hasten on the track of the dapple deer."

He does not trouble himself in regard to the quarry, but he goes about to net and ensnare the huntsman himself. But if he is on the track

---

* Conjecture; the passage is inaudible.

of a scholarly and studious young man, now again he is absorbed in books, his beard grows down to his feet, the scholar's gown is the thing now and a stoic indifference, and endless talk about Plato's numbers and right-angled triangles. At another time, if some easy-tempered man fall in his way, who is a hard drinker and rich, "Then stands forth the wily Odysseus stripped of his tatters;" off goes the scholar's gown, the beard is mowed down like an unprofitable crop; it's wine-coolers and glasses now, bursts of laughter while walking in the streets, and frivolous jokes against the devotees of philosophy. Just so at Syracuse, it is said, after Plato had arrived, and an insane ardor for philosophy laid hold on Dionysius, the king's palace was filled with dust by reason of the multitude of men that were drawing their geometrical diagrams in it: but when Plato fell out of favor, and Dionysius, shaking himself free from philosophy, returned post-haste to wine and women and foolish talk and licentiousness, then grossness and forgetfulness and fatuity seized upon the whole people as though they had undergone a transformation in Circe's house. A further testimony is to be found in the action of the great flatterers and the demagogues, of whom the greatest was Alcibiades. At Athens he indulged in frivolous jesting, kept a racing-stable, and led a life full of urbanity and agreeable enjoyment; in Lacedaemon he kept his hair cropped close, he wore the coarsest clothing, he bathed in cold water; in Thrace he was a fighter and a hard drinker: but when he came to Tissaphernes, he took to soft living, and luxury, and pretentiousness. So by making himself like to all these people and conforming his way to theirs he tried to conciliate them and win their favor. Not of this type, however, was Epameinondas or Agesilaus, who, although they had to do with a very large number of men and cities and modes of life, yet maintained everywhere their own proper character in dress, conduct, language, and life. So, too, Plato in Syracuse was the same sort of man as in the Academy, and to Dionysius he was the same as to Dion.[30]

—That's interesting. You could reread . . . the four criteria?
[A participant rereads the last part of the passage from Plutarch.]
—OK. So, [those] are the criteria of the parrēsiastēs. Well, so, shall we read . . . or? But maybe you have questions to ask.

—Not so much a question, but what we read here is very, very close to page 215 of Seneca, and also where Thucydides[31] writes about Alcibiades.

—What? Where?

— Thucydides writes about Alcibiades and ... in one of the histories, it doesn't give the reference here ... it's just a selection. But his description of Alcibiades corresponds exactly with Plutarch, and also Seneca, on page 215, no, I'm sorry, 217, very close to the bottom.

—Ah, yeah, yeah. I think that this notion of schema, with those very [...] concrete forms are the dresses, the behavior itself, the clothes, the language, life, and the fourth is ... voilà ... that is, dress, conduct, language, life. [...] that's it, that's it: stolē, diaitē, logō, biō. Stolē, that's the dresses, the clothes; diaitē, that is the diet, the regime, that means the way he eats, drinks, sleeps, does exercises, and so on, it's a very technical notion; logos, that means what he says and the way he says what he says; and bios, that is [...];* the existence of a schema, of one schema, of the same schema, in those four domains. And the fact that the schema is always the same throughout his life, that is the proof, the evidence, that your [...] man is a real parrēsiastēs, and not a flatterer.

So I think that idea, this theme, is rather important, because, as you see, the problem of choosing a parrēsiastēs, the problem has two aspects. When you need a parrēsiastēs to help yourself in the care of yourself, [...] first you must be sure that he is sincere and that he says to you what he thinks, but you have also to be sure that he says things which are true, because he could be really sincere and say stupid things. And, you see, this problem never intervenes in Plutarch's text nor in Galien, Galen, never, because he doesn't need to raise this problem, since the bios, the logos, the diaitē, the stolē, all those signs of the way somebody lives, are evidence both of the truth of what he is thinking and of the sincerity of what he is saying. The truth of thinking and the sincerity of the words are the same thing or at least have the same system of evidence. The same thing is a touchstone for the truth of what he is saying and for the sincerity with which he says [it]. And that's the reason why this notion of schema, which has to be

* Passage completely inaudible.

unique in all the domains, which has to be the same throughout life, is so important because it is evidence of the truth and of sincerity: truth in the *logos* and sincerity in his *bios*. And, I think, in the notion of *parrēsia*, that is something very important. It is very important, because, as you see, the reference of what has been said to the speaker [...] is quite clear. The *parrēsiastēs* is the man who says something whose truth is proved by what he is. This reference, [from what he has said] to what he is, is inherent in the parrhesiastic type of being.

As you know very well, in the Latin ... in the Christian confession, [there will] also be this kind of implication. The penitent will be somebody who has to say the truth about what he is. But the relation between the truth of what is being said [...] what the speaker is, this reference is quite different. In one case, the way of living of the philosopher, as a director, is the proof of what he says [...], of the sincerity and the truth of what he says to the directed. In the other case, the case of the penitent, [...] what the directed says must be the disclosure of what he is in reality. So that, you see, the shift which will move the obligation of telling the truth from the director to the directed, this move is also a change in the structure of the relation between the truth of what is said and the reality of what the speaker is. Those two changes, I think, are quite decisive for the story of *parrēsia*. Well, anyway ... Well, is there any question? I don't know if [I have been] very clear on this last point. Yes?

—*Maybe you could back up ... you may have been clear, but I ...*

—Well, maybe because I'm afraid you have to help me in this thing, because my English is not good enough. I would like to know if there is something obscure and what is obscure.

—*I just somehow missed the connection between the shifts in the Christian sacrament and what you were saying prior to that, the concrete forms [of the schema of living].**

—Well, there [are] two shifts, two. First one, the fact that in the ancient direction the one who has to be sincere, the one who has to say whatever he has in [his] mind, this one is the director, is the mas-

---

* Conjecture; the auditor does not finish the sentence; the last phrase has been reconstructed based on context and Foucault's response.

ter. And the pupil, the directed, has nothing to say, or very few things to say. We have seen with Seneca and Serenus how few things Serenus has to say.[32] So the duty of telling the truth, of being a *parrēsiastēs*, is the duty of the master [himself]. Well, in the Christian tradition, in the Christian penance, it could be the reverse. The one who has to say whatever he thinks, whatever he feels, whatever happens inside of his heart, and so on, is the pupil. It's a fact that the notion, the word *parrēsiastēs*, or *parrēsia*, will be changed also, but that's nothing else truly; I'll speak about it later on. You understand this . . .

The second change is this one. What is the proof that the master says the truth? And what is the proof that he is sincere? It is the fact that he has one visible schema for all his behavior throughout his life. So what he is, is the proof of the truth of what he says. OK? In the Christian penance, on the contrary, the penitent has to say whatever he thinks, feels, whatever he has done and so on and so on, he must say everything, but through what he says, and through what he says about himself, what he "is" has to appear. And there will be a problem for the Christian penance, the theory and the practice of Christian penance: how can the director be sure that what the directed says is true? And what are the evidences that he is sincere, that the reality of what he is appears through what he says? So, the answer, there are two answers.

First one is since the penitent, when he shows the depth of his soul to the director, shows it also to God, and since God sees everything, and since God has seen from the beginning of time, the centuries, the soul, the depth of the soul of this man, it doesn't matter if he lies: God, in any case, will know that he lies. So the problems of the signs of the sincerity of the penitent are not very important for Christianism. The problem of choosing a good *parrēsiastēs*, that's something very important in the ancient practices. In the Christian ones, it's not so important, but what's also of great importance is the choice of the *satisfactio*, satisfaction, dependent on what the director thought about the directed. So he had to try to find signs of his sincerity, and there were, you can find in the treatises of confession several signs which are supposed to give indices, indications about the sincerity of the directed, for instance, the way, essentially the way he behaves during the confession, if he flushes, if he cries, if he […] and so on. But anyway that's not really important, since all that happens in front of God, who anyway knows everything, who knows if the man is sincere or not.

— *That would be why rhetoric is so problematical for early Christianity, because if one is in control of rhetoric, one can speak, one can give a false confession, or…*

—Yes, sure.

—*So that Augustine…*

— So, in those treatises, you find some rather amusing indications about the way to recognize if somebody is sincere or not in the confession, but I think it's not really a problem, it's not an ethical or a theological problem.

— *I wonder what happened to the pattern, to the schema, in this shift. If the test of the director is the relation between what he says and the way he lives, if you shift to the directed … in the later Christian church, the schema is Christ's life, I'm thinking of sixteenth and seventeenth century … of the Puritan autobiographies and so on. What about in the early church?*

—Well, you are quite right. All those problems, you find them deeply *renouvelés* … renewed in the sixteenth century with the Puritan or in the Lutheran and Calvinist culture. Sure. In early Christianity, the notion of schema, you find it in the definition of the monastic life. And as you know, "schema" in the monastic literature means both the way of life and the clothes. The technical meaning of schema is both the way of life and the clothes the monk wears. In the beginning of the *Institutes* of Cassian, there is a very beautiful analysis of the spiritual meaning of the schema as clothes, schema as clothes meaning a way of life.[33] So that's where you find the notion of schema. And the directed has to acquire a schema. But the schema is not from the point of view of the distinction … the schema is [no longer] a sign of the sincerity of what somebody says, of the sincerity of the directed. It is what is acquired through the direction.

— *What do you imagine the implications of this change to be? Your presentation makes one ask: What are the implications of this change? And you've been silent about them…*

—What do you mean by implications?

—*Well, I imagine that you might think about why this has happened and in what ways it manifested itself.*

—Well, the first question is, What are the reasons why this . . . well, very hard to say. Well, I think that, first—maybe we can say . . . I can say a few words about it tomorrow—there [were] very important changes in the social-political structure in the early [. . .] Roman Empire, which, I think, can explain the development of this care, the care of the self. And one aspect of the problem is this one: Is this culture of the self related to the [rise]* of an individualistic form of societies, of civilizations?

Most of the time, I think, people confuse individualism and the problem of the self, and I think that we have in the Roman Empire a very good example of a society which was not at all an individualistic society and which developed a very large, very rich culture of the self.[34] It was not at all an individualistic society . . . or what I have told you about the necessary relationship between a director and a directed, the fact also that this direction in its main form, that means the Stoic form, this culture of the self, had as a result the justification of all the social, familial, sexual, relations between people. All that is also evidence that it is not at all the result, that the development of the culture of the self is not at all a result, of an individualistic society. It is the result of something else.

And I think it was the result of the change in what I could call the governing instances in a society, since in a society the governing instances are not only the ruling class, but [rather] there [are] a lot of governing instances inside a society. I think that in Roman society you see, in the Roman Empire, deep changes in the distribution and in the hierarchy, in the organization of all those ruling, of all those governing, instances inside the society. And as a result you have this thing, this culture of the self, which is, I think, the search to find a new form of governing oneself and a new form of governing other people through a new form of rationality, rational means.

The problem of the changes from this kind of society to the Christian one is much more difficult . . . or maybe much easier. Much eas-

---

* Foucault says "raise."

ier insofar as what is visible in this Christian care of the self is what happened inside the small societies which were the monasteries, in this monastic society, which has been very influential in culture, but which has been, in spite of that, rather isolated at least in the fourth and fifth century. Then, we don't have to explain that through general changes in the society. What happened after was the fact that this kind of model which developed inside the monastic institution, why it has developed with considerable changes in the large society throughout the ages as a consequence.

All that is not an answer but an indication, it was to your first question: What are the reasons. What are the consequences? That I cannot answer now. What I can try to do now is to excavate the beginning of this story of the techniques of the self. Well, we go after, I have to . . . What I propose, if you want, will be, tomorrow, we spend the beginning of our session [on] this Galen . . . if you are interested in that, in that text, and the last hour will be for general questions; I think it will be enough. You agree with that? Thank you.

—*Do we have free speech?*

—Yes, you have free speech.

FOURTH MEETING

WE SHOULD START TODAY WITH Galen. Maybe, if you like, I'll say a few things* about Seneca,[1] then free speech for everyone, beginning maybe with questions directly related to the seminar, then questions related to the lectures, then questions related to the world, and then questions related to truth, with no answers! Sure.

So I think you have read or at least you received the xerox of this Galen text. I look like Marlene Dietrich . . .

—*Over there you sound like a frog . . .*†

—So what do you want us to do? Would you like to reread the text? Do you want us to comment without rereading it? What do you prefer?

—*Has everyone read it?*‡

---

* No doubt for lack of time, Foucault does not discuss Seneca again.

† Foucault's voice is audibly hoarse in the recording.

‡ Because Foucault does not have a participant read the text aloud in this case, as he has done in the other meetings of the seminar, we have reproduced the full text of Galen here. As in the other meetings of the seminar, during this meeting the participants had xeroxed copies of the texts in question.

Since errors come from false opinion while the passions arise by an irrational impulse, I thought the first step was for a man to free himself from his passions; for these passions are probably the reason why we fall into false opinions. And there are passions of the soul which everybody knows: anger, wrath, fear, grief, envy, and violent lust. In my opinion, excessive vehemence in loving or hating anything is also a passion; I think the saying "moderation is best" is correct, since no immoderate action is good.

How, then, could a man cut out these passions if he did not first know that he had them? But as we said, it is impossible to know them, since we love ourselves to excess. Even if this saying will not permit you to judge yourself, it does allow that you can judge others whom you neither love nor hate. Whenever you hear anyone in town being praised by many because he flatters no man, associate with that man and judge from your own experience whether he is the sort of man they say he is. First, if you see him going continually to the homes of the wealthy, the powerful, or even monarchs, be sure that you have heard falsely that this man always speaks the truth, for such adulation leads to lies. Second, be equally sure that his reputation is false if you see him greeting these people by name, visiting them, and even dining with them. Whoever has chosen such a life, not only does not speak the truth, but he is wholly evil, because he loves some or all of the following: wealth, rule, honors, reputation.

When a man does not greet the powerful and wealthy by name, when he does not visit them, when he does not dine with them, when he lives a disciplined life, expect that man to speak the truth; try, too, to come to a deeper knowledge of what kind of man he is (and this comes about through long association). If you find such a man, summon him and talk with him one day in private; ask him to reveal straightway whatever of the above-mentioned passions he may see in you. Tell him you will be most grateful for this service and that you will look on him as your deliverer more than if he had saved you from an illness of the body. Have him promise to reveal it whenever he sees you affected by any of the passions I mentioned.

If, after several days, although he has obviously been spending time with you, he tells you nothing, reproach him and again urge him, still

more earnestly than before, to reveal immediately whatever he sees you
doing as the result of passion. If he tells you that he has said nothing
because he has seen you commit no passionate act during this time,
do not immediately believe him, nor think that you have suddenly become free from fault, but consider that the truth is one or the other
of the following. First, the friend whom you have summoned has either been negligent and has not paid attention to you, or he remains
silent because he is afraid to reproach you, or because he does not
wish to be hated, knowing as he does that it is usual, as I might say,
with all men to hate those who speak the truth. Second, if he has not
remained silent for these reasons, perhaps he is unwilling to help you
and says nothing for this or some other reason which we cannot find
it in ourselves to praise.

If you will now believe me that it is impossible for you to have
committed no fault, you will praise (me) hereafter when you see that
every day all men fall into countless errors and do countless things in
passion because they do not understand themselves. Do not, therefore, consider that you are something else and not a human being. But
you do judge that you are something other than a human being if you
mislead yourself into believing that you have done nothing but good
actions for a whole day, much less for a whole month.

If your own choice or some evil disposition has made you disputa-
tious, or if you are naturally disposed to quarrel, perhaps you will re-
but the argument I proposed before by contending that wise men are
something more than human beings. But compare your argument with
mine, which was twofold: first, that only the wise man is entirely free
from fault; second, in addition to the foregoing, if the wise man is free
from fault, neither is he a human being in this respect. This is why you
hear the philosophers of old saying that to be wise is to become like
God. But, surely, you would never suddenly come to resemble God.
When those who have spent their entire lives training themselves to
be free from emotion do not believe that they have perfectly acquired
this goal, you should be all the more convinced that you are not free
from emotion since you have never devoted yourself to this training.

Therefore, you must not believe the man who tells you he has seen
you do nothing in passion; consider that he says this because he is

unwilling to help you, or because he chooses not to observe the wrong you do, or because he wishes to make sure that you do not come to hate him. Perhaps, too, he has seen that you could not endure it in the past when someone censured your errors and passions; hence, he naturally remains silent because he does not believe you are telling the truth when you say that you wish to know every wrong action you commit. But if you will remain silent from the first and utter no complaint against him who would correct you and free you from your deeds (of passion), you will find in a very short time thereafter many men who will give you true correction; this will be all the more likely to happen if you show gratitude to your corrector after you have, thanks to him, removed the harm from yourself. You will find a great advantage in considering whether he is right or wrong in censuring you. If you do this continuously because you have really chosen to become a good and noble man, you will be such.

In the very beginning, even if you find on examination that he has brought a charge against you which is insolent and untrue, do not try to persuade yourself that you have done no wrong; but let this be your first rule of conduct, namely, to be steadfast when treated with insolence. Sometime later, when you see that your passions have been put under restraint, you may undertake to defend yourself against your slanderer. But do not make it clear by the bitterness of your reproof and by the contentiousness of your words that you wish to confound him; rather, give evidence that you are acting to improve yourself. Hence, after he has spoken persuasively and contradicted you, you will win him over to a better understanding, or you will find, after a more extensive examination, that he was in the right. So at any rate Zeno, too, deemed that we should act carefully in all things—just as if we were going to answer for it to our teachers shortly thereafter. For, according to Zeno, most men are ready to censure their neighbors, even if no one urges them to speak.[2]

—Do you want to ask questions or do you want me to give some comments? Well, what I can do is to give you my impressions about this text. And then speak... Yes, I think that this text clearly deals with the problem of *parrēsia*. The word *parrēsia* is not used by Galen in this text, but it is clearly the problem we met, for instance, with Plutarch, in Plutarch's treatise about flattery. Remember that the problem was how to recognize a true *parrēsiastēs* from somebody who is only a flatterer. And I think that the beginning of this treatise by Galen, the beginning answers or intends to answer the question, how to recognize a true *parrēsiastēs*.

What is interesting in this text is the fact that it is very simple. Without too great or apparently without great philosophical pretensions, it is supposed to answer very practical questions: how to find somebody who is able to help you if you want to take care of yourself. In spite of the fact that that it is a very factual analysis, the philosophical background of the text is interesting.

First point, the treatise or those two treatises, one about [...] the diagnosis and cure of passions and [...], in another treatise, the diagnosis and cure of errors, those two treatises ... Excuse me, there are two treatises, and the treatise written about passions, "Diagnosis and Cure of the Soul's Passions," this treatise from which I quoted the text which is xeroxed, which you have, this treatise is an answer written by Galen to an Epicurean treatise about passions. This Epicurean treatise written by Antonius was not preserved, it is lost now, we do not know what this treatise [said], but what is interesting is that Galen objects to this treatise [due to] the fact that it is not clear in Antonius's analysis, it is not clear what he means by the word or the expression or the theme "warding or protecting oneself against passions."

And Galen says: Antonius speaks about warding oneself or protecting oneself against passions, but [...] in this Epicurean treatise, there is no clear analysis, no clear difference between watchfulness, diagnosis, and correction.[3] That means that for Galen there are [...] three specific operations in which consists the guard, the guarding, the protection against the passions: [first,] watchfulness, which is the fact that somebody has to be perpetually, permanently, watchful about himself and his passions; [second,] the specific operation of diagnosis, which is to recognize which are the passions you suffer from, what is the sign of those passions, what are the causes of those passions, and so on; and third, the correction, the cure itself. An attitude, an operation of diagnosis, and a remedy, correction, cure, and so on. Those three things are to be distinguished, and you find this distinction in Galen's treatise. That's the first point.

The second point is as a background of the text the fact that you can find throughout the text, I think, three important ideas. The first one is that passions and errors are different from each other. [...]* Passions and errors are different from each other. This thesis of course is very important. [...] Passions and errors are different from each other, and passions are at the roots of errors. Those two principles, the distinction between passions and errors (passions are not errors, errors are not passions) and [the fact that] the passions are the deep cause, they are the roots of the errors, those two theses, as [...] some of you know very well, those two theses are at the exact opposite of the main Stoic thesis, the main Stoic principle.

At least in the first Stoic philosophy, you know that there [was] no difference between passions and errors and that what we call passions — [that is,] the irrational movements of the soul, which is the classical canonic definition of error in the Stoic philosophy — passions in the Stoic philosophy [...] are the results of errors. Here, in spite of the fact that Galen has been very much influenced by Stoic philosophy, you have those two theses which in fact you can find also in the last forms of Stoicism. At least, as you see, the intellectualist position which was the characteristic of the first Stoicism here disappears; the domain of passion is quite different from the domain of error, and the domain of passion is so deep, so strong, that it is the real cause of the errors. That's the first thing.

The second thing, the second great principle is if passions are not errors, if passions are the cause of errors, in spite of that, knowledge is necessary in order to cure passions. And that must be quite clear, because I think that there is very often confusion about those two ideas. It's quite possible that passions may be independent from errors, it may be that passions constitute [...] a specific domain which is not the domain of errors, and you need the truth in order to cure,

* The recording is inaudible here; Foucault can be heard to say ". . . never . . ."

not only errors, but also passions. Truth is a general medicine, either against errors, of course, and also against passions. And the way [in] which truth is a medicine against errors is not, of course, the way [in] which knowledge, truth is a remedy against passions. Against errors, truth [. . .] may be a cure only by the refutation of errors. For the passions, [the] truth may be a cure insofar as passions may be cured by the *gnōthi seauton*. The knowledge of oneself, self-knowledge, is the way [that] truth may be a medicine against passions. That's the second idea you find in the text, throughout the text.

And the third idea is that this self-knowledge is never possible without the help of somebody else. You cannot know yourself by yourself, but you need always to rely upon somebody else. And the reason why you need somebody else in order to know yourself is that self-love, the love of yourself, makes you blind to your own faults. This necessity of self-knowledge related to self-love is something which is also very important. You couldn't find that in the Socratic or in the Platonic conception, you couldn't find that even in the first Stoic for-mulations, but it is a theme which develops in [. . .] the last forms of Stoicism.

So the difference between passions and errors, necessity of truth as a remedy, as a cure both against errors and against passions, but with the form of self-knowledge as a cure against passions, and the fact that self-knowledge needs the help of somebody else on the ground, that self-love is an obstacle to self-knowledge. So [those] are, I think, the main elements of the background of the text.

Well, in the text which has been xeroxed, I have for my part—after we can have a discussion on that—I have noticed several elements which, I think, are rather important. So I think the xerox starts with "Since errors . . . ," no? Ah yeah. Yes, you will . . . maybe beautiful fal-sifications . . . that have been useful in the *Affaire Dreyfus*! So . . . so, you see, the beginning is "Since errors . . ." and so on, it is these rela-tions, well, the distinction between errors and passions and the fact that passions are the root are the reason why we forge false opinions. And "How then could a man cut out these passions if he did not first know that he had them?"—the necessity of self-knowledge for the cure of passions. "But, as we said, it is impossible to know them, since we love ourselves to excess": relations between self-love and self-knowledge, self-knowledge as cure of self-love. "Even if this saying will not permit you to judge yourself, it does allow that you can judge others whom you neither love nor hate." And I would like to go a little over this last sentence.

So this self-love prevents you [from being] the judge of yourself, but of course it doesn't prevent you [from] being the judge for the others, others "whom you neither love nor hate." That's interesting because, as you . . . maybe you remember that in Plato, in the *Alcibiades*, also in Seneca, and maybe in Plutarch . . . anyway [in] most of those texts you find the idea that the care of the self needs the help of somebody else, but this other person which is necessary for the care of the self has to be a friend, has to have an emotional relation to the one who is supposed to [be guided,]* and the *philia*, the friendship, is the necessary background of the care . . . of the help in the care of the self. The role of the other is linked to friendship. This friendship may take the form of love, of *eros*, or only of friendship in the [current] meaning, say.†

But here [in Galen], you see, there must be a kind of emotional neutrality between the two partners, between the director and the directed. This, as far as I know, is one of the first mentions you can find of this emotional neutrality. You'll find it after in Christian spirituality, but in antiquity, I think that this text, which has been written at the end of the second century, this text is rather new if you compare it to the general thesis that friendship, affective emotional relations, are necessary for the care of the self. I must say that in Epictetus you can find neither the idea that *philia* or *eros* is necessary, nor the idea of an emotional neutrality. [At least], I do not remember anything about the necessity of emotional relations or of emotional neutrality.

[On this] point [. . .] that the care of the self is not linked with *philia* in this text, what can we say? First, of course, it may be related to the disappearance of *philia* as one of the main social relations, and of the main emotional experiences in ancient civilization, culture.

---

* Foucault mistakenly says "to guide."
† Foucault can be heard to say, "I can use the word and so on."

The disappearance of *philia*, of its role, of its social role, of its political role, of its emotional role, is something which has been really
important, and maybe we have there one of the signs of this great
disparition, which has been very important in this culture.[4] Maybe
also the fact that the professionalization of the care of the self is perceptible at this moment. More and more the care of the self is the
fact of people who are professionals, philosophers, teachers, and so
on. But I think that we [...] must be very careful in saying that, because, as you'll see later on, there are no professional requirements
for the choice of the director. So the disappearance of *philia*, friendship, is, I think, quite clear; the [rise] of professionalism is, I think,
not very clear in the text.

"Whenever you hear anyone, in town, being praised by many because he flatters no man, associate with that man and judge from your
own experience whether he is the sort of man they say he is." So, as
you see, and that's something very interesting, I think very new, I
couldn't find it in any other text of this period, the idea that, when
you need somebody to help you in the care of yourself, you have to
fetch him among the people you do not know. It's not among your
friends, it is not among your relatives, the people you can know, etc.;
you have to look in the town somebody who has this ... this credit.
That's something rather strange, it is one of the reasons why I have
chosen this text. And as you see, this man you are looking for, who
will be your director, you have to judge him, you have to try him, you
have to prove, and that's also something very interesting. You remember that Epictetus, for instance, refused to be the director of some
young boys who came and who behaved in such a way that Epictetus did not want them as pupils, he did not want [...]. to take care
of them. Epictetus asks his disciples to give proofs of their attitude,
their ability to be directed by him. Here the situation is the opposite.
Galen gives the advice to the directed to try, to ... *on dit "éprouver"?*
Comment on dit ... prove? No?

— *Try ... to test.*

— ... to test the man. You are here very close to what Plutarch
said in his treatise we spoke about yesterday, his treatise about the
way to distinguish the flatterer from the *parrēsiastēs*. But, as you see,

in Plutarch, it was only a question of deciphering some signs of the *parrēsia*. Here, there is a real game between the director, or the maybe director, and the directed. The directed organizes a set of tests in order to discover if really ... to know, in order to know if the director is really worthwhile, if one can trust him. That's, I think, also very interesting. And when you look at the tests, which the directed or the man who wants to be directed, the tests to which he exposes the director, you see that there is no question of professional competence, nothing is said either about the fact that he knows something about soul, about body, about human nature, and so on, nothing is said about him as a philosopher. The only question is the question of *parrēsia*, of frankness, and all the tests concern frankness. And the tests of frankness are the way the man behaves with rich people, mighty people, if he looks for wealth, rule, honors, reputation, and so on and so on. It is the social behavior of the director which is the real test of his *parrēsia*. Nothing about the competence, nothing about the philosophical background. And so you have this situation which is rather strange: somebody is looking among the people with whom he has no personal relation, no emotional links, emotional relationship, he looks for somebody he does not know but who has the reputation of being a *parrēsiastēs*, he proposes a set of tests and then, you see that in page 33, he asks him to become his *parrēsiastēs*: "Tell him you will be most grateful for this service and that you will look on him as your deliverer more than if he had saved you from an illness of the body."

So, as you see, what is going on between the two partners in this situation is that a relation of service, *officium*, is established between them, and the directed promises that he will consider what the director has done for him as an *officium*, a service—you can say "service?"—a service. And, of course, there is no question of direct reward or there is no direct question of reward, but [...] it's implied by the text; [though] nothing very precise is said about this reciprocity of [...] the reward given by the directed to the director.

Third point on which I would like to insist is the fact that, as you see, the question which is asked by the directed to the director, this question is exactly, One, what or who am I? As you see, the directed has nearly nothing to say. He says a few things: he says that he needs somebody, he asks for the help of the director and he says a few things about himself, but that's enough. And after that, it is the duty, it is the task, of the director to tell to the directed who he is, and that, of course, is very different from what we see in the Christian spirituality.

And of course the last point is—later we can discuss about all that—is the fact that the distrust towards oneself is something which is dominant through all the text. And the game between the director and the directed is dominated by this theme. If the director seems to . . . says that you have no . . . faults, that there is nothing wrong with you, then you must distrust your director. Your director cannot be right if he says that there is nothing . . . because in any case you make mistakes, you make faults, you have passions, and so on. And the game of this . . . You must trust your director insofar as he says that you have . . . faults, that you have passions, and if he says that you don't have any passions and so on, so you must distrust him because you must during all your life be distrustful towards yourself.

And what Galen says, page 34, about the wise man, who is supposed to have no passions and to make no faults, is very interesting. [. . .] I don't know if you have noticed the short passage where he says that of course a wise man does not make any fault, he is entirely free from fault, but the wise man is not a human being; he is not a human being because he is a god or he is close to a god. So, insofar as you are human being, then you have passions and make faults, and then the game between you and the director will be "Tell me the faults you don't . . . I have done, tell me the passions which I suffer from. If you tell me that I make no faults or I have no passions, that may be either that you are not interested in me, or that you are afraid that I will be angry against you because you told me about my faults."

And what is also interesting is on page 35 . . . but I am not sure that the English *traduction* is the good one. As far as I remember, in the French translation . . . the French translation is quite different . . . is rather different, and, as far as I remember, the Greek text . . . well, the French translation is much closer to the Greek text than the English one. But, anyway, I was not able to find the Greek text here. It is [on] page 35, when Galen raises the hypothesis of a director who makes untrue and unjust charges against the directed, and the

directed knows very well that the charges made against him are unjust. And, as far as I remember, the Greek text says: "Well, anyway,
even if the director is wrong, it's a very good test for you to be unjustly
accused." And anyway . . . so, this idea, which is really very close to
one you find in Christian spirituality, is, I think, something very rare
in the traditional culture of the self in antiquity. So. But I am not quite
sure: "But let this be your first rule of conduct, namely, to be steadfast
when treated with insolence." *C'est-à-dire*, steadfast, *ça veut dire* . . .

— *Tenir bon.*

— . . . *oui, tenir bon, résister.* And, as far as I remember, the French
translation is "anyway: it is always a good for you when you are treated
with insolence" or there is a good test . . .

— [. . .]*

— Ah yeah. It is always a *bénéfice* if you . . . That can mean . . . ?
Ah yeah. I am nearly sure that the Greek text means that it is always
a *bénéfice* for you to be unjustly accused. So.

Well, I don't want to say anything more about this text. It is a very
strange text, very curious, very deeply rooted in the Stoic context
of this period, that is, the last form of Stoicism, [. . .] but there are
several elements which are very rare and, I think, very close to what
the main features, or certain of the main features, of the care of the
self later on in Christian spirituality will be. Anyway the technical,
practical picture of this kind of relations is, I think, interesting. So.

— *Do you think that one could say that what the Christian context
does is in some way metaphorically combine the relationship of* philia, *and
then this other relationship that's expressed here, the neutral observer, insofar as the person to whom you confess in Christianity is metaphorically
a brother or a father, and yet in reality is a neutral observer?*

— I think it would be better to say that in Christianity the relationship of *philia*, of friendship, is much more the relation between the
penitent and God, or at least the penitent and Christ, and the neutrality is characteristic of the relations between the penitent and the
confessor. But anyway, in the Catholic cure of soul, in the sixteenth –

---

* The recording is inaudible here, though there seems to be a brief comment on the English translation, which the context would corroborate.

seventeenth centuries, in the Counter-Reformation, then you have a huge amount of texts and so on which refer to spiritual friendship and the problem of spiritual friendship. This practice is something very, very important, it's very influential, but I am . . . we have no specific information about it. But in the confession by itself, I think that there [is] no friendship in confession. Friendship is much more in Christ, as he is a mediator between God and [man]. There are no questions about this text? What were your reactions about this text? No one was surprised?

—*To add to Tim's question, I think we see in this development of the relationship between* philia *to neutrality, we have the status of the other, and it's a very simple other, in relationship [. . .] to Christ or to God, we see a transformation of the relationship of the other as intermediary, as [. . .] a shift changes, or transforms . . .*

—What's your question?

—*Not so much a question . . . I think we see not only a change in the care of the self, but a change in the relationship to others who can be intermediaries or friends or helpers or even antagonists. We see a transformation away from* philia *to neutrality, and this transformation is a defamation of that relationship of* philia *and a very [. . .] grounded transformation. It's just a point, not so much a question . . .*

—Yes, that's a very important question. First, not exactly . . . I have said the disappearance of *philia* . . . it's not a disappearance of *philia*, but *philia* has lost some of its context, of its social grounds and so on, and I think that one of the great problems of Christian ethics and of Christian society was to find a place and a role for friendship. And, of course, brotherhood in Christus, brotherhood in the church, was a way to give to friendship a kind of status, but friendship, as it is a personal and a selective relation—because to be friends with somebody means you are not a friend of others—the personal and selective character of friendship, that is something quite different from the general brotherhood with all Christians or even with anybody in the church. Friendship is not a group structure, it is a personal structure, and the brotherhood in *Christus* is . . . has a group structure.

So I think that Christianity had a lot of problems with this friendship, and it is very interesting to see in the early Christian texts about monasteries how they were ... at which point they were embarrassed with the problem of friendship between monks, or the problem of friendship between the director and the directed, the friendship between the *seniores* and the novices, the friendship between novices, and there you see, developing with this problem of friendship, a very sharp or ... not very sharp, very clear distrust against what would later become homosexuality. On this point, I do not agree exactly with what Boswell has written about Christianity and homosexuality.[5] It is true there [was] no legal prohibition of homosexuality in Christianity before Boswell [says, in the tenth century].* In the monastic structure, you have very clear texts about all of that, very interesting texts about this problem of the status of friendship and whether [the field has shifted between the tenth and twelfth centuries].† Anyway, that was ...

—[...] *I guess it's fairly clear that there's interest on both sides, not only interest on the part of the directee, but also an understandable interest on the part of the director [...]. But now here with Galen we have a case of a text that recommends a procedure of finding themselves [...] in this tradition of frankness. But what's difficult for me is [to understand] what the interest [of the director could be in Galen's text].‡*

—Yeah, yeah, that's very enigmatic in this text. You have both a neutralization which seems to refer to a professionalization of direction, *and* there is nothing about the professional status of [the director]. The single thing, the single element is [on] page 33 at the end of the first paragraph: "Tell him you will be most grateful for this service and that you will look on him as your deliverer more than if he had saved you from an illness of the body." So, it seems here to refer to medical practice. As you know, the physician in the Greek society was unpaid—as he is now—he was supposed to do that only either out of friendship or on the ground of social obligations, and of course he was rewarded by gifts. This kind of relation (neutrality,

---

* Conjecture; the phrase is partially inaudible.

† Conjecture; the end of the sentence is almost completely inaudible.

‡ Conjecture; the end of the sentence is almost completely inaudible and has been reconstructed based on context and Foucault's response.

professionalization, reward, gift) seems to be implicated there, but
nothing is said about personal competence ... On that you find in
the Stoic texts of the same period the idea that only philosophers are
good advisers, and that you mustn't trust in anybody. Nothing like
that [here]. Only *parrēsia* seems to be a requirement for this relation.
That's the main textual structure.

— [*What could the motivation be to render someone this kind of ser-*
vice?]*

—Yeah, we can't see any motivation. Of course, you see that in
Greco-Roman society the relationships which were established on
the grounds of an *officium* means somebody helps somebody else either to get an honor or to marry ... *to constituer une dot ...*

— *To make a dowry.*

— ... or to buy a house, or things like that. So, on the ground of
those purely utilitarian relationships, then, it was a tradition that some
personal relationship could be established, then, and [entails]† a reciprocity and so on. So, of course, for us it's much more strange than
for a person of these centuries, but it is still rather strange. Any ... ?

— *What do you see as the significance of the medical metaphor that*
runs through all these texts?‡

—Yeah, yeah, from Plato, from Democritus. I think that Democritus is considered as the one who has first said that passions need to
be cared for as an illness. Well, you ask me the reason why this metaphor has been said?

— ... *the significance of it.*

—What do you mean by significance? No, no, because really to
deal with this problem, why this metaphor—but not only this metaphor, why this proximity between the care of the self and the medical care—that's, I think, something which cannot be answered in a

* Conjecture; the question is almost completely inaudible and has been
reconstructed based on context and Foucault's response. The auditor can be
heard to say, "Structure [...] a person's motivation [...]."

† Conjecture: the phrase is inaudible.

‡ The rest of the question is inaudible, though the auditor can be heard
to say, "[...] Seneca [...] care of the self [...]."

few sentences. I think that we should look at all the history of Greek medicine, history of the care of the self, history of Greek society, and so on. It's a huge problem.

What is interesting, I think, is that, from the first or second century of our era, the relationships between medical institutions, medical care, and the care of the self became closer and closer, for several reasons. One of them is that [...] the social, the cultural, the scientific, importance of medicine increased in a very perceptible way in the first centuries of the Roman Empire. For instance, the role of Greek medicine in the beginning of the imperial period is something very impressive. And, as you know, there [was] public medical care in the Roman Empire, which [was] supported by public culture. And emperors [defended]* this medical politics. And you see also that people were more and more interested in this aspect of their own lives. Gymnastics and those physical exercises decrease in importance, and, for instance, the young Romans in the imperial period nearly never do those kind of exercises, gymnastics, which was so important for the Greeks, but they were obsessed [with] their health. That's in Seneca and so on. So, and you see, for instance, Epictetus saying that his school is in fact an *iatreion*, a dispensary, a clinic. He does not want people to come to his school to learn something; they have to come in order to be cured from something.⁶ And I think that this proximity between medicine and philosophy, or medicine and philosophy as far as imperial philosophy is a care of the self, this proximity [is] broken by Christianity at a certain point, since Christianity considers [it] the role of the priest to be the one who cares [for] the souls of people [...].† But it is not an answer to the general question which is ...

—*I'm puzzled [...] about what you do with your mentor [if he can say things that are not true].‡ I was interested to know if this has any effect on the notion of* guérison. *What does* guérison *mean then if you can say things that are not true?*

* Conjecture; the phrase is inaudible.
† The end of the sentence is inaudible.
‡ Conjecture; parts of the question are inaudible and have been reconstructed based on context and Foucault's response.

—Well, I think that you have to suppose there that it is not on purpose that the . . . anyway it's not for a bad motive or a bad motivation that the director says things which are not true. Either he thinks that they are true, and he has [made a mistake], or he says things which are untrue as a test for the directed. And that may be, that may be possible, because, as I told you yesterday, *parrēsia* is an art, a technique by which you are free to use the means which are useful for the one you take care of. So you have to choose the occasions, you have to moderate some of your judgments; that's something commonplace in the art of *parrēsia*. Sometimes you have to be very severe and at certain other moments you have to be very mild. And eventually you can imagine that the *parrēsiastēs*, the director, even if he is a *parrēsiastēs*, says something which is much too severe and does not quite conform to reality in order [to test] the directed.

Anyway, that's something which will happen very often in Christian spirituality, at least in early Christianity. Then you see some directors who propose things quite absurd to the directed, and he obeys. For instance, there is the famous . . . the famous test, the famous trial of—I think it was Abbot Johannes, I don't remember exactly—who as a novice was obliged by his master to go and water every day a stick which has been stuck in the desert, and every day he had to water it. And after one year the master was very angry [towards] the novice because there were no flowers on the stick. And then one year more the novice was obliged to water the stick twice a day, and then, at the end of the second year [. . .], a rose flowered.[7] So the fact that the master is able in some circumstances to say something wrong and to give absurd orders to the directed is not, I think, a counterexample of *parrēsia*. It's a way of being a real *parrēsiastēs*. Yes?

—*This is a more general question, and I'm afraid it's a rather complicated question that has to do with the hermeneutics of the subject, the hermeneutics of the self. Hermeneia, as we all know, comes from Hermes, the messenger of the gods, the interpreter of the gods, the bringer of light, [. . .], the lion, but also one whose very presence is a sign, whose very presence is [. . .] a thing to be interpreted. And so, the Greek understanding of signs through hermeneia, in that we don't have signs in language and speech, but there are signs in the world, signs underlying things, signs underlying trees and rivers and so on, and also signs in the body, signs, symptoms, medical symptoms, dispositions, feelings, tics, so that to . . . there seems to be a commonality to the body, language, and the world, such that there is a suppositum hidden underneath, that lies beneath the body, that lies beneath the world [. . .]. Anyway, this suppositum would seem to be that which is continually traversed by the many distinctions that you make between the knowledge of self, the care of the self, the obligation to* parrēsia. *. . . that these continuous traversals and shifts and discontinuities are what constitute the subjects, the subjects who are that [which] lies underneath through discourses. And I was wondering if my understanding of that is close or correct, and then, what then is the nature of this suppositum, what lies beneath the making of subjects?*

—I don't know if I catch exactly your question, but . . .

—*It's really three questions.*

—Anyway I'll . . . You are quite right to say that, for instance, in medicine there were signs, symptoms, in the cure of the self people used signs, symptoms, and so on, and texts also. And that *hermeneia* was the technique through which it was possible to disclose the truth which was hidden under the signs. But I think that the model for this *hermeneia*, the matrix of all that, was not at all the idea of a system of signs. For us, for instance, it is quite clear that the principal model of our hermeneutics is language, the fact that we have verbal signs that we use. But I think that the model for Greek hermeneutics was not at all linguistic, was not at all semiotic or something like that. It was only the fact that the oracles had to be interpreted. I think that the oracle and the religious experience of oracles was a crucial experience. And the oracle does not use signs, he says only obscure things. And the relation is between obscurity and light, or is between the obscure things that have been said and the hidden reality which is said through those obscure sayings. And this model—obscurity to hidden reality—is not exactly the same as [the model of] signs. But of course, at a certain moment, then the Greeks started developing a theory of signs, either medical signs, a general theory of signs in the Stoics, and also the grammarians developed [one]. But I think that the crucial experience is much [more] the oracle than language, than a systems of signs. But I don't know if it is an answer to . . .

—*No, I think it is very much consonant with what I was going after. But the only thing I would add would be that it seems that at this moment . . . I agree with you about the distinction, and about the signs as well, [. . .]. What then becomes of interest is the moment where [. . .] collapses into a* hermeneia *that does have to do with signs, that does have to do with a procedure of signs, and that* hermeneia, *the lines in the body, that it is obscured, and . . . for which we don't have speech or discourse, I think that that* hermeneia *is what we would call the . . . I've lost it, the hermeneutics of the body . . . the hermeneutics of the self. That collapse seems to be very interesting and important.**

—Yeah, yeah. Has any of you ever read the Artémidore book about the *onirocritique?* No? Never? *Onirocritique,* the dream interpretation.

—*Artemidorus.*

—Artemidorus. He was a Greek author, maybe a physician, but nobody knows exactly, who has written, at the end of the second century, a book about the interpretation of dreams. And, as you know, the interpretation of dreams was something very, very common in Greece, and in Rome also. And it is a fact that none of those texts, which were numerous, were preserved. They are all lost, but Artemidorus, who has been . . . which has been translated in English and in French during those last years under the influence of psychoanalysis, of course.[8]

Well, I think that you should read it if you are interested in this problem of *hermeneia.* It was my intention to comment on this text with you but . . .† And it's very interesting, because there you have— the French translation has at least 200 or 250 pages, very, very long, very long text—and you have a lot, dozens and dozens of dreams which are interpreted. And it's interesting because the principle of interpretation is always the principle of analogy, similitude. And either the dream has a complete, an immediate, similitude to what the meaning is, so it is only the announcement of an event—for instance,

---

* The question is partially inaudible.

† The remainder of the sentence is partially inaudible; Foucault can be heard to say, "I think [I may have quoted . . .] No?"

somebody dreams that he is on a boat and that the boat is sinking, and in fact he is on a boat and a few minutes after his dream, the boat sinks. That's a perfect dream. That's the point of departure. And then you have a lot of other dreams, but all the interpretations derive from the same model.

And you have, and there are very interesting chapters: two [or] three chapters about sexual dreams, and it is very interesting to see that Artémidore does exactly the contrary of what Freud has done. Artémidore never gives, or nearly never—maybe two or three times in all the book, say ten times, but there are hundreds and hundreds of dreams—he nearly never gives any sexual interpretation to dreams, but he has dozens and dozens of sexual dreams to which he gives always a social, professional, economical, interpretation. And it is very interesting to see how, and I think that is something which is deeply rooted in the Greek culture, sexual relations are social relations and the truth of sexual relations is there . . . is in the social relations. And the value of the sexual act is due, is related, to the value of the social relations which is put in work in this sexual relations. The truth of sexual behavior is a social truth. And for us it is exactly the contrary: the truth, the deep reality which is hidden in our social relations, is the sexuality, the sexuality. And for Artémidore, it is quite clear that is exactly the contrary: if you want to see, to disclose, what is hidden in a sexual dream, then you find social life. So that's interesting. If you have nothing to do for the weekend, read Artémidore; I am sure it is in the library. The English translation was published in, I think, in 1970 . . . the early '70s . . . '75, I think. Yeah?

—*Another general question. And that is in the general thing that you presented about the reversal of the obligation to speak, [. . .] the obligation onto the directed . . . that reversal, I assume that you made allusion to the relationship of that to social relations in the time between how the relations work in Greek society and in early Christian society [. . .]. I was wondering if you could spell out more this relationship, and to what degree we can even speculate on it, and the ability that provides for types of social relationship . . .*

—Yes, yes, well, you see, I think that you are quite right to raise this type of question. But of course I can . . . I cannot answer this . . .

only this thing that, I think, we need really a pragmatic of discourses,[9] I won't say of speech acts—but, no, it's quite clear, the speech act is a certain level of analysis, what I am trying to do is an analysis, not of speech acts, but of discourses, that means games in which you find of course a lot of speech acts, but the game which consists in discourse is something [other] than a speech act.[10] In those games which characterize discourses, in those games the role of the speaker and the hearer, I think, needs to be analyzed both from a formal point of view, from a technical point of view, and also from a social and a political point of view.

And, for instance, the mere fact that [to] tell the truth about oneself is the task of the other in Greek society and is your own task in Christian society, or our society, is something which needs really, not only the technical explanation that I have tried to give in my lectures, but also a social and historical analysis of those [controls]* and the power relationships which are behind them. And there we find the problem of pastoral power you asked me about this morning, the fact that there are people in Christian society which have as their privilege, their duties, their obligations, to control the behavior of people, not only to control their everyday behavior, but to know who they are, to be familiar with their life, with their conscience, with their depth, with their soul, and so on; that's something which is very important, very crucial, very specific, for our culture, because in Rome or in Greece, for instance, the importance of the care of the self was great, of course, but nobody was obliged to obey somebody like a pastor or like a priest.[11] All those relations were quite entirely voluntary relations, and in Christianity all that becomes an obligation with an authoritarian structure, which characterizes pastorship in Christian society.

In fact there is a huge, huge historical and social background for this problem of "why do I have to speak of myself to somebody else," and why am I obliged to tell the truth about myself to people. That's a political and social problem with very precise, technical [aspects]. You see, the level to which I have . . . where I was in those [presenta-

---

* Conjecture; the phrase is inaudible.

tions]* was only the technical one. I took this problem of the obligation of telling the truth and I tried to see, or to indicate at least, which
techniques were used in this practice, [and what] the implications
are for the formation of the relationship we have to ourselves. But I
put aside all the historical and social background . . .

One thing I would like to say, I think I said a few things about it
yesterday,[12] is the problem [of] the relation between an individualistic society [and the development of the culture of the self].† I think
that it is not at all the [rise]‡ of an individualistic society but all the
reorganization in the structure of the political and social power in
the empire which is behind, or which is the historical context of, this
culture of the self.

—[. . .] *One of the things that struck me about this text [of Galen]
was that at the same time, on the one hand, you have the directed choosing the directors, people they don't know; on the other hand, you get the
sense that within . . . after several days, a very, very short period of time,
the director is supposed to be able to [tell them], almost like a doctor-
patient relationship, but to very quickly [diagnose the directed]§ . . . and
there's no sense of any kind of training on the director's part or any sense
of anything written that will . . .*

—Yes, sure, sure. Nothing was written here, you are quite right,
and it seems to be, it seems to be very quick . . . But you have a lot of
examples in Galen about this quickness of the relationship. For instance, there is a text about the way he discovered that a lady who
was ill was in fact in love with an actor. And he arrives, he looks at
the lady, he sees that she is very pained and so on, he wonders why
it is, and, well, he notices that when he pronounced the name of this
actor she blushes . . . that's it. . . . very, very simple, [. . .] which is
presented as a very great discovery . . . he has done something very
important, very difficult, and what is strange is that you find this text
quoted in the beginning of the nineteenth century by Pinel, and Pinel

---

* Conjecture; the phrase is inaudible.
† Conjecture; Foucault does not finish the sentence.
‡ Foucault says "raise."
§ Conjecture; the phrase is inaudible.

quotes it as a proof of the incredible perspicacity of Galen! Well, yes, yes, you are quite right. There is no training in this relation. He insists very clearly in this text on the necessity of a personal training, a continuous, a permanent, training for the one who is directed and who has to train in all his life, without any interruption[13] and so on, but the master seems to be a kind of abstract point who is supposed to say after a few meetings the truth and that's . . .

— *I have another question, it's a very general one. Maybe you'd say it's too general. I was tempted before when you were asked about hermeneutics, but you've now called it pragmatics, and I'm glad to hear that . . . I guess the point I'd want to make is that a pragmatics can be aimed at doing many different things. So one thing it could aim at is just providing true descriptions. (And I take it that that is the main thrust of speech-act theory, to give true descriptions.) But another thing pragmatics could do, and I guess the clearest example of this is Jürgen Habermas, he does what he calls "universal pragmatics," but it's not only to be true, but to have critical function, that is, to provide a basis for a critique of society, [isolating the unspoken delusions]* of that I suppose, and so on. Now, I think that possibly a better thing to try to do than universal pragmatics is historical pragmatics, which might be one way to describe what you're up to. I wonder if you think about this in another way than just providing true descriptions. So my question is, I guess, this: you're making a lot of claims, which are distinctive in that they're not claims about our subjectivity and self-consciousness, they're not claims about a universal condition of knowledge being true, but rather they're claims about how society would be at a certain time. Do you see that your claims have a critical function? And if so, how is that?*

— Well, yes, you see that it is . . . that [this] was my main objective for the last part of the . . . Well, yes, you are quite right when you say that now I use the word *pragmatic* to characterize what I am doing. I did not use this term before, but I think that, if I have now to die in thirty seconds and to tell exactly what I have done in my life, I would say that I tried to do a pragmatic history of the true discourses, a pragmatic history of truth.[14] When in our society somebody is sup-

---

* Conjecture; the question is partially inaudible.

posed to tell the truth, is accepted as saying the truth, when what he said circulates as truth, what is the pragmatic which is la *racine* . . . the root, or the historical condition?

For instance, when somebody . . . well, in Western civilization, people started to ask themselves: "What is madness? How [can] madness be analyzed as an illness?"—it was not so clear before—when some people were qualified to tell the truth about madness, to decide if somebody has to be put in an asylum or not and so on and so on, what is the historical pragmatic? My problem is not to analyze the psychiatric institutions. Other people do that and much better than I could do. Anyway it's not my thing. My problem is how the real history of those institutions have had as a result the qualification of some people to tell the truth about madness, which kind of discourses [have] been produced, how is the man who has the right to say the truth about madness now qualified, how is the man who is supposed to be mad qualified, and so on and so on.[15] That's a historical pragmatic.

What I [tried] to do in the book about the order of things is a pragmatic of scientific discourse in the seventeenth century, the empirical discourses, empirical scientific discourses in the seventeenth century: What were the conditions [put on] the person who was supposed to tell the truth about economics, about grammatics, about natural sciences? What formal requirements [were] put on him, on his saying, on his way of looking at things, and so on and so on.[16]

Now, my problem is what is the pragmatic which is behind the obligation of telling the truth about oneself and specifically about the problem of sexuality. Why and how are people obliged to tell about their sexual behavior things which are now deeply linked with our sexual experience?[17]

—*[You appear to greatly valorize the culture of the self in Greek society].* Do you think we should return to that, as opposed to the lousier present time . . . [And, on the other hand, what kind of relationship is there between the notion of pleasure and the Greek culture of the self?]*

* The first part of the question is almost completely inaudible and has been reconstructed based on what can be made out in the recording, the context, and Foucault's response.

—Ah yeah, yeah, yeah, it's a very insightful question, and you see, I . . .

—*I'm not talking about a return, but the way the analysis is set up, there seems to be a subtext that anyone confronted with this type of analysis would draw the hasty conclusion that [. . .]. What are the grounds that [. . .]?*

—Well, the first question, I must . . . I would like to make quite clear, that I never wanted to, [and] it was never my purpose, to oppose to this horrible state of things, which is ours, a "lost paradise," the Greek society, and so on.

For instance, when I analyzed the prisons, I tried to show that prisons were without any rational and universal necessity in our societies; it was linked to a very specific situation at a certain moment and so on and so on, and it was not at all a means to say that before prison, [. . .] when everybody was hanged because he had stolen a handkerchief, it was better. No, no lost paradise in such an analysis! When mad people were running through the streets and so on, I am not sure that is better than when they were put in an asylum, but the fact that asylums are not worse does not mean that asylums are a necessity. You see?

I think that we must disconnect those evaluations [from]* another problem, which is the problem of our freedom and of our creativity. What, I think, is very dangerous in those systems of evaluation is the fact that they imprison us, that they prevent us [from being] free for creating something else. If you accept that . . . the present situation [. . .] is better than before, you are exposed to accepting a situation, the actual situation, as if it were definitive. Or if you oppose the horrible present situation to a lost paradise,[18] then I think you deprive yourself of the possibility of a real change in the actual context. So I disconnect the evaluations and I try to make as little evaluation as possible, in order to show how things have been established [. . .] and so on and in order to leave a space free for creativity.

The second question is pleasure and sexuality. That's a problem! Well, what strikes me and what, as far as I understood those changes,

* Foucault says "with."

224 THE SEMINAR, JUNE 1982

is striking in the history of late antiquity and Christianity and so on is that for the Greeks, for instance, the problem of sex and sex regulation was the problem of pleasure. Sex was pleasure. As you know, the Greeks didn't have any word, any specific word to say "sexuality." As you know, the word "sexuality" is a word which has been invented, created, in the beginning of the nineteenth century. And of course the fact that the word has been invented, created, in the beginning of the nineteenth century does not mean that people didn't have any sex before, nor sexual behavior, it doesn't mean exactly that the notion, the field, of sexuality did not exist, but it is a sign of the fact that people didn't have consciousness of their own sexual behavior as belonging to the field of sexuality, and that's something very important.

Well, anyway, yes, the Greeks had a word, and this word is very interesting to analyze. It is *un adjectif pluriel substantivé*. It is *ta aphrodisia*. And *aphrodisia* is the things which belong to Aphrodite, and it means the pleasures, it means the sexual behavior insofar as it is a pleasure. And, I think, one of the things which [was] very important in Christian spirituality, in Christian techniques of the self, [is] the fact that the problem of the pleasure . . . As you saw, in this Greek problematic of *aphrodisia* the main problem was the problem of excess: if those *aphrodisia*, if those pleasures are excessive or not. The second great problem was, In those acts of pleasure, are you active or passive?

Those two problems, the limits, the excess, activity, and passivity, that was the code for the regulation of *aphrodisia* in Greek society.[19] That was the regulation of pleasure: subject or object of pleasure, limit and excess. Then, in the Christian techniques of the self, you see very clearly the problem of desire becoming the main problem, the main notion, and it is here the existence of this desire, called *concupiscentia*, which is the point which we have to analyze.[20] And I think that the development of those techniques of the self and the problematic of *concupiscentia*, desire, is something which took place at the end of antiquity, and you can oppose that to experiences of sexual behavior which were much more dominated by the problem of pleasure, excess, activity, and passivity. And it's very interesting to see that the problem of pleasure, I think, has nearly disappeared in all the analysis of sex, of sexual behavior—till now, even in psycho-analysis, you cannot find anything about pleasure, or very few things. As soon as they meet the problem of pleasure, they translate pleasure in terms of desire.

That's very specific, I think, to Christian and post-Christian civilization. And with this problem of desire, you also see that the main distinction in the sexual behavior and in the sexual ethic is the distinction between the feminine and the masculine role, which is not the distinction between activity and passivity. There is on the passive side you find, you find in the Greek ethics, the passive side, women, sure, boys, for sure, and slaves. Those three categories of sexual objects were on the passive side of pleasure. And the men correspond to the active side. So there [was] a great interdiction ... [There] was scandal [when] a man [kept] the habit of [being] passive. But women, slaves, boys, they were done, they were passive, that was their role, [this was not a] scandal. So that's, I think, the main reason why what we call homosexuality was, as we say, "tolerated," but all that [made no] sense [in] Greek society. But there were very deep, very strict, very strong, very oppressive, if you want, interdictions, prohibitions [on] the passivity of men, since their role was to be active.

Well, anyway, you see, so I think that between the problematic of pleasure, with excess, limit, activity, passivity, and the problematic of desire, you have two very different ways of deciphering, of analyzing pleasure ... no, sexual behavior.

— *There is a moment [later in Neoplatonism] when all the questions that you've just raised come together, and it's not an isolated moment. [...] It offers the possibility of an analysis of a tradition of pleasure in the body which hasn't been sufficiently spoken of. One that would be neither Christian nor purely Neoplatonic in the sense of [fallenness], nor purely Greek [in terms of the social hierarchy ...]. So it's neither the one nor the other [...].**

* The comment is clearly about Neoplatonism, but is often barely audible. We have reproduced the central question here to the fullest extent possible from the recording. The question is prefaced by a series of remarks, in the participant's own terms, on *"the relationship between hermeneutics and*

—Well, sure. You are quite right that . . . the very different things which are put under the name of Neoplatonism had in late antiquity a very . . . a very important role, and [are] very difficult to analyze. One thing I would like to say is first that this rise of Neoplatonism or the new forms of Neoplatonism that you refer to are posterior to the period I have studied. I studied the first and second centuries.

— *They may or may not be. As you know, it's a very complex history itself [. . .]*

—Yeah, anyway, anyway, in the two first centuries, you cannot find any text, Neoplatonic text in the meaning you refer to. So, of course, I know very well that just now there are several people either in Switzerland, in Germany, or even in France, who try to raise this very important and interesting question of what became of Platonism besides the traditional Academy, with the skeptical trends [of the Academy]; what became of Platonism between Plato and the Neoplatonism. And you know that Gigante in Italy, several years ago, has invented, created, what he called the *Aristotele perduto*[21] and he tried to explain a lot of things in the history of philosophy by this existence of an Aristotle *perduto*, and people, I think, are trying now to write a Plato *perduto*. Gaiser has written a very interesting book about that,[22] but in fact we do not have evidence of the existence of a Neoplatonism at this period. The problem of Neoplatonism, the rise, the development of Neoplatonism at the third, fourth, fifth, century is something very interesting, very important, which is at the borderline of pagan philosophy, of non-Christian religions, of Christianity, of the Oriental and dualistic influences over Christianity in this period, that's, of course, a huge cultural figure, very obscure, very interesting, and, of course, I didn't speak about that because it's not, that is not my historical field, and . . .

---

signs, the question of the relationship between signs of the self in a medical context, signs in the world, which was related to the question of artificial making, astrology, interpretation of [. . .] and signs of texts, which was [. . .] in its relation to prophecy and dreams, over which there was always a certain amount of anxiety [. . .]."

—[...] *there are earlier trends* [...]

—But you can't say that it is Neoplatonist, it's not Neoplatonist. That's exactly what the historians call the Gnostic or pre-Gnostic or ... that's not Neoplatonism.

—*It's a difficult issue, what the relationship is ...*

—No, no.

—[...] *but these traditions, it seems to me, are not entirely different ...*

—Yes, sure. But my point is that it is quite different. What I wanted to show was, in pagan society, Greco-Roman society in the two first centuries, the existence of a very manifest, very well-known, very familiar care of the self with its techniques, its institutions, its philosophy, and so on and so on, and in spite of the fact that we have the texts, or some of the texts, in spite of the fact that we have all the testimonies in the witnesses, it is much more forgotten than the Neoplatonism about which so many thousands of books have been written. And what I want to show, to make appear, is the existence of those techniques which are not Neoplatonic, which are not Platonic, which are not Aristotelian, and so on. And you can follow the history of those techniques through late antiquity and you can find them also in Christian spirituality, the monastic institutions, and so on. Some of the texts are really ... have been recopied, or you can find the same metaphor, the same idea, for instance, this principle, which is so important, since you find it from Epictetus to Cassian, from Cassian to Freud, the idea of the money changer: we are the money changers of our thoughts. And each time thought appears in the consciousness, there is, or Freud says there is, a censorship. Cassian and Epictetus said we have to be the censors of our thought and to ... to test this [money]. That's what's interesting. And that was my point. And I didn't say either Neoplatonism doesn't exist or Neoplatonism was not important, I said there was something quite different from all that, which had its existence, its institutions, its witnesses, its effects, and so on. For sure.

—*[But I still ask myself the question ...]*

—No, no, no, it is not a [question], but ... you are quite right to say that the question of Neoplatonism is very important, but I think that my point was to show something quite different from this Neo-platonism.

—*I have one final question, and I think it builds on some of what you've been saying, although in a different way. I want to take the example of Saint Augustine. It seems to me that Augustine's importance, for example, lies not so much in his thought, but in its re-readability, and the possibility of Augustine's text to be reread, recopied, recuperated into a different discourse . . . is that true?*

—The problem of Augustine is very difficult, very difficult. I should say, but maybe . . . I think that at least for the problem of sexual behavior, we can say that Augustine was the first one who has succeeded in translating in juridical words, in juridical terms, this kind of spiritual experience which was linked to early Christian spirituality. And my hypothesis—but maybe I am wrong, I am working on that field now—my hypothesis is that Augustine is most of the time for us the one who . . . well, he is interpreted as a witness of a spiritual experience which is quite different from the juridical framework of the church, of the Middle Ages church. And it's a fact that when, during the Reformation, in the sixteenth century, people have tried to get rid of those very strict, very strong juridical structures, they referred to Augustine, to Augustine as the master of spirituality against the juridical structures of the church. That was the case of Luther and so on and so on.

But I think that when you read the things on the other side, from late antiquity to Augustine, then you see that Augustine has been, of course, inheritor of those first spiritual experiences, but I think that he has, first, created the theology—Origen is of course a problem—but even if Augustine is not exactly the creator of the theology, he [was] the first great theologian, at least recognized by the church, [celebrated] by the church. And he [was] also the one who gave the juridical translation of some of those spiritual themes which . . . and this juridical transcription, translation, has given to the church the possibility of organizing this ethics as a social ethics, as a pastoral ethics, and to give to this ethics the roots, or at least the institutional guarantees, the institutional framework . . . It's at least very, very clear for the problem of sexual behavior, marriage, and so on and so on.

Marriage, for instance, the problem of virginity, marriage, sexual behavior, was a problem of spirituality, at least it was an important problem, a difficult problem in the framework of the spiritual . . . spiritual experience from Methodius of Olympus in the fourth century to Gregory of Nyssa and so on, and it started to become the code for the sexual behavior of married people with Augustine.[23] Augustine was really the first one who invented, created, a sexual code of behavior for married people. When we compare, for instance, Clement of Alexandria, who in chapter 10 of the second book of the *Pedagogus*[24] gives also a sexual code for married people. Clement of Alexandria doesn't do anything else than repeating word for word what you find in Musonius Rufus, in Seneca, in others. It's not at all Christianity's, the Christian sexuality, it's the pagan one, repeated word for word at the beginning of the third century, reference by reference. Two centuries later [. . .] after the great spiritual movements of the third–fourth century, Augustine arrives and works on this material and gives the first properly, really Christian code of sexual behavior, marriage, and [. . .] which was the root, the basis, the framework, of all the Christian ethics for sexual behavior until Pope John Paul II.

— *I wonder if I might ask you about what we might call the political implications of this pragmatic analysis, to follow up your remark in the last lecture about the possibility of a creative politics of the self. And I wonder which direction this would take, either a specific choice of a particular way, a particular technology of the self, which could be politically valorized, or whether the political project would be, in the other direction, one of problematizing the general enterprise of the technology of the self. Whether a creative politics would be a new choice of another technology or the problem of the self in general.*

— Well, I think that it is . . . well, I think that *technē* and technology are constitutive features of our behavior, our rational behavior, and that's the reason why I won't say that my project will be to get rid of any kind of technology. But since the self is nothing more and nothing less than the relation we have to ourselves, the ontological status of the self is nothing other than the relation that we have to ourselves.[25] This relation is maybe, and anyway is always, the object, the theme, the basis, the target, and so on of a technology, of a technical behavior, a *technē*. And the problem is to know how we can imagine, create, innovate, or change the relations to ourselves through those techniques? I don't think that we have to . . . I know very . . . I feel that your question arises from a Heideggerian point of view, with the question of the *technē*, but we can discuss that later. Even if we accept the status or the meaning Heidegger gives to the *technē*, from the political point of view—I don't speak now of the philosophical one—from the political point of view, the technology of the self is something which has to be created, re-created, renovated, changed, and so on. But that does not prevent us from raising the question of what those technologies are, what technologies of the self are in general, and what the status of *technē* is, the philosophical status of *technē*, which has also political implications.

But I don't think that we have to put aside all those problems, political problems of technology of the self, for the reason that *technē* has to be philosophically put in question from a Heideggerian point of view. Concretely, you can really change what, for instance, the asylum is in raising the question of what madness is in our civilization, but taking care of not . . . Well, the philosophical implications of those political questions, those philosophical implications are present, I think, in the political questions, in the political debate, in the political struggle, but the political struggle must not await the solution of philosophical question.

— *In relation to that, I was wondering about two things you said, one in your third lecture and one in the sixth . . .*

—I am . . . I feel really intimidated!

— *I'm not trying to use it against you, I'm just trying to put something together. You have spoken of revolution and the possibility of liberating the self. [Are you] saying that certain ideas of revolution and ideas of the possibility of liberating the self have an oppressive, rather than liberatory, character? . . . Is that the case? Is that what you're implying?*[*]

---

[*] The question is only intermittently audible and has been pieced together here based on the audible portions of the exchange, the context, and Foucault's response. At some point, the participant seems to ask whether the idea of revolution *"has been [concerned with] domination rather than the*

—Not exactly. When I spoke about the revolution, it was only from a theoretical or historical point of view. It was the fact that people now are studying revolution as a phenomenon which belongs typically to our nineteenth century, or eventually nineteenth and a half, twentieth century, but it is now a historical figure much more than an actual possibility or than an actual threat. Well, considering revolution as a historical figure, I think that it would be very interesting to relate revolution to this problem of the techniques of the self. The revolution has not been only social movements or political movements. The attractiveness . . . the attraction of revolution over people links, I think, to the fact that, for the care of the self, for the status of the self, for the changing of the self, for *askēsis*, revolution has been something really very important.[26] And I think that people . . . if people were so anxious to make revolution, it was not only for [. . .]*

---

definition of power," though the full question is unclear. Note that it is here in a mostly inaudible portion of the question that the participant seems to reference the sixth lecture of the series, which could not be recovered: *"Where you talked about the effect of the [. . .] revolution on [. . .] and then in the sixth lecture you talked about the possibility of liberating the self as being perhaps technically [. . .]."*

* The recording ends here; the final words of the discussion have been lost.

NOTES

INTRODUCTION

1. Records and a statement by Foucault at the end of section 3 of Lecture I (see *infra*, p. 12) indicate that he had planned to give six lectures. Similarly, in the fragmentary audio of the final question posed to Foucault at the end of the fourth meeting of the seminar, the participant seems to reference a "sixth lecture" (see *infra*, pp. 230–31n). However, no trace of the sixth lecture could be found in the archives. For more details, see the "Note on the Reconstruction of the Text" in this volume.

2. This is most likely the English translation given by the organizers of the Summer Institute of the French title that Foucault originally proposed: "Dire-vrai sur soi-même." Since this translation does not seem to capture what Foucault had in mind, we decided to give this volume a title that more appropriately translates the French one.

3. For a record of these remarks, see R. Joseph, "An Encyclopedia of Semiotics: ISISSS '82 in Review," *Semiotica* 45, nos. 1–2 (1983): 103–13.

4. See *HS*.

5. See *GSO*; *CT*; *DT*.

6. See *P*.

7. "Technologies of the Self," in *EW* 1, 16–49.

8. See *La culture de soi*, in *CCS*, 81–109.

9. *La culture de soi*, 84.

10. See *UP*; *CS*.

11. *CS*, 37–68. In the original French edition, chapter 2 is titled *La culture

de soi, or "The Culture of the Self"; the English edition mistranslates this title as "The Cultivation of the Self."

12. *Infra*, p. 6.

13. *ABHS*, 21. (A previous version, which included numerous errors which have been corrected in the Chicago edition, was published as Michel Foucault, "About the Beginning of the Hermeneutics of the Self: Two Lectures at Dartmouth," *Political Theory* 21, no. 2 [1993]: 201.)

14. *La culture de soi*, 84. See also "What Is Enlightenment?," in *EW* 1, 312, 15, 18; *GSO*, 19–21.

15. See Arnold I. Davidson and Daniele Lorenzini, introduction to *CCS*, 21–26.

16. *GL*, 99–102.

17. See *AC*.

18. For a concise introduction to the principal themes of Foucault's thought in the 1980s, see Daniele Lorenzini, Ariane Revel, and Arianna Sforzini, "Acualité du 'dernier' Foucault," in *Michel Foucault: Éthique et vérité, 1980–1984*, ed. Daniele Lorenzini, Ariane Revel, and Arianna Sforzini, Problèmes et controverses (Paris: Vrin, 2013), 7–28.

19. *ABHS*, 27n*.

20. See *ABHS*.

21. *Infra*, p. 12.

22. *Infra*, pp. 81–86. See also Foucault, "Technologies of the Self," 34–35; "The Ethics of the Concern for the Self as a Practice of Freedom," in *EW* 1, 271–72; "Self Writing," in *EW* 1, 210; *HS*, 243–44, 317–27, 331–33.

23. *Infra*, p. 86.

24. *Infra*, p. 87. See also *ABHS*, 36: "The term *gnome* designates the unity of will and knowledge; [. . .] the type of subject which is proposed as a model and as a target in the Greek or in the Hellenistic or Roman philosophy is a gnomic self, where the force of the truth is one with the form of the will."

25. *Infra*, pp. 58, 71–72.

26. *Infra*, p. 71. Foucault revisits the problem of "the change from pagan asceticism to Christian asceticism" in his final lecture of his final course at the Collège de France; see *CT*, 317–21.

27. Regarding *exagoreusis*, see especially *ABHS*, 73–76; *GL*, 288–313; *P*, 3; "Technologies of the Self," 43–49; *WDTT*, 163–91.

28. *Infra*, pp. 13–14.

29. *HS*, 1–2.

30. *HS*, 372.

31. See *P*.

32. With the publication of the Toronto seminar in the present volume, Foucault's interventions on the subject of *parrēsia* are now available in their entirety.

33. See again *GSO*; *CT*; *DT*.

34. See *DT*, 62, 67–68, 223–24; *GSO*. See also Davidson and Lorenzini, introduction, 25.

NOTE ON THE RECONSTRUCTION OF THE TEXT

1. *Infra*, p. 12.

2. Yet, according to something said by one of the seminar participants (see *infra*, pp. 230–31), it seems possible that Foucault did in fact give six lectures in all.

3. BnF NAF 28730, boxes 29 and 76.

4. Foucault reused some of this material in his course description for his 1982 Collège de France course on the hermeneutics of the subject. See Foucault, "The Hermeneutics of the Subject (Course Summary)," in *EW* 1, 93–106.

5. See "Technologies of the Self." The Toronto manuscript appears to be a first draft of the Vermont lectures.

LECTURE I

1. See *HIST*, 59–61, 69–70.

2. Foucault traced the history of the role played by avowal in juridical institutions and procedures from the Middle Ages to the twentieth century in his May 13 and 20, 1981, lectures at Louvain; see *WDTT*, 163–229.

3. Foucault went into much greater detail regarding this history in the February 19, 1975, lecture of *Abnormal*, as well as in the May 13 of *Wrong-Doing, Truth-Telling*. See *AB*, 183–94; *WDTT*, 172–77.

4. See Foucault, "Technologies of the Self," 245–49; *GL*, 288–320; *WDTT*, 23–24, 125–52, 163–68; *ABHS*, 62–74; *P*, 3; "Sexuality and Solitude," in *EW* 1, 182–83; "The Battle for Chastity," in *EW* 1, 193–96.

5. Regarding this question, see *HS*, 421–22; *CS*, 142–43; *ST*, 281–89.

6. Foucault, "Technologies of the Self," 224.

7. See *OT*.

8. See *BC*.

9. See *DP*.

10. For an analogous introduction to the themes of techniques and technologies of the self, see *ABHS*, 24–26; Foucault, "Sexuality and Solitude,"

177–78; "Technologies of the Self," 224–25. For more on this theme, see *UP*, 10–12; Foucault, "Subjectivity and Truth (Course Summary)," 87–88; *ST*, 35, 275; *WDTT*, 23–24.

11. See *PP*.

12. See *ABHS*, 25–26.

13. At the bottom of the manuscript page, Foucault noted "Toronto 1."

14. The notion of *epimeleia heautou* (care of the self) constitutes the heart of Foucault's analyses in *HS* (2ff.) and across the majority of his final works, up to the appearance of the appropriately titled *History of Sexuality*, vol. 3, *The Care of the Self.*

15. In French in the original English manuscript.

16. See Jean Defradas, *Les thèmes de la propagande delphique* (Paris: Librairie G. Klincksieck, 1956), 268–83.

17. Foucault is alluding to the interpretation of W. H. Roscher, "Weiteres über die Bedeutung des E zu Delphie und die übrigen *grammata Delphika*," *Philologus* 60 (1901): 81–101. See also *HS*, 4.

18. Xenophon, *Memorabilia*, in *Memorabilia, Oeconomicus, Symposium, Apology*, trans. E. C. Marchant, O. J. Todd; rev. Jeffrey Henderson, Loeb Classical Library (Cambridge, MA: Harvard University Press, 2013).

19. Plato, *The Apology*, in *The Collected Dialogues of Plato*, ed. Edith Hamilton and Huntington Cairns (Princeton: Princeton University Press, 1961), 28a–31c (pp. 14–17).

20. Gregory of Nyssa, *On Virginity*, in *Saint Gregory of Nyssa: Ascetical Works*, The Fathers of the Church, vol. 58 (Washington, DC: The Catholic University of America Press, 1967), ch. 13, "That Release from Marriage Is the Beginning of Caring for Oneself," 46–48.

21. Gregory of Nyssa, *On Virginity*, ch. 12, "That the One Who Has Purified Himself Will See the Divine Beauty in Himself; Also on the Cause of Evil," 42–46.

22. Luke 15:8–10.

23. "Let no one when young delay to study philosophy, nor when he is old grow weary of his study. For no one can come too early or too late to secure the health of his soul. And the man who says that the age for philosophy has either not yet come or has gone by is like the man who says that the age for happiness is not yet come to him, or has passed away. Wherefore both when young and old a man must study philosophy, that as he grows old he may be young in blessings through the grateful recollection of what has been, and that in youth he may be old as well, since he will know no fear of what is to

come. We must then meditate on the things that make our happiness, seeing that when that is with us we have all, but when it is absent we do all to win it." Epicurus, *Letter to Menoeceus*, in *The Extant Remains* (Oxford: Oxford University Press, 1926), 122 (p. 83).

24. See Marcello Gigante, "Philodème, sur la liberté de parole," in *Actes du VIIIe Congrès de l'Association Guillaume Budé (Paris, 5–10 avril 1968)* (Paris: Belles Lettres, 1969), 196–217.

25. Philo of Alexandria, *On the Contemplative Life, or Suppliants*, in *Philo*, vol. 9, trans. F. H. Colson, Loeb Classical Library (Cambridge, MA: Harvard University Press, 1941).

26. "When someone inquired why they put their fields in the hands of the Helots, and did not take care of them themselves, he said, 'It was by not taking care of the fields, but of ourselves, that we acquired those fields.'" Plutarch, "Sayings of Spartans," in *Moralia*, vol. 3, trans. Frank Cole Babbit, Loeb Classical Library (Cambridge, MA: Harvard University Press, 1931), 217A (p. 97).

27. See E. R. Dodds, *Les grecs et l'irrationnel* (Paris: Flammarion, 1977), 140–78; J.-P. Vernant, "Aspects mythiques de la mémoire" (155) and "Aspects de la personne dans la religion greque" (1960), in *Mythe et pensée chez les Grecs* (Paris: La Découverte, 1996), 109–36, 355–70.

28. Plato, *Symposium*, in *Lysis, Symposium, Gorgias*, trans. W. R. M. Lamb, Loeb Classical Library (Cambridge, MA: Harvard University Press, 1925), 220a–b (pp. 33–35). In the lecture, Foucault misspeaks and references the battle of Mantinea; however, the episode in question, referenced in the *Symposium*, took place at the battle of Potidaea. Foucault also makes this mistake in Lecture III below; see *infra*, p. 65.

29. Plato, *Symposium*, 217a–19e (pp. 23–33).

30. *Symposium*, 174e–75e (pp. 89–93).

31. See Xenophon, *Oeconomicus*, in *Memorabilia, Oeconomicus, Symposium, Apology*, trans. E. C. Marchant, O. J. Todd; rev. Jeffrey Henderson, Loeb Classical Library (Cambridge, MA: Harvard University Press, 2013).

32. See *HM*.

33. See *DP*.

34. On this problem, see Foucault, *La culture de soi*, 97–98; *HS*, 4–9.

35. "Maybe the problem of the self is not to discover what it is in its positivity, maybe the problem is not to discover a positive self, or the positive foundation of the self. Maybe our problem is now to discover that the self is nothing else than the historical correlation of the technology built in our history. Maybe the problem is to change those technologies. And in this case,

one of the main political problems would be nowadays, in the strict sense of the word, the politics of ourselves." *ABHS*, 76.

LECTURE II (SECOND ENGLISH VERSION)

1. We have reproduced only the "second English version" of Lecture II here because it is this version that Foucault corrected himself to present at Toronto. As noted above, the first English version is a translation of Foucault's French manuscript by an unknown third party, which contains both numerous interpretive errors and departs from Foucault's style. The second English version is nearly identical but includes numerous corrections and several extra manuscript pages. Foucault reused pages 11–16 of the manuscript in his lectures on the culture of the self at the University of California, Berkeley in April 1983.

2. Plato, *Alcibiades I*, in Plato, *Charmides, Alcibiades I and II, Hipparchus, The Lovers, Theages, Minos, Epinomis*, trans. W. R. M. Lamb, Loeb Classical Library (Cambridge, MA: Harvard University Press, 1964). Foucault provides a detailed analysis of the *Alcibiades* through the framework of the care of the self in *HS*. See *HS*, 30–47, 51–59, 65–78, and passim. See also Foucault, "Technologies of the Self," 228–31; *La culture de soi*, 89–91; *CT*, 125–27, 158–60, 246.

3. Regarding the question of the Neoplatonic ordering of Plato's works, Foucault notably relies upon A.-J. Festugière, "L'ordre de lecture des dialogues de Platon au Vᵉ-VIᵉ siècles," in *Études de philosophie grecque* (Paris: Vrin, 1971), 535–50. For Foucault's remarks on the Neoplatonic commentaries on the *Alcibiades*, see *HS*, 169–73.

4. Foucault gives a detailed commentary on this passage of the *Alcibiades* in the first meeting of the seminar in the present volume; see *infra*, pp. 117–29.

5. Regarding the prominent characteristics of the "culture of the self" in the imperial period, see Foucault, "The Hermeneutics of the Subject (Course Summary)," 95–99; *La culture de soi*, 91–97; *HS*, 81ff.; *CS*, 44–45.

6. See Epictetus, *Discourses, Books I and II*, trans. W. A. Oldfather, Loeb Classical Library (Cambridge, MA: Harvard University Press, 1956); *Discourses, Books III and IV*, trans. W. A. Oldfather, Loeb Classical Library (Cambridge, MA: Harvard University Press, 1952). Regarding the relationship of Epictetus to Socrates, see Foucault's commentary on Book III, Discourse I, "Of Personal Adornment," §§16–23 (pp. 11–13) at the end of the first meeting of the seminar; *infra*, pp. 132–37.

7. The manuscript reads "the second book of the *Discourses*," but this is a typo in the English manuscript; Foucault is referring to Book I, Discourse XVI,

"Of Providence," in Epictetus, *Discourses, Books I and II*, pp. 109–13. "Marvel not that the animals other than man have furnished them, ready prepared by nature, what pertains to their bodily needs—not merely food and drink, but also a bed to lie on,—and that they have no need of shoes, or bedding, or clothing, while we are in need of all these things." Foucault comments on this text in the second meeting of the seminar; see *infra*, pp. 148–50.

8. Epicurus, *Letter to Menoeceus*, 122 (p. 83).

9. Reported in Plutarch, "On the Control of Anger," in *Moralia*, vol. 6, trans. W. C. Helmbold, Loeb Classical Library (Cambridge, MA: Harvard University Press, 1939), 453D (p. 97): "One of those excellent precepts of Musonius which I remember, Sulla, is: 'He that wishes to come through life safe and sound must continue throughout his life to be under treatment.'"

10. Regarding these expressions of Seneca, see *HS*, 85–86; *CS*, 46.

11. Dio Chrysostom, *Discourse 20*, "On Retirement," in *Discourses 12–30*, trans. J. W. Cohoon, Loeb Classical Library (Cambridge, MA: Harvard University Press, 1962), 246–69.

12. "A man does everything, for many years in succession, that he may become a good physician, or public speaker, or grammarian, or geometer. Is it a disgrace for you to toil for a long time that you may one day be a good man?" Galen, *On the Passions and Errors of the Soul*, trans. Paul W. Harkins (Columbus: Ohio State University Press, 1963), 41.

13. See Philo of Alexandria, *On the Contemplative Life, or Suppliants*.

14. Lucian, *Philosophies for Sale (Vitarum Auctio)*, in Lucian, vol. 2, trans. A. M. Harmon, Loeb Classical Library (Cambridge, MA: Harvard University Press, 1960), 449–512.

15. Lucian, *Hermotimus, or Concerning the Sects*, in Lucian, vol. 6, trans. A. M. Harmon, Loeb Classical Library (Cambridge, MA: Harvard University Press, 1959), 259–416.

16. Regarding the crucial role of writing in the culture of the self, and the *hupomnēmata* and correspondence in particular, see *HS*, 360–67; Foucault, "Self Writing," 207–22.

17. Seneca, *Epistles*, vol. 1, *Epistles 1–65*, trans. Richard M. Gummere, Loeb Classical Library (Cambridge, MA: Harvard University Press, 1917); vol. 2, *Epistles 66–92*, trans. Richard M. Gummere, Loeb Classical Library (Cambridge, MA: Harvard University Press, 1920); vol. 3, *Epistles 93–124*, trans. Richard M. Gummere, Loeb Classical Library (Cambridge, MA: Harvard University Press, 1925).

18. Pliny the Younger, *Letters*, vol. 1, *Books 1–7*; vol. 2, *Books 8–10*; *Panegyricus*, trans. Betty Radice, Loeb Classical Library 55, 59 (Cambridge, MA: Harvard University Press, 1969).

19. Marcus Aurelius, "Miscellaneous Letters of Marcus Aurelius," in *Fronto: Correspondence*, vol. 2, trans. C. R. Haines, Loeb Classical Library (Cambridge, MA: Harvard University Press, 1920). Foucault comments on several of these letters at the end of the second meeting of the seminar; see *infra*, pp. 164–70.

20. Aelius Aristides, *The Sacred Tales*, in *The Complete Works*, vol. 2, *Orations XVII–LIII*, ed. C. A. Behr (Leiden: E.J. Brill, 1981). See also Foucault, "Technologies of the Self," 242; *La culture de soi*, 97.

21. See *supra*, p. 238, note 5.

22. Epicurus, *Letter to Menoeceus*, 122 (p. 83).

23. See again Plutarch, "On the Control of Anger," 453D (p. 97): "One of those excellent precepts of Musonius which I remember, Sulla, is: 'He that wishes to come through life safe and sound must continue throughout his life to be under treatment.'"

24. "For each of us needs almost a lifetime of training to become a perfect man. Indeed, a man must not give up trying to make himself better even if, at the age of fifty, he should see that his soul has suffered damage which is not incurable but which has been left uncorrected. Even if a man of this age should find his body in poor condition, he would not give it over entirely to its poor health, but he would make every effort to make himself more vigorous, even if he could not have the bodily strength of a Hercules. Therefore, let us continue striving to make our souls more perfect, even if we cannot have the soul of a wise man. If from our youth we take thought for our soul, let us have the highest hope that we will one day have even this, namely, the soul of a wise man. If the fact is that we have failed in this, let us see to it that, at least, our soul does not become thoroughly evil." Galen, *On the Passions and Errors of the Soul*, 37.

25. See Seneca, *De tranquillitate animi*, in *Moral Essays*, vol. 2, trans. John W. Basore, Loeb Classical library (Cambridge, MA: Harvard University Press, 1932).

26. See Seneca, *Epistles*, vol. 1, *Epistles 1–65*; vol. 2, *Epistles 66–92*; vol. 3, *Epistles 93–124*.

27. Marcus Aurelius, *The Meditations*, in *Marcus Aurelius*, ed. C. R. Haines, Loeb Classical Library (Cambridge, MA: Harvard University Press, 1916), Book III, §14 (p. 63).

28. Regarding the distinction between three forms of "conversion" (Platonic *epistrophē*, Hellenistic and Roman conversion, and Christian *metanoia*), see *HS*, 201–17. Regarding the *epistrophē eis heauton* as common objective of practices of the self in the imperial period, see *CS*, 64–66.

29. *Inaestimabile bonum est suum fieri.* (And it is a priceless good to be master of oneself.) Seneca, *Epistle* 75, "On the Diseases of the Soul," in *Epistles*, vol. 2, §18 (p. 147).

30. Regarding the three functions of the care of the self in the imperial period (the critical function, the function of struggle, and the therapeutic function), see *HS*, 93–97, 229, 321–22; Foucault, "The Hermeneutics of the Subject (Course Summary)," 97; *La culture de soi*, 93–95.

31. Plutarch, "Advice about Keeping Well," in *Moralia*, vol. 2, trans. Frank Cole Babbitt, Loeb Classical Library (Cambridge, MA: Harvard University Press, 1928), 122E (p. 22). Regarding the direct correlation between medicine and the care of the self, see also *CS*, 54–58.

32. "Men, the lecture-room of the philosopher is a hospital; you ought not to walk out of it in pleasure, but in pain. For you are not well when you come; one man has a dislocated shoulder, another an abscess, another a fistula, another a headache. And then am I to sit down and recite to you dainty little notions and clever little mottoes, so that you will go out with words of praise on your lips, one man carrying away his shoulder just as it was when he came in, another his head in the same state, another his fistula, another his abscess?" Epictetus, *Discourses, Books III and IV*, Discourse III, Chapter 23, §§31–32 (p. 181).

33. "If you ask me now, 'Are our syllogisms useful?' I will tell you that they are, and, if you wish, I will show how they are useful. 'Have they, then, helped me at all?' Man, you did not ask, did you? whether they are useful to you, but whether they are useful in general? Let the man who is suffering from dysentery ask me whether vinegar is useful; I will tell him that it is useful. 'Is it useful, then, to me?' I will say, 'No. Seek first to have your discharge stopped, the little ulcers healed.' So do you also, men, first cure your ulcers, stop your discharges, be tranquil in mind, bring it free from distraction into the school; and then you will know what power reason has." *Discourses, Books I and II*, Discourse II, Chapter 21, §§21–22 (p. 391).

34. Galen, *On the Passions and Errors of the Soul*, 40–41, 54–56.

35. Regarding the thesis that there is a progressive "disconnection" of the care of the self and the erotic over the course of Greco-Roman history, see *ST*, 183–98; *HS*, 58–59, 347–48; *CS*, 190–232. Regarding the problematiza-

tion of the relation between pedagogy and the erotic in classical Greece, see *ST*, 90–95.

36. Seneca, *Epistle* 52, "On Choosing Our Teachers," in *Epistles*, vol. 1, §§1–3 (p. 345).

37. "How, then, could a man cut out these passions if he did not first know that he had them? But as we said, it is impossible to know them, since we love ourselves to excess." Galen, *On the Passions and Errors of the Soul*, 32.

38. Regarding the figure of Demetrius, see *HS*, 142–43, 230–31; *CT*, 193–95, 205–6; *DT*, 158, 183.

39. Seneca, *De Consolatione ad Helvium*.

40. Plutarch, "On Tranquility of Mind," in *Moralia*, vol. 6, trans. W. C. Helmbold, Loeb Classical Library (Cambridge, MA: Harvard University Press, 1939), 464E–65A (p. 167). (The recipient of the letter is in fact Paccius, not Fundanus.)

41. See Foucault's remarks regarding amorous relations between Marcus Aurelius and Fronto at the end of the second meeting of the seminar; *infra*, p. 56.

LECTURE II (RECORDED VERSION)

1. Regarding the prominent characteristics of the "culture of the self" in the imperial period, see *HS*, 81ff.; Foucault, "The Hermeneutics of the Subject (Course Summary)," 95–99; *La culture de soi*, 91–97; *CS*, 43–44.

2. See Clement of Alexandria, *Christ the Educator*, trans. Simon P. Wood, The Fathers of the Church (New York: The Catholic University of America Press, 1954).

3. See *Stromateis, Books 1–3*, trans. Simon P. Wood, The Fathers of the Church (New York: The Catholic University of America Press, 1991).

4. Epictetus, *Encheiridion*, in *Discourses, Books III and IV*.

5. The *Patrologiae Cursus Completus*, Series Latina is an imposing collection of texts of the early church fathers and other ecclesiastics from Tertullian to Innocent III, published under the direction of the abbé Jacques-Paul Migne in 221 volumes between 1844 and 1864.

6. See Foucault, *La culture de soi*, 88.

7. Plato, *Alcibiades I*. See also *supra*, p. 238, note 2.

8. Regarding the question of the Neoplatonic ordering of Plato's works, Foucault notably relies upon Festugière, "L'ordre de lecture des dialogues de Platon au Vᵉ-VIᵉ siècles," 535–50. For Foucault's remarks on the Neoplatonic commentaries on the *Alcibiades*, see *HS*, 169–73.

9. *Epimeleisthai allois*: here, "care for others" or "care of others."

10. Book I, Discourse XVI, "Of Providence," in Epictetus, *Discourses, Books I and II*, pp. 109–13. Foucault comments on this text in the second meeting of the seminar; see *infra*, pp. 147–60.

11. Epicurus, *Letter to Menoeceus*, 122 (p. 83).

12. See Plutarch, "On the Control of Anger," 453D (p. 97).

13. Regarding these expressions of Seneca, see *HS*, 85–86; *CS*, 46.

14. See Chrysostom, *Discourse* 20, "On Retirement," 246–69.

15. See Galen, *On the Passions and Errors of the Soul*, 41.

16. The typescript reads instead "or, for an example at once celebrated and mysterious, at the frontier of Greco-Roman culture, the 'Therapeutes' described by Philo of Alexandria." See Philo, *On the Contemplative Life, or Suppliants*.

17. Of Euphrates the philosopher, Pliny says, "I made intimate acquaintance with this person in my youth, when I served in the army in Syria and took some pains to gain his affection; though that indeed was nothing difficult, for he is exceeding open to access, and full of that humanity which he professes." See *Letter X, To Attius Clemens*, in *Letters*, vol. 1, *Books 1–7*, 33. See also *HS*, 151–52; *CS*, 43.

18. Regarding the figure of Demetrius, see *HS*, 142–43, 230–31; *CT*, 193–95, 205–6; *DT*, 158, 83.

19. Lucian, *Hermotimus, or Concerning the Sects*, 259–416.

20. See also *WDTT*, 134; *HS*, 398. Although Foucault invokes this statement on multiple occasions, the source of this proverb is unclear, as it seems to be either a paraphrase or a composite of two passages from the Psalms. These difficulties are laid out in detail by Bernard Harcourt and Fabienne Brion in *WDTT*, 154n17.

21. See *infra*, p. 140.

22. Regarding the crucial role of writing in the culture of the self, and the *hupomnēmata* and correspondence in particular, see *HS*, 360–67; Foucault, "Self Writing," 207–22.

23. Foucault seems to be referring to *Epistle* 99, though the citation that Foucault reads does not appear in this letter. See Seneca, *Epistle* 99, "On Consolation to the Bereaved," in *Epistles*, vol. 3.

24. See Marcus Aurelius, "Miscellaneous Letters of Marcus Aurelius."

25. Foucault comments on several of these letters at the end of the second meeting of the seminar; see *infra*, pp. 164–70.

26. Aristides, *The Sacred Tales*. See also Foucault, "Technologies of the Self," 242; *La culture de soi*, 97.

27. Aelius Aristides, "Regarding Rome," trans. C. A. Behr, in *The Complete Works*, vol. II, *Orations XVII–LIII*, ed. C. A. Behr (Leiden: E.J. Brill, 1981), 73–97.

28. Epicurus, *Letter to Menoeceus*, 122 (p. 83).

29. See Plutarch, "On the Control of Anger," 453D (p. 97).

30. See Galen, *On the Passions and Errors of the Soul*, 37.

31. Marcus Aurelius, *The Meditations*, Book III, §14 (p. 63).

32. Regarding the distinction between three forms of "conversion" (Platonic *epistrophē*, Hellenistic and Roman conversion, and Christian *metanoia*), see *HS*, 201–17. Regarding the *epistrophē eis heauton* as common objective of practices of the self in the imperial period, see *CS*, 64–66.

33. See, for example, Seneca, *Epistle* 75, "On the Diseases of the Soul," in *Epistles*, vol. 2, §18 (p. 147): "And it is a priceless good to be master of oneself." (*Inaestimabile bonum est suum fieri.*)

34. "Your parents, to be sure, asked other blessings for you; but I myself pray rather that you may despise all those things which your parents wished for you in abundance. Their prayers plunder many another person, simply that you may be enriched. Whatever they make over to you must be removed from someone else." *Epistle* 32, "On Progress," in *Epistles*, vol. 1, para. 4 (p. 233).

35. Here Foucault is referring to two different passages in Epictetus. See Epictetus, *Discourses, Books III and IV*, Discourse III, Chapter 23, §§31–32 (p. 181); *Discourses, Books I and II*, Discourse II, Chapter 21, §§21–22 (p. 391). See also *supra*, p. 241, notes 32, 33.

36. Galen, *On the Passions and Errors of the Soul*, 40–41, 54–56.

37. See *supra*, p. 242, note 41.

LECTURE III (FIRST ENGLISH VERSION)

1. On the Greek notion of *askēsis*, see *UP*, 30, 72–77, 126; *HS*, 315–21, 422; *ST*, 33–34; *DT*, 193–95.

2. See Musonius Rufus, "Which Is More Effective, Theory or Practice?," in *Musonius Rufus, "the Roman Socrates,"* ed. and trans by Cora E. Lutz (New Haven: Yale University Press, 1947), 49–53. See also *HS*, 426–28.

3. "Well, the *paraskeuē* could be called both an open and an orientated preparation of the individual for the events of life. What I mean is this: In the ascesis, the *paraskeuē* involves preparing the individual for the future, for a future of unforeseen events whose general nature may be familiar to us, but which we cannot know whether and when they will occur. It involves, then, finding in ascesis a preparation, a *paraskeuē*, which can be adapted to what

may occur, and only to this, and at the very moment it occurs, if it does so."
HS, 320–21.

4. "'Just as,' he [Demetrius the Cynic] says, 'the best wrestler is not one
who is thoroughly acquainted with all the postures and grips of the art, which
he will seldom use against an adversary, but he who has well and carefully
trained himself in one or two of them, and waits eagerly for the opportunity to
use them—for it makes no difference how much he knows if he knows enough
to give him the victory—, so in this effort of ours there are many points that
are interesting, few that are decisive.'" Seneca, *De beneficiis*, in *Moral Essays*,
vol. 3, trans. John W. Basore, Loeb Classical Library (Cambridge, MA: Harvard University Press, 1935), Book VII, 1, 4 (p. 457).

5. *Epistles* 90 and 91, in *Epistles*, vol. 2, pp. 394–445.

6. "For as savage dogs become excited at every strange cry and are soothed
by the familiar voice only, so also the passions of the soul, when they are
raging wild, are not easily allayed, unless customary and familiar arguments
are at hand to curb the excited passions." Plutarch, "On Tranquility of Mind,"
465C (p. 169).

7. "These are the things that my friend Demetrius says the tiro in philosophy must grasp with both hands, these are the precepts that he must never let
go, nay, must cling fast to, and make a part of himself, and by daily meditation
reach the point where these wholesome maxims occur to him of their own
accord, and are promptly at hand whenever they are desired, and the great
distinction between base and honourable action presents itself without any
delay." Seneca, *De beneficiis*, Book VII, 2, 2 (p. 459).

8. Foucault does not return to this subject in the seminar, perhaps because
of lack of time. However, he does develop analyses of these themes in his lectures of March 3 and 24, 1982, on the hermeneutics of the subject (*HS*, 331–
70, 453–90). See also Foucault, "Technologies of the Self," 235–39.

9. Plutarch, "On Listening to Lectures," in *Moralia*, vol. 1, trans. Frank Cole
Babbitt, Loeb Classical Library (Cambridge, MA: Harvard University Press,
1927), Book I, 2 (pp. 207–11).

10. Philo of Alexandria, *On the Contemplative Life, or Suppliants*, 77 (p. 161).

11. On the "art of listening," see Foucault, "Technologies of the Self," 236;
HS, 340.

12. Regarding the role of writing in the culture of the self, and the *hupomnēmata* and correspondence in particular, see *HS*, 360–67; Foucault, "Self
Writing," 207–22.

13. Regarding the practice of *anachōrēsis*, see "The Hermeneutics of the

Subject (Course Summary)." See also *CS*, 60–62; Foucault, "Débat au Département de Français de l'Université de Californie à Berkeley"; *DT*, 220.

14. Frances Yates, *The Art of Memory* (London: Routledge and Kegan Paul, 1966).

15. Regarding the process of the "subjectivation of the truth," see Foucault, "The Ethics of the Concern for the Self as a Practice of Freedom," 286; "Technologies of the Self," 238; "Self Writing," 210; *HS*, 233, 315–27, 332–33.

16. Regarding this distinction, see Foucault, "Technologies of the Self," 239–41; *HS*, 425–26.

17. For a more detailed analysis of the *praemeditatio malorum*, see *HS*, 463–73.

18. Seneca, *Epistle* 91, "On the Lesson to be Drawn from the Burning of Lyons," in *Epistles*, vol. 2, 430–45. See also *Epistle* 24, "On Despising Death," in *Epistles*, vol. 1, §2 (p. 167).

19. Plato, *Symposium*, 220a–b (pp. 33–35). In the lecture, Foucault misspeaks and references the battle of Mantinea; however, the episode in question, referenced in the *Symposium*, took place at the battle of Potidaea. Foucault also makes this mistake in Lecture I; see *supra*, p. 11 and p. 237, note 28.

20. Plutarch, "On The Sign of Socrates," in *Moralia*, vol. 7, trans. W. C. Helmbold, Loeb Classical Library (Cambridge, MA: Harvard University Press, 1959).

21. Seneca, *Epistle* 18, "On Festivals and Fasting," in *Epistles*, vol. 1, §§1–5 (p. 117).

22. On the examination of representations in Epictetus, see *DT*, 211–15; "The Hermeneutics of the Subject (Course Summary)," 103; *HS*, 298–301; Foucault, "Débat au Département de Français de l'Université de Californie à Berkeley," 166–67; "Technologies of the Self," 239–40.

23. Epictetus, *Discourses, Books III and IV*, Discourse III, Chapter 12, "Of Training," §15 (p. 85).

24. *Discourses, Books I and II*, Discourse I, Chapter 20, "How the Reasoning Faculty Contemplates Itself," §§7–9 (p. 139).

25. On the examination of the self in the first centuries of Christianity, especially in Cassian, see Foucault, "Technologies of the Self," 246–48; "The Battle for Chastity," 193–94; *HS*, 299; *GL*, 300–309; *WDTT*, 145–50; *ABHS*, 64–70; *DT*, 213.

26. Epictetus, *Discourses, Books III and IV*, Discourse III, Chapter 8, "How Ought We to Exercise Ourselves to Deal With the Impressions of Our Senses?," §§1–3 (p. 61).

27. Epictetus, *Discourses, Books III and IV*, Discourse III, Chapter 3, "What Is the Subject-Matter with Which the Good Man Has to Deal; and What Should Be the Chief Object of Our Training?," §§14–16 (p. 33).

28. See *supra*, p. 245, note 6.

29. Regarding the *meletē thanatou*, see *HS*, 477–80; Foucault, "The Hermeneutics of the Subject (Course Summary)," 104.

30. Seneca, *Epistle* 12, "On Old Age," in *Epistles*, vol. 1, §9 (p. 71).

31. Marcus Aurelius, *The Meditations*, Book VII, §69 (p. 195).

32. *The Meditations*, Book II, §5 (p. 31).

33. Epictetus, *Discourses, Books III and IV*, Discourse III, Chapter 5, §§5–6 (p. 41).

34. "I shall leave it to Death to determine what progress I have made. Therefore with no faint heart I am making ready for the day when, putting aside all stage artifice and actor's rouge, I am to pass judgment upon myself,—whether I am merely declaiming brave sentiments, or whether I really feel them; whether all the bold threats I have uttered against fortune are a pretense and a farce." Seneca, *Epistle* 26, "On Old Age and Death," in *Epistles*, vol. 1, §5 (p. 189).

LECTURE III (SECOND ENGLISH VERSION)

1. "Since a human being happens to be neither soul alone nor body alone, but a composite of these two things, someone in training must pay attention to both." Musonius Rufus, *Lectures & Sayings*, trans. Cynthia King (Scotts Valley, CA: CreateSpace Independent Publishing Platform, 2011), 36.

2. *HS*, 426–28.

3. In the final lecture in the series "The Courage of Truth," Foucault takes up the problem of the passage from pagan (and notably Cynic) asceticism to Christian asceticism, and their mutual relationship, without, however, returning to the distinction between an "asceticism oriented towards reality," and "asceticism oriented towards truth." Alongside several features in common on the level of ascetic practice, forms of endurance, and modes of exercise, Foucault insists on two major differences between pagan and Christian asceticism. On the one hand, "in Christian asceticism there is of course a relation to the other world (*l'autre monde*), and not to the world which is other." That is to say that "in Christianity that the aim of the other life (*la vie autre*) to which the ascetic must dedicate himself and which he has chosen, is not simply to transform this world—again, notwithstanding the theme of the catastasis or apocatastasis—but is also and above all to give individuals,

possibly all Christians, the entire Christian community, access to an other world (*un monde autre*)." On the other hand, at the heart of Christian asceticism is an unprecedented principle, one that we do not find in pagan ascetic practice: the "principle of obedience to the other (obedience to the other in this world, obedience to the other which is at the same time obedience to God and to those who represent him)." It is in this way that Christianity inaugurates "a new style of relation to self, a new type of power relations, and a different regime of truth." *CT*, 319–20.

4. Friedrich Wilhelm Nietzsche, *On the Genealogy of Morality* (Cambridge: Cambridge University Press, 2008); Max Weber, *The Protestant Ethic and the Spirit of Capitalism*, trans. Talcott Parsons (London: Routledge, 2001).

5. Foucault would not ultimately develop this project. However, in the second hour of the February 29, 1984, lecture in the series "The Courage of Truth," within his analysis of Cynicism as "an historical category which, in various forms and with diverse objectives, runs through the whole of Western history," he raises the idea of revolution not as political project, but as a "form of life" that raises the question of "an other life, which is the true life." *CT*, 174, 184.

6. At the beginning of the first meeting of the seminar, which took place between the second and third lectures, a participant suggested that Foucault explicate the reasons for his interest in antiquity, which some auditors were having trouble understanding. Foucault promised to do so in the third lecture, and engages that question here. See the first meeting of the seminar, *infra*, p. 109.

7. On the theme of old age in the ancient culture of the self, see especially *HS*, 108–11 and passim.

8. Cicero, *On Old Age*, in *On Old Age, On Friendship, On Divination*, trans. W. A. Falconer, Loeb Classical Library (Cambridge, MA: Harvard University Press, 1923).

9. See Seneca, *Epistle* 12, "On Old Age," in *Epistles*, vol. 1.

10. In an article written for the first issue of the review *Le Gai Pied* in 1979, on what might be called an "art of suicide," Foucault affirms that "one has the chance to have at one's disposal this absolutely singular moment [the moment of death]: of all it is the one which merits the greatest care: not at all to worry oneself or to reassure oneself, but for a pleasure that is singular, of which the patient, unabated preparation for something no longer fated, will illuminate all of one's life." Michel Foucault, "Un plaisir si simple," in *DE II*, no. 264, p. 779 (trans. D. Wyche).

11. Seneca, *Epistle* 12, "On Old Age," in *Epistles*, vol. 1, §8 (p. 71).

12. From this point to the end of the lecture, the text comes from two pages of a second version of the typescript, identical to the first, but typed on a different machine. The typescript suggests that Foucault began directly at the second paragraph. Further, it seems that from this point, Foucault more closely follows the text of section 2 of the first English version of Lecture III, "*Askēsis* as Preparation" (see above). However, the text is incomplete, and we do not know how similar the end of this version of the lecture is to the first manuscript.

13. The manuscript breaks off here. However, Foucault does begin the lecture by saying that following his discussion of the *épreuves* and tests he will treat the examination of the self. It is possible that this part of the lecture did or would have resumed his analyses of Seneca's *De ira* (as he would at the University of Vermont in October 1982; see Foucault, "Technologies of the Self," 237, 245 and *De tranquillitate animi* (already presented at the University of California, Berkeley, and at Dartmouth College in October and November 1980); see *ABHS*, 33–36). A remark about Seneca and Serenus in the third meeting of the seminar seems to confirm this hypothesis; see *infra*, p. 195. For further commentary on *De ira*, see *DT*, 195–200; *HS*, 162, 481–84; *CS*, 61–62; *GL*, 239–41, 253; *WDTT*, 97–100. For further commentary on *De tranquillitate animi*, see *DT*, 200–210; *HS*, 89, 131–35, 156–57; *GL*, 239; *WDTT*, 100–103.

LECTURE IV

1. *DP*, 135–36, 151–54, 162–69, and passim.

2. See the second version of the third lecture in the present volume; *supra*, pp. 70–73.

3. For a detailed analysis of the concept of *metanoia*, see *HS*, 211–17; *GL*, 128–35, 144–46, 176–77, 226. See also L. Cremonesi, A. I. Davidson, O. Irrera, D. Lorenzini, and M. Tazzioli, in *ABHS*, 84n25.

4. Regarding the notion of *ēthopoiēsis*, see *HS*, 237; Foucault, "Self Writing," 209; *DT*, 236n34.

5. Foucault remarks that "the term *gnome* designates the unity of will and knowledge; it designates also a brief piece of discourse through which truth appears with all its force and encrusts itself in the soul of people." *ABHS*, 36. Regarding this concept, see also *ABHS*, 36–37; Foucault, "Débat au Département de Français de l'Université de Californie à Berkeley," in *CCS*, 162; *WDTT*, 132. See also L. Cremonesi, A. I. Davidson, O. Irrera, D. Lorenzini, and M. Tazzioli, in *ABHS*, 49n35.

6. In his lectures at Dartmouth in 1980, Foucault traced the opposition

between a "gnomic self," in which "the force of the truth is one with the form
of the will," and "gnoseologic self," which poses the problem of discovering
and deciphering the secret truth of the self through a hermeneutic labor. See
ABHS, 13, 36–38, 76–77. These two historical configurations of the "self" seem
to correspond in a precise way to what Foucault calls here "gnomic knowledge of the self" and "hermeneutic knowledge of the self." However, in the
lectures given at UC-Berkeley in October 1980, Foucault complicated this binary schema by introducing a "gnostic self, which "has to be discovered inside
of the individual, but as a part, as a forgotten sparkle, of the primitive light."
ABHS, 55n, 76n. At Toronto, on the other hand, the third form of knowledge
of the self in Western culture is this "critical self-knowledge," which is to say,
"knowledge of the structural or transcendental conditions which make us able
to know the truth," as inaugurated by Cartesian and Kantian modernity. In
the manuscript of Lecture V, Foucault rather presents Gnosticism as one of
the permanent "temptations" within Christianity, "which consists in bringing together, as if they were the same process, the Revelation of truth and the
discovery of our own reality." See *infra*, p. 105.

7. The manuscript does not indicate any specific references to the text of
Marcus Aurelius that Foucault mentions here. However, he is very likely referring to a passage from the *Meditations* on the retreat into oneself found
in Book IV, §3: "Men seek out retreats for themselves in the country, by the
seaside, on the mountains, and thou too art wont to long intensely for such
things. But all this is unphilosophical to the last degree, when thou canst at a
moment's notice retire into thyself. For nowhere can a man find a retreat more
full of peace or more free from care than his own soul above all if he have that
within him, a steadfast look at which and he is at once in all good ease, and by
good ease I mean nothing other than good order. Make use then of this retirement continually and regenerate thyself. Let thy axioms be short and ele-
mental, such as, when set before thee, will at once rid thee of all trouble, and
send thee away with no discontent at those things to which thou art returning.

"For with what art thou discontented? The wickedness of men? Take this
conclusion to heart, that rational creatures have been made for one another;
that forbearance is part of justice; that wrong-doing is involuntary; and think
how many ere now, after passing their lives in implacable enmity, suspicion,
hatred, and at daggers drawn with one another, have been laid out and burnt
to ashes think of this, I say, and at last stay thy fretting. But art thou discontented with thy share in the whole? Recall the alternative: Either *Providence
or Atoms!* and the abundant proofs there are that the Universe is as it were a

state. But is it the affections of the body that shall still lay hold on thee? Bethink thee that the Intelligence, when it has once abstracted itself and learnt its own power, has nothing to do with the motions smooth or rough of the vital breath. Bethink thee too of all that thou hast heard and subscribed to about pleasure and pain. But will that paltry thing, Fame, pluck thee aside? Look at the swift approach of complete forgetfulness, and the void of infinite time on this side of us and on that, and the empty echo of acclamation, and the fickleness and uncritical judgment of those who claim to speak well of us, and the narrowness of the arena to which all this is confined. For the whole earth is but a point, and how tiny a corner of it is this the place of our sojourning! and how many therein and of what sort are the men who shall praise thee!

"From now therefore bethink thee of the retreat into this little plot that is thyself. Above all distract not thyself, be not too eager, but be thine own master, and look upon life as a man, as a human being, as a citizen, as a mortal creature. But among the principles readiest to thine hand, upon which thou shalt pore, let there be these two. One, that objective things do not lay hold of the soul, but stand quiescent without; while disturbances are but the outcome of that opinion which is within us. A second, that all this visible world changes in a moment, and will be no more; and continually bethink thee to the changes of how many things thou hast already been a witness. 'The Universe—mutation: Life—opinion.'" Marcus Aurelius, *The Meditations*, Book IV, §3 (pp. 67–71).

Foucault had prepared a commentary on this passage from Marcus Aurelius for the sixth and final meeting of the seminar on *parrēsia* at the University of California, Berkeley in October and November 1983. Although he did not have time to present the material there, the manuscript has been preserved. That commentary can perhaps provide a sense of what Foucault discussed during this lecture at Toronto.

8. On the practice of *anachōrēsis*, see Foucault, "The Hermeneutics of the Subject (Course Summary)." See also *CS*, 60–62; Foucault, "Débat au Département de Français de l'Université de Californie à Berkeley"; *DT*, 220.

LECTURE V

1. Foucault inscribed the problem of the will to truth (Why do we desire to know the truth? Why do we prefer the truth to error?) at the heart of his first courses at the Collège de France. See "The Discourse on Language," in *The Archeology of Knowledge and the Discourse on Language* (New York: Pantheon Books, 1972); *LWL*. Foucault never abandons this problem, which, reformulated in terms of the question of the obligation to speak the truth and

the historical forms of true speech, constitutes the guiding thread of his researches in the 1980s.

2. See *HM*.

3. See *DP*.

4. See *HIST*.

5. See *supra*, pp. 13–14 and p. 235, note 3.

6. For some analogous descriptions of "truth obligations" in Christianity, see Foucault, "Technologies of the Self," 223–24; *WDTT*, 92, 166–78; *ABHS*, 54–56. In his Collège de France lectures on the government of the living, Foucault presents this same duality in terms of what he calls "regimes of truth." *GL*, 93–102.

7. "For behold, thou hast loved truth, and he that doth it, cometh to the light." Augustine, *Confessions*, vol. 2, *Books 9–13*, trans. W. Watts, Loeb Classical Library (Cambridge, MA: Harvard University Press, 1912), Book X, §1 (p. 75).

8. See Epictetus, *Encheiridion*, in *Discourses, Books III and IV*.

9. John Cassian, *The Institutes*, trans. Boniface Ramsey, O.P., Ancient Christian Writers (New York: The Newman Press, 2000).

10. John Cassian, *The Conferences*, trans. Boniface Ramsey, O.P., Ancient Christian Writers (New York: The Newman Press, 1997).

11. Cassian, *The Conferences*, Conference XIV, The First Conference of Abba Nestoros: On Spiritual Knowledge, VIII.1–7 (pp. 509–11).

VIII.1. But let us return to discussing the knowledge that was spoken of at the beginning. As we said previously, the πρακτική is dispersed among many professions and pursuits. The θεωρηθική is divided into two parts—that is, into historical interpretation and spiritual understanding. Hence, when Solomon had enumerated the different forms of grace in the Church, he added: "All who are with her are doubly clothed." Now there are three kinds of spiritual knowledge—tropology, allegory, and anagogy—about which it is said in Proverbs: "But you describe those things for yourself in threefold fashion according to the largeness of your heart."

2. And so history embraces the knowledge of past and visible things, which is repeated by the Apostle thus: It is written that Abraham had two sons, one from a slave and the other from a free woman. The one from the slave was born according to the flesh, but the one from the free woman by a promise." The things that follow belong to allegory, however, because what really occurred is said to have prefigured the form of another mystery. "For

these," it says, "are two covenants, one from Mount Sinai, begetting unto slavery, which is Hagar. For Sinai is a mountain in Arabia, which is compared to the Jerusalem that now is, and which is enslaved with her children." 3. But anagogy, which mounts from spiritual mysteries to certain more sublime and sacred heavenly secrets, is added by the Apostle: "But the Jerusalem from above, which is our mother, is free. For it is written: Rejoice, you barren one who do not bear, break out and shout, you who are not in labor, for the children of the desolate one are many more than of her who has a husband." Tropology is moral explanation pertaining to correction of life and to practical instruction, as if we understood these same to be covenants as πρακτική and as theoretical discipline, or at least as if we wished to take Jerusalem of Zion as the soul of the human being, according to the words: "Praise the Lord, O Jerusalem; praise your God, O Zion."

4. The four figures that have been mentioned converge in such a way that, if we want, one and the same Jerusalem can be understood in a fourfold manner. According to history it is the city of the Jews. According to allegory, it is the church of Christ. According to anagogy it is that heavenly city of God "which is the mother of us all." According to tropology it is the soul of the human being, which under this name is frequently either reproached or praised by the Lord. Of these four kinds of interpretation the blessed Apostle says thus: "Now, brothers, if I come to you speaking in tongues, what use will it be to you unless I speak by revelation or by knowledge or by prophecy or by instruction?"

5. Now, revelation pertains to allegory, by which the things that the historical narrative conceals are laid bare by a spiritual understanding and explanation. Suppose, for example, that we tried to make clear how "all our fathers were under the cloud, and all were baptized in Moses in the cloud and in the sea, and [how] all ate the same spiritual food and drank the same spiritual drink from the rock that followed them. But the rock was Christ." This explanation, which refers to the prefiguration of the body and blood of Christ that we daily receive, comprises an allegorical approach.

6. But knowledge, which is also mentioned by the Apostle, is tropology, by which we discern by a prudent examination everything that pertains to practical discretion, in order to see whether it is useful and good, as when we are ordered to judge for ourselves "whether it befits a woman to pray to God with unveiled head." This approach, as has been said, comprises a moral understanding.

Likewise, prophecy, which the Apostle introduced in the third place, bespeaks anagogy, by which words are directed to the invisible and to what lies in the future, as in this case: "We do not want you to be ignorant, brothers, about those who are asleep, so that you may not be saddened like others who have no hope. For if we believe that Christ has died and has arisen, so also God will bring those who have fallen asleep in Jesus with him. For we say this to you by the word of the Lord, that we who are alive at the coming of the Lord shall not anticipate those who have fallen asleep in Christ, for the Lord himself shall descend from heaven with a command, with the voice of an angel and with the trumpet of God, and the dead who are in Christ shall arise first."

7. The figure of anagogy appears in this kind of exhortation.

But instruction lays open the simple sequence of a historical exposition in which there is no more hidden meaning than what is comprised in the sound of the words, as in this case: "I delivered to you first what I also received, that Christ died for our sins according to the Scriptures, that he was buried, that he rose on the third day, and that he was seen by Cephas." And: "God sent his Son, made of a woman, made under the law, to save those who were under the law." And this: "Hear, O Israel: the Lord your God is one Lord."

12. Cassian, *The Conferences*, Conference XIV, The First Conference of Abba Nestoros: On Spiritual Knowledge, I.2–3 (p. 505). "There are indeed as many kinds of knowledge in this world as there are different sorts of arts and disciplines. But, although all are either completely useless or contribute something of value only to the present life, still there is not one that does not have its own order and method of instruction by which it can be grasped by those who are interested in it. 3. If, then, those arts follow their own defined principles when they are taught, how much more does the teaching and profession of our religion, which is directed to contemplating the secrets of invisible mysteries rather than to present gain and which seeks instead the reward of eternal prizes, consist in a defined order and method. The first kind is πρακτική, or practical, which reaches its fulfillment in correction of behavior and in cleansing from vice. The other is θεωρηθική, which consists in the contemplation of divine things and in the understanding of most sacred meanings."

13. Cassian, *The Conferences*, Conference XIV, The First Conference of Abba Nestoros: On Spiritual Knowledge, VII (pp. 508–9).

14. Cassian, *The Conferences*, Conference XIV, The First Conference of Abba Nestoros: On Spiritual Knowledge, III.2–3 (p. 506). "Yet we should

know that we must exert ourselves twice as hard to expel vice as to acquire virtue. We do not come to this by our own guesswork, but we are taught by the words of him who alone knows the ability and intelligence of what he has made: 'Behold,' he says, 'today I have set you over nations and over kingdoms, to root up and to pull down and to disperse and to scatter and to build and to plant.' 3. He has pointed out that four things are necessary for expelling what is harmful—namely, rooting up, pulling down, dispersing, and scattering. But for perfecting the virtues and for acquiring what pertains to righteousness there are only building and planting. Hence it is quite clear that it is more difficult to pluck out and eradicate the ingrown passions of body and soul than it is to gather and plant spiritual virtues."

15. For further specification and elaboration of this point, see *GL*, 290–97.

16. On the definition of *logismos*, see *GL*, 298–99. "The history of this word is very interesting, because what did *logismos* designate in classical Greek? It designated reasoning, that is to say the way *logos* is employed in order to arrive at the truth. Now in the vocabulary of Christian spirituality [. . .] *logismos* is not the positive use of a positive *logos* enabling one to arrive at truth. *Logismos* is thought that comes to the mind along with all the uncertainties of its origin, nature, and content, and consequently of what one can extract from it."

17. Cassian, *The Conferences*, Conference II, The Second Conference of Abba Moses: On Discretion, I–VII (pp. 83–89). See also Conference I, The First Conference of Abba Moses: On the Goal and End of the Monk, XVI–XXIII (pp. 56–64).

18. See again Conference XIV, The First Conference of Abba Nestoros: On Spiritual Knowledge, IX.4 (p. 512).

19. In the first hour of the February 17, 1982, lecture of the series "The Hermeneutics of the Subject," Foucault speaks of an "exegetical model" that the Christian church developed in order to bring about a clear caesura in relation to the "Platonic model," organized around the theme of recollection, as the latter had been taken up by the Gnostic movements. The effect of this exegetical model "within Christian spirituality was not to give knowledge of the self the memorial function of rediscovering the subject's being, but rather the exegetical function of detecting the nature and origin of internal impulses produced within the soul." *HS*, 257.

20. On *gnōsis* and its relation to Christianity, see *HS*, 16, 256–57, 421; *GL*, 310; *ABHS*, 55, 76, 80n6.

21. The manuscript of the lecture ends abruptly here. It corresponds to the first part, up to the break; the second part could not be recovered. However,

on the last sheet, in handwriting that is not Foucault's, someone recorded the English version of the text of Cassian (Conference XIV, III.3) that Foucault alludes to (see *supra*, p. 254, note 14). Note that the translation here is different from the Ramsey version we have referenced: "He designated four things necessary in the removal of that which is evil; they are: to tear out and to destroy, to throw down and to dissipate; but only two things, to edify and to implant, in rendering oneself perfect in virtue and in acquiring that which is attendant to justice. From which it follows obviously that it is more difficult to tear out and uproot the inveterate vices of the body and the soul than to edify and to implant spiritual virtues." See Cassian, *The Conferences*, Conference XIV, The First Conference of Abba Nestoros: On Spiritual Knowledge, III.3 (p. 506).

THE SEMINAR: FIRST MEETING

1. The beginning of Lecture II is devoted to the *Alcibiades*; see *supra*, pp. 15–20, 34–41.

2. Foucault elaborates on this at the beginning of Lecture III; see *supra*, p. 74 and p. 248, note 6.

3. Regarding the argument that the "culture of the self" during the imperial period is not "the manifestation of a growing individualism," but the "apogee" of a long-standing phenomenon which corresponds to an intensification and valorization of the relationship of the self to itself, see *CS*, 95. See also Foucault, *La culture de soi*, 88–89.

4. Ramsay MacMullen, *Roman Social Relations, 50 B.C. to A.D. 284* (New Haven: Yale University Press, 1981) (*Les rapports entre les classes sociales dans l'Empire romain, 50 av. J.-C.-284 ap. J.-C.*, trans. A. Tachet [Paris: Seuil, 1986]).

5. "When someone inquired why they put their fields in the hands of the Helots, and did not take care of them themselves, he said, 'It was by not taking care of the fields, but of ourselves, that we acquired those fields.'" Plutarch, "Sayings of Spartans," 217A (p. 97).

6. Sarah B. Pomeroy, *Goddesses, Whores, Wives, and Slaves: Women in Classical Antiquity* (New York: Schocken Books, 1975).

7. On this point, see *ST*, 227–43; *CS*, 75–77, 147–85.

8. Plato, *The Apology*, 36b–e, 37 (p. 22).

9. *The Republic* (Cambridge: Cambridge University Press, 2018), Book 9, 591c–92b (pp. 311–12).

10. Foucault is alluding to a passage in Book III, Discourse I, "Of Personal Adornment," in Epictetus, *Discourses, Books III and IV*, §20 (p. 11), which he comments on later in the seminar; see *infra*, pp. 125–26.

11. See Plato, *The Apology*, 30a–b (p. 16).

12. Foucault is referencing Lecture I; see *supra*, pp. 9–11.

13. Dodds, *Les grecs et l'irrationnel*, 140–78; Vernant, "Aspects mythiques de la mémoire" (155) and "Aspects de la personne dans la religion greque," (1960).

14. Plato, *Alcibiades I*, 129b–30b (pp. 95–99). We have included the full text of the passages that Foucault cites here.

15. *Phaedrus*, in Plato, *Euthyphro, Apology, Crito, Phaedo, Phaedrus*, trans. Harold North Fowler, Loeb Classical Library (Cambridge, MA: Harvard University Press, 1914), 246b (pp. 471–73).

16. *Alcibiades I*, 133c (pp. 211–13).

17. On this theme, see *HS*, 70–73 and passim.

18. Book III, Discourse I, "Of Personal Adornment," in Epictetus, *Discourses, Books III and IV*, §§16–23 (pp. 11–13). See also *HS*, 8, 96.

19. Book III, Discourse I, "Of Personal Adornment," §§1–4 (p. 5).

20. "Someone said to him: I have often come to you, wishing to hear you and you have never given me an answer; and now, if it be possible, I beg you to say something to me." Book II, Discourse XXIV, "To One of Those Whom He Did Not Deem Worthy," in Epictetus, *Discourses, Books I and II*, §§1–29 (p. 421).

21. Foucault says "another dialogue" here, but is still referencing Book II, Discourse XXIV, "To One of Those Whom He Did Not Deem Worthy." See also *P*, 25–26; *HS*, 347–48; *GSO*, 320.

22. "Show me, then, what I shall accomplish by a discussion with you. Arouse in me an eagerness for it. Just as suitable grass when shown to the sheep arouses in it an eagerness to eat, whereas if you set before it a stone or a loaf of bread, it will not be moved to eat, so we have certain moments of natural eagerness for speech also, when the suitable hearer appears, and when he himself stimulates us." Book II, Discourse XXIV, "To One of Those Whom He Did Not Deem Worthy," §§12–18 (p. 425). The Greek word *probaton*, which denotes small livestock, is translated "goat" in the English version that Foucault references, and by *brebis* (sheep) in the French version; it also appears as "sheep" in the Loeb edition cited here.

THE SEMINAR: SECOND MEETING

1. This is an allusion to the fact that Paul Bouissac, who invited Foucault to Toronto, was very interested in circuses; see Paul Bouissac, *Circus and Culture: A Semiotic Approach* (Bloomington: University of Indiana Press, 1976).

2. Plato, *Alcibiades I*, 134e (p. 217).

3. *Alcibiades I*, 134d–e (p. 217).

4. The Loeb edition reads as follows: "—Soc. Then do you know how you may escape from the condition in which you now find yourself? Let us not give it a name, where a handsome person is concerned!—Alc. I do.—Soc. How?—Alc. If it be your wish, Socrates.—Soc. That is not well said, Alcibiades.—Alc. Well, what should I say?—Soc. If it be God's will.—Alc. Then I say it. And yet I say this besides, that we are here to make a change in our parts, Socrates, so that I shall have yours and you mine. For from this day onward it must be the case that I am your attendant, and you have me always in attendance on you." *Alcibiades I*, 135d–e (p. 221).

5. The Loeb edition reads as follows: "—Soc. Ah, generous friend! So my love will be just like a stork; for after hatching a winged love in you it is to be cherished in return by its nestling.—Alc. Well, that is the position, and I shall begin here and now to take pains over justice.—Soc. I should like to think you will continue to do so; yet I am apprehensive, not from any distrust of your nature, but in view of the might of the state, lest it overcome both me and you." *Alcibiades I*, 135e (pp. 221–23).

6. "His audience listen with ears pricked up and eyes fixed on him always in exactly the same posture, signifying comprehension and understanding by nods and glances, praise of the speaker by the cheerful change of expression which steals over the face, a difficulty by a gentler movement of the head and by pointing with a finger-tip of the right hand. The young men standing by show no less." Philo of Alexandria, *On the Contemplative Life, or Suppliants*, 77 (p. 161).

7. The sentence is partially inaudible, but the auditor is most likely referring to Katherine Frances Mullany, *Augustine of Hippo: The First Modern Man* (New York: Frederick Pustet, 1930).

8. Book I, Chapter XVI, "Of Providence," in Epictetus, *Discourses, Books I and II*, §§1–5 (p. 109). See also Foucault, *La culture de soi*, 87; *HS*, 457–58; *CS*, 47.

9. Plato, *Protagoras*, in *Laches, Protagoras, Meno, Euthydemus*, trans. W. R. M. Lamb, Loeb Classical Library (Cambridge, MA: Harvard University Press, 1924), 320c–21e (p. 129).

10. Book I, Chapter XVI, "Of Providence," §§6–8 (pp. 109–10).

11. Book I, Chapter XVI, "Of Providence," §§9–14 (p. 111).

12. See Lecture IV, *supra*, p. 87 and p. 250, note 7.

13. On the relationship of Cynic philosophers to nature, see *CT*, 171, 206, 254–55.

14. Book I, Chapter XVI, "Of Providence," 15–21 (p. 113).

15. Plato, *The Apology*, 29c–30a (pp. 15–16).

16. "I am the same sort of thing as red in a mantle." Book III, Discourse I, "Of Personal Adornment," in Epictetus, *Discourses, Books III and IV*, §23 (p. 13). See also *supra*, pp. 125–26.

17. Cleanthes, "Hymn to Zeus," in *Hellenistic Religions*, ed. Frederick C. Grant (New York: Bobbs-Merrill, 1953), 152–54.

18. The auditor is referring to Book I, Chapter I, "Of the Things Which Are Under Our Control and Not Under Our Control," in Epictetus, *Discourses, Books I and II*, §§1–3 (p. 7). Foucault passes over this text in favor of reading the Marcus Aurelius materials.

19. The full passage reads: "Among the arts and faculties in general you will find none that is self-contemplative, and therefore none that is either self-approving or self-disapproving. How far does the art of grammar possess the power of contemplation? Only so far as to pass judgement upon what is written. How far the art of music? Only so far as to pass judgement upon the melody. Does either of them, then, contemplate itself? Not at all. But if you are writing to a friend and are at a loss as to what to write, the art of grammar will tell you; yet whether or not you are to write to your friend at all, the art of grammar will not tell. The same holds true of the art of music with regard to melodies; but whether you are at this moment to sing and play on the lyre, or neither sing nor play, it will not tell. What art or faculty, then, will tell? That one which contemplates both itself and everything else. And what is this? The reasoning faculty; for this is the only one we have inherited which will take knowledge both of itself—what it is, and of what it is capable, and how valuable a gift it is to us—and likewise of all the other faculties." Book I, Chapter I, "Of the Things Which Are Under Our Control and Not Under Our Control," 1–6 (pp. 7–9).

20. See Lecture IV, *supra*, p. 87 and pp. 250–51, note 7. Here Foucault announces his intention to talk about two texts of Marcus Aurelius, though analysis of only one (*The Meditations*, Book IV, §3) could be found in the materials conserved from Lecture IV.

21. Plato, *Alcibiades I*, 127e–30c (pp. 87–203). For further commentary on the term *chrēsis*, and the verb *chresthai*, see HS, 56.

22. On the notion of *kairos* within ancient ethics and "the use of pleasures" (*chrēsis aphrodisōn*) specifically, see Foucault, "Débat au Département de Français de l'Université de Californie à Berkeley," 112–14; *UP*, 32, 36, 53–54; *CS*, 130–31, 138. On the importance of this notion in the practice

of *parrēsia,* see *DT,* 122, 160; *P,* 22–24; *HS,* 383–85, 387–89; *GSO,* 217–18, 224–25.

23. Regarding the crucial role of writing in the culture of the self, and the *hupomnēmata* and correspondence in particular, see *HS,* 360–67; Foucault, "Self Writing," 207–22.

24. Fronto to Marcus as Caesar (A.D. 145–147), in Marcus Cornelius Fronto, *Correspondence,* vol. 1, trans. C. R. Haines, Loeb Classical Library (Cambridge, MA: Harvard University Press, 1919), 219–24.

25. See Dodds, *Les grecs et l'irrationnel,* 37–70.

26. See Foucault, "Débat au Département de Français de l'Université de Californie à Berkeley," 172.

27. Foucault seems to be referring to the letter referenced above in note 24; see Fronto to Marcus as Caesar (A.D. 145–147), in Fronto, *Correspondence,* vol. 1, 219–24.

28. Marcus Aurelius to Fronto (A.D. 144–145?), in Fronto, *Correspondence,* vol. 1, 181–83. Foucault also comments on this letter in *HS,* 157–64

THE SEMINAR: THIRD MEETING

1. This discussion of *parrēsia* is very similar to the lecture that Foucault gave several weeks earlier at the University of Grenoble; see *P.* The latter already represents a significant development with regard to Foucault's analyses of *parrēsia* in the context of the care of the self in the March 10, 1982, lecture on the hermeneutics of the subject; see *HS,* 371–409. Foucault devoted his final two courses at the Collège de France and his cycle of lectures at the University of California, Berkeley in the fall 1983 to in-depth analyses of the notion of *parrēsia;* see *GSO; DT; CT.*

2. Foucault most clearly describes the successive steps of this evolution in *DT.*

3. "One could not find a political system and principle so favorable to equality and freedom of speech, in a word so sincerely democratic, as that of the Achaean league." Polybius, *The Histories,* vol. 1, *Books 1–2,* trans. W. R. Paton, rev. F. W. Walbank, Christian Habicht, Loeb Classical Library (Cambridge, MA: Harvard University Press, 2010), Book II, 38, 6 (p. 337).

4. Foucault cites from an English translation of Plutarch's *On Exile,* which reproduces the dialogue from Euripides in question. See Plutarch, *On Exile,* in *Moralia,* vol. 7, trans. Phillip H. De Lacy, Benedict Einarson, Loeb Classical Library 405 (Cambridge, MA: Harvard University Press, 1959), 605F–606A (p. 559).

5. Euripides, *Phoenician Women*, 388-93. We have reproduced the English version from the Loeb edition of Plutarch, because Foucault and the seminar participants are reading from an excerpted version of the dialogue in Plutarch. It is not clear if Foucault is using the Loeb translation at this time, but he repeats the last line of the dialogue, "The folly of the mighty must be borne," verbatim in the recording as it is rendered in the Loeb edition of Plutarch, which suggests that this may be the translation in use here. See also Euripides, *Helen, Phoenician Women, Orestes*, ed. and trans. David Kovacs, Loeb Classical Library (Cambridge, MA: Harvard University Press, 2002).

6. "Say on, for I will do nothing to hurt you: [one ought not to be angry with just men.]" Euripides, *Bacchae*, in *Bacchae, Iphigenia at Aulis, Rhesus*, ed. David Kovacs, Loeb Classical Library (Cambridge, MA: Harvard University Press, 2003), 666-73 (p. 77).

7. On this notion of the "parrhesiastic pact," see *P*, 31-32; *GSO*, 162-63, 176-77, 203; *CT*, 12-13; *DT*, 53, 74. See also Henri-Paul Fruchaud and Daniele Lorenzini, in *DT*, 223n20.

8. "For, save I find her who gave life to me, my life is naught. If one prayer be vouchsafed, of Athens' daughters may my mother be, that by my mother, may free speech be mine. The alien who entereth a burg of pure blood, burgher though he be in name, hath not free speech: he bears a bondsman's tongue." Euripides, *Ion*, in *Euripides in Four Volumes*, vol. 4, ed. and trans. Arthur S. Way, Loeb Classical Library (Cambridge, MA: Harvard University Press, 1912), 669-75 (pp. 69-71).

9. "Me—friends, 'tis even this dooms me to die. That never I be found to shame my lord, nor the sons whom I bare: but free, with tongues unfettered, flourish they, their home yon burg of glorious Athens, blushing ne'er for me. For this cows man, how stout of heart soe'er, to know a father's or a mother's sin." *Hippolytus*, in *Euripides in Four Volumes*, vol. 4, ed. and trans. Arthur S. Way, Loeb Classical Library (Cambridge, MA: Harvard University Press, 1912), 421-25 (p. 197).

10. Aeschines, *The Speech against Timarchus*, in Aeschines, *Speeches*, trans. C. D. Adams, Loeb Classical Library (Cambridge, MA: Harvard University Press, 1919).

11. "But I know that it is hazardous to oppose your views and that, although this is a free government, there exists no 'freedom of speech' except that which is enjoyed in this Assembly by the most reckless orators, who care nothing for your welfare, and in the theatre by the comic poets." Isocrates, *On The Peace*, in Isocrates, vol. 2, *On the Peace, Areopagiticus, Against the Sophists, Antido-*

sis, Panathenaicus, trans. George Norlin, Loeb Classical Library (Cambridge, MA: Harvard University Press, 1929), 15.

12. "For those who directed the state in the time of Solon and Cleisthenes did not establish a polity which in name merely was hailed as the most impartial and the mildest of governments, while in practice showing itself the opposite to those who lived under it, nor one which trained the citizens in such fashion that they looked upon insolence as democracy, lawlessness as liberty, impudence of speech as equality." *Areopagiticus,* 115.

13. "For when men are in private life, many things contribute to their education: first and foremost, the absence of luxury among them, and the necessity they are under to take thought each day for their livelihood; next, the laws by which in each case their civic life is governed; furthermore, freedom of speech and the privilege which is openly granted to friends to rebuke and to enemies to attack each other's faults; besides, a number of the poets of earlier times have left precepts which direct them how to live; so that, from all these influences, they may reasonably be expected to become better men. Kings, however, have no such help; on the contrary, they, who more than other men should be thoroughly trained, live all their lives, from the time when they are placed in authority, without admonition; for the great majority of people do not come in contact with them, and those who are of their society consort with them to gain their favor." *To Nicocles,* in Isocrates, vol. 1, *To Demonicus, To Nicocles, Nicocles or the Cyprians, Panegyricus, To Philip, Archidamus,* trans. George Norlin, Loeb Classical Library (Cambridge, MA: Harvard University Press, 1928), 2–4 (pp. 41–43).

14. Nicocles was the son of Evagoras, who founded the kingdom of New Salamis in Cyprus. (See Norlin's introduction to Isocrates, vol. 1, pp. 38–39.)

15. "Regard as your most faithful friends, not those who praise everything you say or do, but those who criticize your mistakes. Grant freedom of speech to those who have good judgement, in order that when you are in doubt you may have friends who will help you to decide." *To Nicocles,* 28 (pp. 55–57).

16. "Let us attend then. When the Persians, under Cyrus, maintained the due balance between slavery and freedom, they became, first of all, free themselves, and, after that, masters of many others. For when the rulers gave a share of freedom to their subjects and advanced them to a position of equality, the soldiers were more friendly towards their officers and showed their devotion in times of danger; and if there was any wise man amongst them, able to give counsel, since the king was not jealous but allowed free speech and respected those who could help at all by their counsel,—such a man had the oppor-

tunity of contributing to the common stock the fruit of his wisdom. Consequently, at that time all their affairs made progress, owing to their freedom,
friendliness and mutual interchange of reason." Plato, *Laws*, vol. 1, *Books 1–6*,
trans. R. G. Bury, Loeb Classical Library (Cambridge, MA: Harvard University Press, 1926), Book III, 694a–b (p. 225).

17. "Soc. If my soul had happened to be made of gold, Callicles, do you
not think I should have been delighted to find one of those stones with which
they test gold, and the best one; which, if I applied it, and it confirmed to me
that my soul had been properly tended, would give me full assurance that I
am in a satisfactory state and have no need of other testing? — Call. What is
the point of that question, Socrates? — Soc. I will tell you. I am just thinking
what a lucky stroke I have had in striking up with you. — Call. How so? — Soc.
I am certain that whenever you agree with me in any view that my soul takes,
this must be the very truth. For I conceive that whoever would sufficiently
test a soul as to rectitude of life or the reverse should go to work with three
things which are all in your possession—knowledge, goodwill, and frankness." Plato, *Gorgias*, in *Lysis, Symposium, Gorgias*, trans. W. R. M. Lamb, Loeb
Classical Library (Cambridge, MA: Harvard University Press, 1925), 486d–
87a (p. 395).

18. Plutarch, "Precepts of Statecraft," in *Moralia*, vol. 10, trans. W. C. Helmbold, Loeb Classical Library (Cambridge, MA: Harvard University Press,
1936).

19. Philostratus, *Life of Apollonius of Tyana*, vol. 1, *Books 1–4*, trans. Chris-
topher P. Jones, Loeb Classical Library (Cambridge, MA: Harvard University
Press, 2005); vol. 2, *Books 5–8*.

20. "Buddhism is […] essentially a technique of the self, much more so
than a religion, much more than a morality properly speaking." Foucault, "Débat au Département de Français de l'Université de Californie à Berkeley," 172.
For more on Foucault's understanding of Zen and Buddhism more generally,
especially in relation to Christian techniques, see "Sexuality and Solitude,"
178. "La scène de la philosophie," interview with M. Watanabe, in *DE II*, no.
234, pp. 592–93; "Michel Foucault et le zen: Un séjour dans un temple zen,"
in *DE II*, no. 236, p. 621; *GL*, 186, 192n; *ABHS*, 50, 80. On the "ars erotica" in
the "East," insofar as it is opposed to the "scientia sexualis" of the "West," see
"Débat au Département de Histoire de l'Université de Californie à Berkeley," 145–46; *HIST*, 57–71; "L'Occident et la vérité du sexe," in *DE II*, no. 181,
p. 104; "Sexualité et pouvoir," interview with C. Nemoto and M. Watanabe,
in *DE II*, no. 230, pp. 556–57.

21. Peregrinus died in 165 CE; for an analysis of the figure of Peregrinus, see *CT*, 181, 195, 254.

22. "From there, thus equipped, he set sail for Italy and immediately after disembarking he fell to abusing everyone, and in particular the Emperor, knowing him to be mild and gentle, so that he was safe in making bold. The Emperor, as one would expect, cared little for his libels and did not think fit to punish for mere words a man who only used philosophy as a cloak, and above all, a man who had made a profession of abusiveness. But in our friend's case, even from this his reputation grew, among simple folk anyhow, and he was a cynosure for his recklessness, until finally the city prefect, a wise man, packed him off for immoderate indulgence in the thing, saying that the city had no need of any such philosopher. However, this too made for his renown, and he was on everybody's lips as the philosopher who had been banished for his frankness and excessive freedom, so that in this respect he approached Musonius, Dio, Epictetus, and anyone else who has been in a similar predicament." Lucian, *The Passing of Peregrinus*, in Lucian, vol. 5, trans. A. M. Harmon, Loeb Classical Library (Cambridge, MA: Harvard University Press, 1936), 18 (p. 21).

23. "From his boyhood felt the stirring of an individual impulse toward the higher life and an inborn love for philosophy, so that he despised all that men count good, and, committing himself unreservedly to liberty and free-speech, was steadfast in leading a straight, sane, irreproachable life and in setting an example to all who saw and heard him by his good judgment and the honesty of his philosophy." *Demonax*, in Lucian, vol. 1, trans. A. M. Harmon, Loeb Classical Library (Cambridge, MA: Harvard University Press, 1913), 3–4 (p. 145).

24. Philodemus, *Philodemi peri parresiae libellus* (Leipzig: B.G. Teubner, 1914).

25. Foucault is referencing the work of Marcello Gigante, specifically Gigante, "Philodème, sur la liberté de parole," in *Actes du VIIIe Congrès de l'Association Guillaume Budé (Paris, 5–10 Avril 1968)* (Paris: Belles Lettres, 1969).

26. Plutarch, "How to Tell a Flatterer from a Friend," in *Moralia*, vol. 1, trans. Frank Cole Babbitt, Loeb Classical Library (Cambridge, MA: Harvard University Press, 1927), pp. 261–396.

27. Among the letters of Seneca that Foucault references here, he is certainly including *Epistle* 75, "On the Diseases of the Soul." Foucault commented on this text extensively in the March 10, 1982, lecture on the hermeneutics of the subject, and in the lecture on *parrēsia* at Grenoble. See *HS*, 401–7; *P*, 30.

28. Giuseppe Scarpat, *Parrhesia: Storia del termine e delle sue traduzioni in*

latino (Brescia: Paideia, 1964). (A new revised edition was published by Brescia in 2001 as *Parrhesia greca, parrhesia cristiana*.)

29. Giuseppe Scarpat, *Il pensiero religioso di Seneca e l'ambiente ebracio e cristiano* (Brescia: Paideia, 1983).

30. Plutarch, "How to Tell a Flatterer from a Friend," 52A–F (pp. 281–85).

31. See Thucydides, *History of the Peloponnesian War*, vol. 3, *Books 5–6*, trans. C. F. Smith, Loeb Classical Library (Cambridge, MA: Harvard University Press, 1921); vol. 4, *Books 7–8*, trans. C. F. Smith, Loeb Classical Library (Cambridge, MA: Harvard University Press, 1923).

32. Seneca, *De tranquillitate animi*, §§4–15 (pp. 205–11).

33. Cassian, *The Institutes*.

34. See *supra*, p. 256, note 3.

THE SEMINAR: FOURTH MEETING

1. Although Foucault does not return to Seneca here, he references *Epistle 75*, "On the Diseases of the Soul," on several occasions. Foucault commented on this text extensively in the March 10, 1982, lecture on the hermeneutics of the subject, and in the lecture on *parrēsia* at Grenoble. See *HS*, 401–7; *P*, 30.

2. Galen, *On the Passions and Errors of the Soul*, 31–36.

3. "Surely it would have been best for Antonius himself to have told us clearly what meaning he wishes to convey by the term 'guarding,' [etc.]" Galen, *On the Passions and Errors of the Soul*, 27.

4. On this *disparition* and its connections to the social, economic, and medical problematization of homosexuality in the modern era, see "Michel Foucault, une interview: Sexe, pouvoir et la politique de l'identité," in *DE II*, no 358, pp. 1563–64.

5. John Boswell, *Christianity, Social Tolerance, and Homosexuality: Gay People in Western Europe from the Beginning of the Christian Era to the Fourteenth Century* (Chicago: University of Chicago Press, 1980). See also Foucault, "Entretien avec Michel Foucault," interview with J.-P. Joecker, M. Oeurd, and A. Sanzio, in *DE II*, no. 311, pp. 1109–11; and Foucault, "Sexual Choice, Sexual Act," in *EW* 1, 140–56.

6. Epictetus, *Discourses, Books III and IV*, Discourse III, Chapter 23, §§31–32 (p. 181).

7. Cassian, *The Institutes*, Book IV, XXIV (p. 90). In the version of this story recounted by Cassian, the branch does not flower or take root at all. On this subject, see M. Senellart, in *GL*, 282n46.

8. *The Interpretation of Dreams (The Oneirocritica of Artemidorus)*, trans. R. J. White (Park Ridge, NJ: Noyes Press, 1975). For Foucault's other commentaries on Artemidorus, see "Rêver de ses plaisirs: Sur l'*Onirocritique* d'Artémidore," in *DE II*, no. 332, pp. 1281–1307; *ST*, 257–97; *CS*, 3–36.

9. If Foucault, inspired by J. L. Austin here, refers to his own work in terms of a "pragmatics of discourse" here (see also *P*, 15), in the January 12, 1983, lecture on the government of self and others several months later, he explicitly detaches it from this perspective, and speaks instead of a "dramatics of discourse." See *GSO*, 61–69. See also H.-P. Fruchaud and Daniele Lorenzini, in *DT*, 236n34.

10. Foucault addressed this point in Michel Foucault, *The Archaeology of Knowledge*, World of Man (London: Tavistock Publications, 1972), 80ff. See also Jocelyn Benoist, "Des actes de langage à l'inventaire des énoncés," *Archives de Philosophie* 79 (2016): 55–78.

11. On the absence of "pastoral power" in Greco-Roman antiquity, see *STP*, 135–47; see also "'Omnes et Singulatim': Toward a Critique of Political Reason," in *Power: Essential Works of Michel Foucault, 1954–1984*, vol. 3 (New York: New Press, 1997).

12. See *supra*, p. 197.

13. "For each of us needs almost a lifetime of training to become a perfect man." Galen, *On the Passions and Errors of the Soul*, 37.

14. See *supra*, p. 266, note 9.

15. See *HM*.

16. See *OT*.

17. See *HIST*.

18. See Michel Foucault, "Nietzsche, Genealogy, History," in *Aesthetics, Method & Epistemology*, ed. Paul Rabinow (New York: The New Press, 1998).

19. On *aphrodisia* and the problematization of pleasures in ancient Greece, see *ST*, 76–97 and passim; *UP*, 36–52 and passim.

20. On Christian concupiscence, see Foucault, "The Battle for Chastity," 192–224; *AB*, 171–81.

21. The hypothesis that Epicureanism was influenced by lost treatises of Aristotle actually predates Gigante, and was formulated for the first time by Ettore Bignone in *L'Aristotele perduto e la formazione filosofica di Epicuro* (Florence: La Nuova Italia, 1936).

22. See Konrad Gaiser, *Platons ungeschriebene Lehre: Studien zur systematischen und geschichtlichen Begründung der Wissenschaften in der platonischen Schule* (Stuttgart: Ernst Klett, 1963).

23. For a brief discussion of Augustine's *De bono conjugali*, see *SV*, 231–32.

24. Clement of Alexandria, *Christ the Educator*.

25. "The self is nothing more than our relation to ourselves. The self is a relation. It is not something structured which is given from the beginning. It is a relation to oneself." Foucault, "Débat au Département de Philosophie de l'Université de Californie à Berkeley," 117 (trans. D. Wyche).

26. See *supra*, pp. 73–74 and p. 248, note 5.

INDEX OF NAMES